When Cobb Met Wagner

When Cobb Met Wagner

The Seven-Game World Series of 1909

DAVID FINOLI *and*
BILL RANIER

McFarland & Company, Inc., Publishers
Jefferson, North Carolina, and London

ALSO OF INTEREST: *When the Bucs Won It All: The 1979 World Champion Pittsburgh Pirates*, by Bill Ranier and David Finoli (McFarland, 2005); *For the Good of the Country: World War II Baseball in the Major and Minor Leagues*, by David Finoli (McFarland, 2002)

LIBRARY OF CONGRESS CATALOGUING-IN-PUBLICATION DATA

Finoli, David, 1961–
    When Cobb met Wagner : the seven-game World Series of 1909 / David Finoli and Bill Ranier.
        p.   cm.
    Includes bibliographical references and index.

    ISBN 978-0-7864-4837-1
    softcover : 50# alkaline paper ∞

    1. World Series (Baseball) (1909)   2. Cobb, Ty, 1886–1961.
3. Wagner, Honus, 1874–1955.   4. Pittsburgh Pirates (Baseball team)— History — 20th century.   5. Detroit Tigers (Baseball team)— History — 20th century.   6. Baseball — United States — History — 20th century.   I. Ranier, Bill, 1960–   II. Title.
GV878.4.F56   2011
796.357'640974886 — dc22   2010048326

British Library cataloguing data are available

Front cover: World Series baseball game at Bennett Park, October 11, 1909; Honus Wagner (both Library of Congress); Ty Cobb (Classic Photos)

Manufactured in the United States of America

McFarland & Company, Inc., Publishers
    Box 611, Jefferson, North Carolina 28640
    www.mcfarlandpub.com

From David:
To my loving wife Viv
whom I've had the honor to spend
the last 25 years of my life with. Happy Anniversary.

Also to the memory of Evelyn Aikens who was
an inspiration throughout her life helping
those who needed it most. Rest in peace.

From Bill:
To my beautiful "Big Three" ...
my wonderful wife Marge
and my darling daughters, Sarah and Meghan.

TABLE OF CONTENTS

ACKNOWLEDGMENTS

From Dave:

I'd like to thank the greatest children a father could ask for, Tony, Matt and Cara. They make me proud to be their father every day. I'd also like to thank one of the most knowledgeable baseball historians I've ever had the honor to meet, and my friend for over 30 years starting when the Pirates were actually a championship-caliber team, Bill Ranier. Bill not only did an outstanding job helping with this book as he has with the ones we have combined on in the past, but was an incredibly valuable resource.

I've been lucky enough to always have a supportive family no matter what I've done in life, and I'd like to thank them also. My father Domenic, mother Eleanor, my sister Mary and her husband Matt, my brother Jamie, my nieces Brianna and Marissa and finally all my aunts, uncles, cousins and my wonderful in-laws Viv and Sam Pansino.

From Bill:

I'd like to thank my wife Marge who has to put up with my baseball mania and my daughters Sarah and Meghan who I hope someday will share a passion for going to ballgames to watch the action rather than to enjoy cotton candy and slushies. Also, for their continued support and love, thanks to my mother, Marcella, my brother Fran and his family, Josephina, Stefanie and Steven, my sister Debbie and her husband Ken and son Matt, my brother Tim and my in-laws Ray and Joan Borkowski. Finally, thank you to my great friend and collaborator, David Finoli, who encouraged me to join him in this enjoyable project.

We'd both like to give a special thank you to Jim Trdinich and the Pittsburgh Pirates, who were kind enough to donate several photos we used for this project.

PREFACE

Sitting at PNC Park for what has become an almost 40-year ritual, author Bill Ranier and I were enjoying the local baseball festival that is Opening Day for the Pittsburgh Pirates. Mired in a record 17-year streak of futility, we nonetheless enjoyed the surroundings discussing as we have for the better part of four decades, the magnificent history that the Pirates have enjoyed throughout the years.

During this particular opening day, the subject du jour was the 100th anniversary of the first of Pittsburgh's five world championships, the 1909 World Series.

Through the years, especially during the past decade when together we researched and wrote two books on the team, one of our favorite subjects was the magnificent Honus Wagner and the dominant Pirate teams of the 20th century's first decade. He was, according both to those who saw him and to the historians and statisticians of the recent past, as incredible a shortstop as has ever played the game as well a consummate gentleman and teammate off the field.

As I came home from the game — a shutout win for the Bucs! — I decided to have a look at some of the 1909 issues old of *The Sporting News'* and *New York Times* and maybe to dip into some books, hoping to read a little more about that memorable World Series. I was fascinated by what that Series meant to Wagner and the city of Pittsburgh, and intrigued by their opponents, the Detroit Tigers. It was a match-up that might have been the most highly anticipated of the decade by the sporting public.

The Tigers during that time were the dominant team in the American League, winning three consecutive junior circuit crowns. With the likes of Ty Cobb, Sam Crawford, Wild Bill Donovan, and Matty McIntyre on the roster, the Tigers had plenty of talent. But they never found a way to translate that talent into the ultimate joy, a world championship, losing three consecutive

World Series between 1907 and 1909. And like the A's of the early 1970s, the Tigers had loads of personality but seemed at their core to be angry, disgruntled. The difference being that while the A's focused their anger at owner Charlie Finley, the Tigers directed it at themselves — most famously in the person of Ty Cobb.

Cobb the man might have been the polar opposite of Wagner, but on the field he was a match for the great shortstop. Good arguments can be made — and have been — that each is the greatest player of not only his time but all others. Their showdown in the 1909 Series was, understandably, heavily hyped As Bill and I discussed the Series in more depth, we decided that it was worth bringing the story back to life.

While the events of the regular season are not the focus of this book, they are the subject of its first two chapters. Bill and I both felt this was important in laying the foundation for how each team came to meet on these fall afternoons in the 1909 Series. For the Bucs it was the end of the most successful decade in team history; for the Tigers, it was a search for the missing ingredient for a world championship.

After that, thanks to the fabulous Society for American Baseball Research's lending library, from which we secured microfilm for *The Sporting News* of 1908 through 1910, and the various web sites that have begun to tackle the monumental task of digitizing America's newspapers and magazines, we were able to re-create each exciting contest of this topsy-turvy World Series. With the research material at our fingers, we were able to not only create a play-by-play account of each game but also bring the players to life. We did this not only in chapters 3 through 9, each devoted to one Series game, but at the end of the book, where chapters 14 and 15 provide career sketches for each player of the 1909 Pirates and Tigers.

As we did at the beginning of the story, we end the book with a synopsis of what happened to each franchise in the years immediately following 1909. We did this in hopes of explaining why, after all the success both clubs had in the century's first decade, neither would make it back to the Fall Classic with the core of these championship players.

It was a Series that captivated the sporting nation in 1909 like no World Series had before, and our hope is that the chapters in this book recapture some of the excitement the country felt over this match-up 102 years ago.

INTRODUCTION

It was a World Series in which two of the game's greatest players took the field battling for the game's greatest honor, world champions of baseball. The Detroit Tigers' Ty Cobb faced the Pittsburgh Pirates' Honus Wagner in the 1909 World Series. These two titans of diamond together made for one of the most memorable clashes in the history of the fall classic.

There was little similar between the two men. Cobb, a southerner from Narrows, Georgia, was disliked by fans and teammates alike. Controversies both off and on the field seemed to follow the Tiger great wherever he went. One such situation occurred earlier in the 1909 campaign when Cobb got into a violent confrontation with a house detec-

Honus Wagner came into the 1909 World Series looking to make up for a poor showing in 1903, when he hit only .222 in a Series loss to the Boston Americans (courtesy the Pittsburgh Pirates).

tive in Cleveland, one that would affect his performance greatly during the World Series against the Pirates.

Wagner on the other end was respected and admired by teammates and

3

Ty Cobb had varied success in the Tigers' first two trips to the World Series. The Hall of Famer hit .200 in 1907 before rising to .368 a year later against the Cubs (courtesy of Library of Congress, Bain Collection, Prints & Photographs Division, 8006u).

friends alike. He seemed loyal to a fault, turning down a huge offer by Washington of the new American League because of his loyalty to Barney Dreyfuss and the Pittsburgh Pirates. Honus was not only the type of player fans respected, but also the type of man they did. The reason his 1909 baseball card is considered the Holy Grail of cards (it sold for $2.35 million in 2007) is that he had the card pulled because the sponsor of the card was a tobacco company and he didn't want to be seen as supporting smoking for children (although he did chew tobacco and smoke cigars).[1] Legend has it that Wagner paid the tobacco company for its losses in already printing the card.

There was very little these men had in common when their worlds collided in the fall of 1909, but one thing that they did share was their immense baseball talent. Cobb was as brilliant on the field as he was hated off it. He won a record 12 batting titles, including nine in row, a feat no player has ever matched. His .366 career average has never been topped either and his 4,189 hits makes him one of only two men in the annuls of the sport to have eclipsed the 4,000-hit plateau. In 1909 he was at his best by winning the American League Triple Crown with a .377 average, 9 homers and 107 RBIs.

Wagner was almost his equal. The Flying Dutchman, as he was called, stood atop the leaderboard in the National League's batting average race eight times in his phenomenal career. While he is considered one of the premiere defensive shortstops ever to step on the diamond, many contemporaries said that he was among the greatest defensive players at every position he ever played (Wagner also played first, second, third and the outfield during in his career). During the Bucs' fourth National League championship run in 1909, he won his seventh bat-

Two titans of the game, Ty Cobb (center) and Honus Wagner (right), faced off against each other in the 1909 World Series. Cobb had won his third consecutive American League batting title with a .377 mark coming into this fall classic, while Wagner had captured his seventh National League crown by hitting .339 (courtesy of Library of Congress, Bain Collection, Prints & Photographs Division, 3a29628).

ting crown with a .339 mark and led the senior circuit in slugging percentage, on-base percentage, total bases, doubles, RBIs and extra-base hits. While not being able to join Cobb and all-time hit leader Pete Rose in the 4,000-hit club, Wagner nevertheless is eighth all time with 3,415 hits.

In addition to being members of the initial Hall of Fame class in 1936, these two titans of the diamond had another major thing in common: 1909 was each player's last chance to erase a black spot from an otherwise impeccable career by winning a World Series title. Wagner had been scarred by his poor performance in the initial fall classic in 1903, hitting only .222 while being widely blamed for Pittsburgh's upset loss to the Boston Americans. Cobb had

The 1909 season was the end of a very successful decade for Honus Wagner. He was the leader in all significant batting categories during the decade, except for triples and home runs. The 1909 World Series was his crowning achievement in his very successful decade (courtesy of the Pittsburgh Pirates).

played in the two previous Series in 1907 and 1908 with mixed personal results, although both occurred in five-game losses to the Chicago Cubs. One of these baseball giants was to end up with the exultation of finally putting an exclamation point of his career with a championship; the other would be saddled with another championship defeat.

The ironic thing about this clash of the titans was that neither player would make the biggest difference in the series. That honor fell to a 27-year-old rookie from Tipton, Indiana, by the name of Charles "Babe" Adams, who got a very surprising start in Game 1 and ended up winning a Series record three games in leading the Bucs to their first World Series championship.

While neither Cobb or Wagner would be the single pivotal player in this titanic match-up, it is the fact they entered the field of battle together that made this seven-game classic so important in the history of the national pastime, perhaps even in the annuls of sport itself. Only three times have batting champions met in a fall classic, once when Chick Hafey of the Cardinals squared off against Al Simmons of the A's in 1931, a second when Willie Mays and Bobby Avila in 1954 and the other was this famed 1909 affair.[2] Despite the fact that the previous five fall classics were met with excitement from the sporting world, it was the Cobb vs. Wagner aspect that took the 1909 spectacular to a new level. It wasn't just a sporting event, it was theater, the precursor to the future championship clashes in sports such as Montana vs. Marino and Bird vs. Magic. Those match-ups were memorable not for the teams that played, but by the legendary greats that squared off. In 1909, the great, anticipated matchup of Cobb versus Wagner lived up to its expectations, as it was the first World Series to extend to its maximum length with a final decisive game.

◆ 1 ◆

THE PIRATES' REGULAR SEASON

The beginnings of the Pirates' championship run in 1909 actually began the year before. While history remembers the classic 1908 National League pennant race between the New York Giants and Chicago Cubs, few recall that the Bucs had a chance to capture the senior circuit crown on the final day of the season.

It was a pennant race that was muddled further by the famous Merkle Boner game, where the Giants apparently had won an important contest against the Cubs, 2–1, when Al Bridwell's hit seemed to score Moose McCormick with the winning run. However, Merkle, the runner on first base, started for second base before McCormick scored, but stopped when the crowd took to the field. There were several stories how Chicago got a hold of the ball, but the bottom line was they found a ball and got it to Johnny Evers, who tagged second base for a force out to negate McCormick's score.

Amid the chaos, with dusk coming quickly, the game was declared a 1–1 tie. The next day National League President Harry G. Pulliam decided that the game would be replayed. The Cubs won the replayed game, capturing the National League pennant and the 1908 World Series, the last world championship the Cubs would win to date. The thing about the Merkle Boner, had the Pirates won the last game of the season against the Cubs, Pittsburgh would have won the senior circuit crown and not Chicago.

Pittsburgh's rush to contention began on Sunday, September 19, when they began the day five games out of first place with two weeks left in the season. After defeating the Giants, 6–2, that day, Pittsburgh won 13 of their next 14 games putting them a half game ahead of the Cubs and a game and a half in front of the Giants. The *Chicago Tribune* described the incredible race as "thinner than the ham in the sandwiches at the Philadelphia Ball Park."[1] When the Pirates met the Cubs on October 4, a win combined with a Giant loss, who had three games left plus the replay of the Merkle game, would mean a World Series would come to the Smoky City.

The 1909 Pirates were perhaps the greatest team in the history of the Pittsburgh franchise. They won a franchise-record 110 games, while winning their first world championship (courtesy of the Pittsburgh Pirates).

The game was tense from the outset as Pittsburgh tied the score, 2–2, in the sixth inning, but the Cubs scored three more to retake the lead, 5–2. In the ninth inning, Honus Wagner stood at first base with Ed Abbaticchio at bat. The former football great from Latrobe hit a mammoth shot into the right-field crowd. Unfortunately, umpire Hank O'Day called the ball foul, to the chagrin of the Pirates. The whole team dashed onto the field to argue the call, to no avail. After the Bucs' arguments fell on deaf ears, the Cubs' Three Finger Brown retired them and their championship hopes by winning the game, 5–2, and eventually the pennant by a game over both Pittsburgh and the Giants. There was a story that circulated later on about a woman saying the ball that Abbaticchio hit hurt her. Her ticket stub showed she was sitting in fair territory when the ball hit her.[2] A tall tale perhaps, but controversy or not, the Pirates fell one game short of their goal and went into the offseason trying to figure out how to make it up.

There were murmurs that some of the Pirate performances over the second half of the season were marred by excessive drinking, especially that of pitcher Lefty Leifield. Pirate boss Barney Dreyfuss denied the allegations stating, "One or two members of the Pittsburg team have been accused of being drunkards and bums. These accusations have been basely false. Lefty Leifield has, for some reason or another, come in for more censure from the fans than

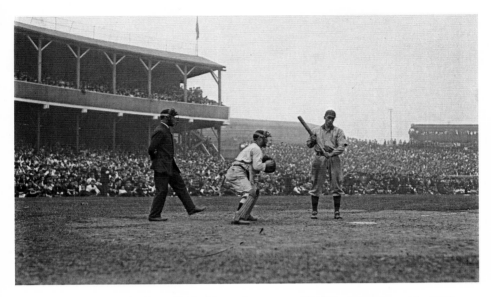

The Pirates meet the New York Giants in a game during the memorable 1908 National League pennant race. Both teams finished one game behind the pennant-winning Cubs (courtesy of Library of Congress, Bain Collection, Prints & Photographs Division, 2289u).

any other member of the team, but I am positive as I am of anything that the St Louis boy has not touched a drop of intoxicating liquor since last June. He never did it to excess, but when he saw that his taking a drink of beer was starting ugly stories about his habits, he cut it out altogether. And I did not ask him to do it either."[3]

An impassioned Dreyfuss further went on to say "I never demand that my players be teatotalers — never did demand it. All that I ask is that they keep themselves in condition to play ball. There never was a more earnest ball player than Leifeld, and I am at a loss to understand why the fans should have seen fit to roast them as they have done. He is always willing to do work. If I needed a man for some extra task, I always called on 'Lefty' because I knew I would not be turned down."[4]

There was reason for concern, since after winning 20 games in 1907, Leifeld fell to 15–14 in 1908. The Pirates would need him at his best the following year if they wanted to halt the three-year hold the Cubs had on the National League crown.

Perhaps the biggest news of the offseason was the plan for a new facility. Exposition Park, where the team currently played, was a wooden structure located off the banks of the city's three rivers that had a tendency to flood

Pitcher Howie Camnitz had marquee season in 1909 for the Pirates, going 25–6 with a league-leading .806 winning percentage (courtesy of Library of Congress, Bain Collection, Prints & Photographs Division, 15679u).

often. Dreyfuss bought land far from the shore, about three miles from it to be exact, in the Oakland section of the city, where he planned to built a spectacular monument to baseball in Pittsburgh that would be ready in July 1909. He named it Forbes Field, after the famous British general from the French and Indian War, John Forbes. The first steel and concrete facility in the National League would give more fans a chance to see the Bucs, as Forbes Field would house over 30,000 fans compared to just 6,500 at Exposition Park.

The construction of the stadium was expected to be a financial boom for the club, following a year in 1908 when the city of Pittsburgh fell on some hard times. Attendance was disappointing at Exposition Park due to an economic downturn that hit Western Pennsylvania especially hard, forcing many mills to close down for much of the year. With the election of William Howard Taft as U.S. president in 1908, the situation looked to improve, with the mills expected to reopen. Combined with the fact that the city was about to get baseball's premiere park, one could see why Dreyfuss was excited about the possibilities of 1909.

With the Pirate owner busy planning his majestic stadium, there was plenty of fanfare about his team in the offseason. Howie Camnitz was incensed when a newspaper reporter wrote a story claiming he was drinking too much and should go home to prepare for the upcoming season. An angry Camnitz, threatened to visit his office and show him how upset he was. Manager Fred Clarke came to his defense, claiming he never forbid his players from drinking and would never demand control of them in the offseason.

There were also rumors, unfounded ones, that the American Association and the American League were both looking seriously at Pittsburgh to place a team to compete with the Pirates.

Honus Wagner was at the base of some rumors also, regarding an investment in an oil well that was about to come through. According to *The Sporting News*, "Wagner told his friends to go with him and he would show them something. A large party visited the farm where the oil was pouring forth in large quantities, and it is said that the prospects are that the company with which Wagner is identified has made a rich strike."[5]

While the fortunes in the Wagner household were beaming in the offseason, those for his teammate Tommy Leach, unfortunately, were not. He lost his wife, who passed away after suffering from ill health for many years, leaving behind her husband as well as the couple's young son Nathan.

Rumors aside, player decisions still needed to be made in order for the Pirates to battle the Cubs for the National League crown. One area the Bucs looked for a big improvement was first base. Manager Clarke was looking to

6-foot, 185-pound Bill Abstein, who had spent the summer of 1908 with Providence of the Eastern League hitting .272 with five homers.

In 1908, four men tried to solidify the first base position, including Harry Swacina, Jim Kane, Warren Gill and Alan Storke. Storke came the closest to permanently securing the job at first, with a .252 mark. There were also reports that the Pirates were interested in picking up Cincinnati first baseman John Ganzel, who had been waived by the Reds in the offseason. Dreyfuss did not consider the 34-year-old first baseman, who had doubled as the Reds manager in 1908, as an upgrade from what he already had, so he passed on the opportunity to pick him up. It was Abstein, though, who Dreyfuss thought would finally be his person at first, as both he and Clarke made no deals for a more established player there.

The outfield was also somewhat of a weak link for Pittsburgh in 1908, as 35-year-old Fred Clarke had an unusually poor season for the .312 lifetime hitter, with a below average .265 mark, the lowest in his career at that point. Rookie Chief Wilson hit only .227, but improved as the year went on, while Roy Thomas, who was purchased from Philadelphia in June, added some stability. The 34-year-old was not the long-term answer though. It was thought that Thomas would either be released or retire in the upcoming season. Spike Shannon, who was selected off waivers from the Giants after leading the National League in runs in 1907, Danny Moeller and Beals Becker added little help off the bench as all three reserve outfielders hit below .197. Clarke thought about moving Storke to third base, which would make room for Abstein to be the regular at first and send Tommy Leach to the outfield to combine with Clarke and Chief Wilson. Leach would then replace Thomas who cooled off in 1908 as the year went on. The offseason thoughts, though, were put on hold for the time being.

There were some positive prospects for 1909. It was thought that Wilson would continue his improvement from his rookie campaign and become a solid contributor. The Bucs also had three very intriguing outfield prospects. Ham Hyatt was purchased from Vancouver before the 1909 campaign began. Nicknamed the "Washington Giant," Hyatt was thought to be an outstanding fielder with an accurate arm. A Seattle writer believed Hyatt to be "a counterpart of the famous Sam Thompson for many years right fielder of the Philadelphia club, with the exception that is he faster on his foot and starts out quicker for fly balls. Given a fair chance, he will make good anywhere."[6] Also in the fold to try and take Thomas' spot was Hughie Tate, who hit .320 with Marion in the Ohio State League, and George Landreth, who hit .300 with Topeka and Louisville in 1908.

As the spring went on, Hyatt began to fade; he was not only never going to be the heir apparent to Thomas, but he would struggle to make the final roster. Ward Miller showed enough talent to start the season at center, but quickly was sent to the bench in favor of Leach. While Tate and Landreth did not make the team, neither of the young outfielders impressed Clarke, who eventually was forced to move Leach into center between Wilson and Clarke as he thought about earlier. The move did make a weak situation in 1908 look very strong for the upcoming season, but it also completely muddled the situation at third.

With Leach in center, it pushed Dreyfuss and Clarke to look at potential options at third. One such player was a 19-year-old from Elmira of the New York State League by the name of Jimmy Esmond. Esmond hit only .213 in 1908, but *The Sporting News* claimed that he could be the next coming of Johnny Evers.[7] The Bucs management decided that while Esmond seemed more mature than they had originally thought, they would send him back to the minors to get more experience, fully expecting him to wear a Pirate uniform sometime in the future.

Another option that the Bucs were seriously considering was a proposed deal with the Cardinals swapping Storke for feisty third baseman Bobby Byrne. The deal reportedly fell through in 1908, but was apparently still alive in spring training.

With the rumored trade still unfulfilled, Dreyfuss inked another third baseman with major league experience. Jap Barbeau played briefly with Cleveland in 1905 and 1906 before hitting .282 with Toledo of the American Association in 1908. Barbeau felt if he didn't make it at third, he could compete for Abbatacchio's slot at second or be a backup at short. With Esmond being sent down and the trade for Byrne still on hold, Clarke opted for Barbeau to start at third after Miller failed in center and Leach moved to there to replace him.

At second base, rumors were going around that Clarke and Dreyfuss were trying to replace Ed Abbaticchio. The 31-year-old had held the spot for the Bucs in 1907 and 1908, hitting .262 and .250, respectively. *The Sporting News* reported that, despite the rumors, "Abbaticchio played excellent ball all season and ranked high among second basemen. He was a consistent performer, although many of the fans failed to give him the credit that was coming to him. There is no doubt that he will be found covering second base for the Buccaneers in 1909."[8] What would be in doubt was whether or not the veteran second baseman would sign with the club, as he was reportedly unhappy with Dreyfuss' first offer. Dreyfuss refuted the reports claiming he had yet to make Abbaticchio an offer. The second baseman ended all questions by quickly signing a contract with the club.

While all seemed well at the time, as he was in the fold, there was some doubt that Abbatacchio would be able to keep his starting job. In January, the team announced that it had signed a young second baseman by the name of John B. "Dots" Miller, who was thought to be a good player but not a finished one at this point. As the spring went on, Miller seemed to be the one new player that made the best impression on Pirate management. In the off-season, Dreyfuss had a dispute with Cleveland of the American League in regards to signing Miller. The case went to the National Commission, which sided with the Pirates. Both he and Clarke seemed very pleased that they had won that battle as they decided to keep Miller on the final roster. The young rookie quickly developed a rapport with Hall of Fame shortstop Wagner, who took him under his wing and roomed with Miller on the road. Wagner was very impressed with his skills. While Abbatacchio kept his starting job at second base, Miller was ready in case the veteran slipped.

There were no such controversies at shortstop as the Bucs possessed one of the greatest players ever to take the diamond in Wagner. The only such controversy came in rumors that occurred in the offseason. The first was the Wagner would retire. Then when he didn't show up at spring training in Hot Springs, Arkansas, there were tales he was attending to his businesses in Carnegie. Finally there was one that he had broken his arm in a basketball game, which was also unfounded.[9] He finally announced that he would miss most of spring training, opting to join the team on April 11 when they stopped in Terre Haute, Indiana, right before the season would begin.

Behind the plate, George Gibson was in complete control of the catcher position, getting ready in the offseason by chasing jackrabbits. Behind Gibson was more of a question, with Clarke having to decide whether or not to release veteran Eddie Phelps and go with Pat O'Connor as Gibson's main backup.

On the mound, rumors persisted that one of the greatest hurlers the franchise had or would know, Deacon Phillippe, had seen his last days on the mound and would not return for the 1909 campaign. The 1903 World Series hero, who was 36 years old and had pitched for nine seasons, winning 20 games or more on six occasions during that time period, seemed to be at the end of his career, only tossing 12 innings in 1908. Phillippe recanted, claiming he was feeling better than he had in the previous two seasons and wanted to give the game another shot as long as he felt he could still pitch. The other components to a great starting rotation seemed to be in order with Sam Leever, Howie Camnitz, Nick Maddox and Vic Willis all coming off solid campaigns.

Willis, like Wagner, was also rumored to be considering retirement, claiming that he was tiring of the game. A letter was said to be circulating around from Willis concerning this, but Dreyfuss was unaware that a letter existed and expected Willis to sign. Even though the veteran hurler didn't retire, he went on a prolonged holdout; he was the last Pirate to sign a contract, sending it back to Dreyfuss with a letter explaining the compensation was not enough. The Pirate president reportedly offered Willis $4,100, a raise of $200 over his 1908 pay comprised of $3,500 in a base salary plus a $400 bonus he received in the fall. The future Hall of Famer held out for $5,000 and did not report for spring training. He claimed he would not give in, which is exactly the same attitude Dreyfuss had. Angry with Willis, Dreyfuss pulled his offer, lowering it to the $3,500 base salary of 1908. Finally after both sides held firm, Willis gave in and accepted the sum, saving Dreyfuss $600 from his original offer.

With Willis now in camp, things were looking very positive for the Bucs pitching staff. Leifield showed up to camp especially early and reportedly looked in exceptional shape in his attempt to shake off his less than stellar 1908 performance. Maddox was a player who in the past did not go out of his way to get in shape during spring training. He decided this year to follow Leifield's lead and got into reportedly the best shape of his career. A young Sam Frock also looked impressive early on. The 26-year-old right-hander, whom the Bucs purchased from Providence of the Eastern League, had one year of major league experience with Boston in 1907 and was trying to secure a spot on the Pirate staff. The other two prospects on the mound that impressed Clarke were Phillip Sitton and Bill Powell. Powell, who played basketball for Homestead in the offseason to keep in shape, had an impressive curve, which helped him make the staff along with both Frock and Sitton.

There was one other hurler that seemed to have a step up on making the opening day roster. He was a rookie pitcher that had a taste in the majors with the Cardinals in 1906 and Pirates in 1907 by the name of Babe Adams. Adams looked like he had impressive stuff to Clarke. In just a few months Adams would go from a man who had hoped to make the final cut of the Bucs roster to a legend in Pirate lore.

The season began on April 14 at the Palace of the Fans on Cincinnati, with Howie Camnitz shutting down the Reds, 3–0. Pittsburgh lost the next three and stood at 6–6 following an 8–2 trouncing of the Cardinals in St Louis on April 28.

When Ed Abbatacchio played poorly, both at the plate and in the field, Clarke decided to insert his rookie second baseman Dots Miller into the starting lineup. This proved to be a master stroke as Miller held on to the starting position throughout the rest of the campaign.

What also bothered the Bucs at the end of April was the weather. Rains proved very clearly why Forbes Field was a necessity when the rivers reached their flood levels, entering the outfield of Exposition Park to cause the cancellation of a three-game series with the Cubs. While this hurt the club financially, costing Dreyfuss potentially big gates with the defending world champions coming to town, it also gave the struggling club a sorely needed break. After the break, Pittsburgh reeled off seven consecutive victories, sweeping a four-game series at Chicago before winning the first three games against St. Louis at home.

Clarke had decided to keep 12 pitchers on his roster early on and needed them often, especially in the series against the Cardinals when they won two consecutive 6–5 decisions. Babe Adams also showed Clarke just what a special pitcher he was going to be, tossing a 1–0 gem against the Cubs in his first start for the Bucs, pitching out of very tough situations on a few occasions to secure the impressive shutout. Adams' second start did not go as well. The Cardinals ended the Bucs seven-game win streak by crushing the rookie hurler, 8–0, dropping their home record at Exposition Park to 4–3.

Things also looked bleak at first base where Abstein, who looked good early on, came down with a case of tonsillitis. Clarke thought about having Hyatt take over first in the St. Louis native's absence. Instead he looked towards a player who was working on his studies at Harvard Law School at the time, who had hit .252 for the Bucs in 219 at-bats during the 1908 campaign, Alan Storke. Storke had signed a contract in December, but asked Dreyfuss if he could have time off in June to take his law exams. Fearing that Storke couldn't give 100 percent to both school and baseball until his exams were over, he originally suggested to Storke that he stay at Harvard until his exams were done.

Despite the illness to Abstein, the club continued to have an extremely successful May with a 20–6 mark for the month, pushing their overall record to 26–12. After defeating the Cubs in a doubleheader on May 30, they moved into first place following a one-day stop in second. The team would hold first place for the rest of the season.

With the team moving along so well Clarke decided he no longer needed so many pitchers and decided to sell Charlie Wacker to Milwaukee of the American Association. They also sold Phil Sitton, who never pitched a game for the club in his short time in Pittsburgh, to Jersey City. The offense started to roll as Abstein returned to the lineup and Dots Miller continued to surprise the National League with his early success, making Abbatacchio an afterthought at second. The relationship between the new double-play combination of Wagner and Miller continued to be close as Miller now was staying at the Wagner household during the year. The Hall of Fame shortstop took pride in teaching Miller the proper way to play the game, which helped the young rookie to continue to succeed in the major leagues.

With the new players playing well, Pittsburgh continued to succeed in June on the strength of a 14-game win streak. Their once meager 4–4 record at Exposition Park now stood at 16–4. After Sam Frock defeated the Dodgers, 8–2, on June 15, the team stood at 36–12, five games ahead of defending-champion Chicago.

Dreyfuss also was looking for another southpaw to complement Lefty Leifield so he sent Ward Miller to Cincinnati for Kid Durbin. Durbin, who won 32 games for Joplin of the Western Association in 1906 and spent a season with the Cubs in 1907, wasn't the answer the Pirate president was looking for and was cut by the end of July.

While Bucs were doing extremely well as a team, Abstein once again came up lame with a sore right shoulder. Clarke made an appointment for him with a doctor when it appeared that the arm was getting no better. When the doctor found that there was a displaced ligament in the arm, Abstein sat once again. This time Hyatt was sent in as his replacement.

At the beginning of the year Hyatt was a candidate for a starting spot in the outfield and when Chief Wilson started off poorly, it was thought he might get a shot in rightfield. Wilson eventually improved at the plate and in the field, giving the Bucs a solid trio in the outfield, keeping Hyatt on the bench. By the end of the season, Wilson became one of the Bucs most relied-upon players as his weakness of 1908, his offensive capabilities, now became a strength.

Jap Barbeau had also been a pleasant surprise to the club at third base. The once erratic fielder was now more consistent.

Pennant fever was alive in Pittsburgh, but Clarke warned Pirate fans and reporters there was still a long way to go. He also pointed out to all, including his players, that the joy, could in fact, be a fleeting thing, saying "We now have won 10 straight games and they are calling us heroes, but if we dropped three or four in a row, the hammers would begin to swing."[10]

As the club forged ahead, the opening of Forbes Field was only a few days away. Track and field star Martin Sheridan was in Pittsburgh with a contingent of other runners, visited the construction area before he left, and deems Forbes Field "the greatest plant of its kind in the world. It's far bigger and better than the Shepard's Bush Stadium in London where the Summer Olympics were held last summer."[11]

The days of the flood-ridden wooden stadium on the city's northside were coming to an end. The Bucs sent out Exposition Park on a high note, by winning 16 of the last 17 games it played at the outgoing facility, finishing its last year in the park at 20–5 following Lefty Leifield's masterful 8–1 triumph over the Cubs on June 30. The next day, 30,338 ecstatic fans filled the

In 1909, Pirate owner and president Barney Dreyfuss took his team into the twentieth century when he opened a spectacular new stadium, Forbes Field, the first steel and concrete stadium built in the National League (courtesy of the Pittsburgh Pirates).

new architectural marvel, four times more than Dreyfuss could fit into his former stadium, only to see the Cubs win, 3–2.

Despite all the fanfare, the team had dropped three of its first four games at Forbes Field, and following the Fourth of July defeat at the hands of the Reds, were 1–4 in the first five games of the month. Even with the early July troubles, the Cubs had only cut a 7½ game deficit that the Bucs held on June 29, to 5½ games on Independence Day. The Pirates quickly returned the lead to 7½ two days later when Leifield once again defeated the Cubs, this time 6–2, on the Cubs' return trip to Pittsburgh for the club's fourth consecutive win in their new stadium.

Dreyfuss found Forbes Field to be a financial boon, drawing almost 110,000 people in its first seven contests, a remarkable figure for the time. The team also once again picked up steam on the field, led by Wagner who was flirting with .400 at this point of the season. As Wagner was succeeding, Abstein's injury problems continued to mount as he was forced out of the lineup with a spilt finger on his throwing hand. Storke came back to fill in at first as the Bucs seemingly did not miss their big first baseman while he recovered. On the mound, Maddox and Leifield were inconsistent, but the rest of the staff was strong, including Phillippe who was enjoying some success after a less-than-stellar 1908 campaign. With everything seemingly operating so smoothly, the Pirates ended July on a high note, beating the Giants, 3–1, to extend their record to an incredible 65–24.

Despite the fact the team had seemingly no weakness at this point, it didn't stop Dreyfuss from sending out scouts to continue to find talent. One such scout, Tom O'Rourke, who had signed Hyatt, found another highly rated outfielder in Aberdeen, Washington, by the name of Vin Campbell. The 6-foot outfielder with tremendous speed would not help the Bucs in 1909, but he would have a fine season in the Smoky City in 1910, hitting .326 in 282 at-bats.

As July ended, two Pirates began to falter as their rookie second baseman Dots Miller was mired in a bad slump and pitcher Howie Camnitz fell ill after the club left Boston. He returned against the Dodgers on August 3, picking up where he left off with a 9–1 defeat of Brooklyn.

Another poor note at the end of July came with the news of the death of Barney Dreyfuss's dear friend Harry Pulliam. Pulliam, who was president of the National League and was at one time a partner of Dreyfuss at both Louisville and the Pirates before being selected as the head of the league. He committed suicide in New York on July 29, shooting himself in the head. It was a moment that would affect the Pirate president deeply and took the luster off what was turning out to be a very special season.

The beginning of August saw the club's injury problems get worse when their best player, Honus Wagner, was sidelined. Wagner had slumped severely shortly before the injury, which occurred sliding into home. Abbatacchio replaced him, and while he did well, was not the equal of his Hall of Fame teammate. There were some reports that the Bucs shortstop would be out for the season with heart problems, but the Pirate faithful were relieved when Wagner returned for the final pennant run.

Despite the injuries, Pittsburgh continued to win, capturing seven in a row to begin August. By the end of the month, they finished with a six-game streak which gave them an 87–32 mark, a 6½ game lead over the Cubs, and a new third baseman.

After almost a year of rumors, Dreyfuss finally put the finishing touches on the deal that brought Bobby Byrne to the club. He sent Storke and Barbeau, who had been by benched by Clarke for two weeks earlier and had been erratic throughout the season, to St Louis. Byrne was an upgrade as Barbeau was hitting a mere .220 at the time of the deal. The Bucs' new third baseman was hitting only .214 himself with the Cardinals, but found new life in Pittsburgh, with a .256 mark the remainder of the year.

The Pirates hit a bump in the road in early September, losing three out of four to the Cubs at Forbes Field. The September 7 contest, the lone Pirate victory, saw one of the great controversies of the season, when Abstein hit a long shot into the left-field corner. Umpire Bill Klem called the hit a home run, to the dismay as the Cubs, which descended upon Klem in a wild manner. Johnny Evers had been suspended the day before for three days due to a rhubarb he had with Klem. In this game, John Heydler, who took over the reigns as president of the National League after the untimely death of Pulliam and was in Pittsburgh for this important series fearing there would be issues, fined Joe Tinker and Frank Chance $50 each and Harry Stienfeldt $25 for their part in attacking Klem in this contest.

Despite the controversy, the Cubs had picked up two games in their trip to Pittsburgh, slicing the Pirate first-place advantage to five games. However, that would be as close as it would get. The Pirates reeled off 16 wins in a row to put away their first pennant in six years and earn themselves a trip to the World Series.

The club hoped the Athletics would win the American league pennant. Since Shibe Park in Philadelphia and Forbes Field were by far the largest two facilities in baseball, such a series could produce large crowds, thus pushing the receipts to record amounts, giving each player quite a payday for their efforts.

When Philadelphia was unable to overcome the Tigers, the Bucs instead had to face Ty Cobb and the three-time defending American League champions. The Pirates took fine credentials into the fall classic, winning what still remains a club record 110 wins. Wagner ended the season with yet another batting title, his seventh, hitting .339. On the mound Pittsburgh was even more impressive with Willis and Camnitz both registering 20 wins, with 22–11 and 25–6 marks, respectively. Leifield came back nicely following his subpar 1908 campaign finishing 19–8 while Phillippe proved he was not done yet at 8–3. Adams gave Clarke a great effort in his rookie campaign ended the year at 12–3 with a miniscule 1.11 ERA.

As the World Series began, Clarke would pass by his more experienced hurlers to make Adams a Pirate legend, as Forbes Field was about to host a World Series in its inaugural season, one that would go down in Pirate lore as one of its most successful and memorable in its long and illustrious history.

1909 Pirates Regular Season Stats

POS	Player	G	AB	R	H	2B	3B	HR	RBI	BB	HBP	SH	SB	AVG	OBP	SLG
C	George Gibson	150	510	42	135	25	9	2	52	44	2	15	9	.265	.326	.361
1B	Bill Abstein	137	512	51	133	20	10	1	70	27	4	27	16	.260	.302	.344
2B	Dots Miller	151	560	71	156	31	13	3	87	39	3	29	14	.279	.329	.396
3B	Jap Barbeau	91	350	60	77	16	3	0	25	37	4	8	19	.220	.302	.283
SS	Honus Wagner	137	495	92	168	39	10	5	100	66	3	27	35	**.339**	**.420**	**.489**
LF	Fred Clarke	152	550	97	158	16	11	3	68	80	6	24	31	.287	.384	.373
CF	Tommy Leach	151	587	126	153	29	8	6	43	66	2	27	27	.261	.337	.368
RF	Chief Wilson	154	569	64	155	22	12	4	59	19	6	20	17	.272	.303	.374
3B	Bobby Byrne	46	168	31	43	6	2	0	7	32	4	2	8	.256	.387	.315
13	Alan Storke	37	118	12	30	5	2	0	12	7	1	5	1	.254	.302	.331
S2	Ed Abbaticchio	36	87	13	20	0	0	1	16	19	0	1	2	.230	.368	.264
01	Ham Hyatt	49	67	9	20	3	4	0	7	3	0	1	1	.299	.329	.463
OF	Ward Miller	15	56	2	8	0	1	0	4	4	1	1	2	.143	.213	.179
C	Mike Simon	12	18	2	3	0	0	0	2	1	0	3	0	.167	.211	.167
C3	Paddy O'Connor	9	16	1	5	1	0	0	3	0	0	0	0	.313	.313	.375
UT	Kid Durbin	1	0	0	0	0	0	0	0	0	0	0	0	—	—	—
P	Vic Willis	39	103	6	14	1	1	0	2	7	0	6	0	.136	.191	.165
P	Howie Camnitz	41	87	8	12	1	0	0	6	12	0	9	0	.138	.242	.149
P	Lefty Leifield	32	73	2	14	1	3	0	8	3	0	2	1	.192	.224	.288
P	Nick Maddox	31	67	6	15	1	2	0	7	7	0	4	2	.224	.297	.299
P	Deacon Phillippe	22	42	1	3	1	0	0	4	1	0	1	0	.071	.093	.095
P	Babe Adams	25	39	0	2	0	1	0	1	2	0	5	0	.051	.098	.103
P	Sam Leever	19	24	2	4	0	0	0	1	3	0	0	0	.167	.259	.167
P	Sam Frock	8	14	1	2	0	0	0	1	0	0	0	0	.143	.143	.143
P	Chick Brandom	13	10	2	1	0	0	0	0	0	0	0	0	.100	.100	.100
P	Bill Powell	3	3	0	1	0	0	0	0	0	0	0	0	.333	.333	.333
P	Harry Camnitz	1	2	0	0	0	0	0	0	0	0	0	0	.000	.000	.000
P	Gene Moore	1	1	0	0	0	0	0	0	0	0	0	0	.000	.000	.000
P	Charlie Wacker	1	0	0	0	0	0	0	0	0	0	0	0	—	—	—
	Total		1564	5128	701	1332	218	92	25	585	479	36	217	185	.260	.327	.353

Player	G	GS	CG	SHO	GF	SV	IP	H	BFP	HR	R	ER	BB	SO	W	L	ERA
Vic Willis	39	35	24	4	4	1	289.2	243	1141	3	84	72	83	95	22	11	2.24
Howie Camnitz	41	30	20	6	11	3	283	207	1057	1	75	51	68	133	25	6	1.62
Nick Maddox	31	27	17	4	1	0	203.1	173	801	2	72	50	39	56	13	8	2.21
Lefty Leifield	32	26	13	3	4	0	201.2	172	810	4	76	53	54	43	19	8	2.37
Deacon Phillippe	22	13	7	1	7	0	131.2	121	496	2	41	34	14	38	8	3	2.32
Babe Adams	25	12	7	3	11	2	130	88	475	0	25	16	23	65	12	3	1.11
Sam Leever	19	4	2	0	12	2	70	74	286	0	30	22	14	23	8	1	2.83
Chick Brandom	13	2	0	0	7	2	40.2	33	149	0	12	5	10	21	1	0	1.11
Sam Frock	8	4	3	0	2	1	36.1	44	154	0	19	10	4	11	2	1	2.48
Bill Powell	3	1	0	0	1	0	7.1	7	31	0	6	3	6	2	0	1	3.68
Harry Camnitz	1	0	0	0	1	0	4	6	18	0	2	2	1	1	0	0	4.50
Gene Moore	1	0	0	0	1	0	2	4	14	0	4	4	3	2	0	0	18.00
Charlie Wacker	1	0	0	0	1	0	2	2	6	0	2	0	1	0	0	0	0.00
Total	236	154	93	21	63	11	1401.2	1174	5438	12	448	322	320	490	110	42	2.07

◆ 2 ◆

THE TIGERS' REGULAR SEASON

The defending American League champions were having a much tougher time defending their 1907 title than they may have expected as the '08 campaign was winding down. The Tigers were baseball's version of a dysfunctional family and it all started with their superstar Ty Cobb. In 1908 he showed exactly how unreliable he could be as he left the club in the heat of the race for five days so he could get married.

Fellow Hall of Famer Sam Crawford expressed what many Tigers must have thought, "He just walked out on us and left us flat in mid-season."[1] Crawford further went on to say how most felt about Cobb "He never had a friend in baseball. That's a terrible thing — to play up there twenty years and never have a friend."[2]

Despite some of the controversies that the troubled superstar caused the club, manager Hughie Jennings seemed to be doing a great job trying to keep everything together to get the Tigers into their second consecutive fall classic. Unfortunately, after holding onto first place since July 13, Detroit found itself looking up at Cleveland in the standings on September 21 when the Tigers fell into second place after losing to the Red Sox, 4–3. Two days later, Boston completed its three-game sweep as the Tigers record fell to 79–61, a mere 30–29 on their home field, Bennett Park. They now were in third place behind the Naps (Indians) and White Sox, 2½ games out with only fourteen games left.

These Tigers may have been dysfunctional, but like the Oakland A's in the early 1970s, they figured out a way to put aside their differences to play championship ball. Detroit came out of its slump in a big way by sweeping Philadelphia to begin a ten-game winning streak, moving the club back into first place on September 29. With the pennant in sight, they lost to the St. Louis Browns twice, keeping the Tigers magic number at two with the final three games of year coming up in Chicago.

The White Sox were in third place, but only 2½ games back. Sweep Detroit, and they had a shot at the pennant. The Tigers, on the other hand, just needed one win, a feat that would be easier said than done. Doc White and Ed Walsh silenced the Detroit bats in the first two contests, 3–1 and 6–1, setting up a one-game match for the American League crown.

October 6, 1908, would see Wild Bill Donovan of Detroit face White for a spot in the World Series. White had pitched two games earlier, creating a fear he may be tired. The decision came down to him or Frank Smith, who had tossed six innings three days earlier. Smith looked to be the favorite, since he seemed fresher and had stats such as hits per innings and ERA that were superior to White's. Also, White had walked out on the team earlier in year. Chicago's stern manager Fielder Jones was not one to forget such act of desertion. Despite all that, Jones curiously turned the ball over to White who proceeded to show the huge throng at South Side Park that the White Sox manager did in fact make the wrong decision. The Tigers beat up on Chicago early and often crushing White, 7–0, for the American League crown.

They won the title amidst controversy. Both Cleveland and Detroit had the same amount of wins, but the Tigers were unable to make up a game against the Senators that was rained out. In 1908 teams were not required to make up a rainout that had implications on the pennant. While the league would change that rule a year later, requiring the game to be made up, for now there was no such rule so the Tigers would face the Cubs in the World Series with a chance at retribution for Chicago's one-sided victory in 1907.

Even though the Tigers were able to win at least one game this time, they still went down meekly to the Cubs, who captured what turned out to be their final championship in the franchise's history to date. For the Tigers, they had to regroup in the offseason to make adjustments, in order to take that next step, winning the illusive world championship that the Tigers sorely wanted. Jennings was confident that Detroit could earn themselves another shot at the Series, and promised exactly that to a collection of 200 Tiger patrons who gathered at a dinner for $6 a plate at the Pontchartrain Hotel shortly after their one-sided loss to the Cubs. The players scattered around the country after the dinner when it was learned that their exhibition series against the New York Giants had been cancelled, leaving Jennings and Tiger president Frank Navin to concentrate on what additions needed to be made in the offseason.

Detroit had one of the most dominant outfields in baseball with Crawford, Cobb and Matty McIntyre, who hit .311, .324 and .295, respectively. Reserve outfielder Davy Jones, another fine player, had been inked to a three-year contract following the 1908 campaign. While there were trades rumors mentioned, like McIntyre for George Stone of the Browns, with all their riches in the outfield, Navin and Jennings were likely to leave this area alone.

One thing that the Tigers hierarchy was not counting on was the sudden issue of McIntyre's health. In January, the Detroit outfielder was reported to be suffering from appendicitis, which required McIntyre to go under the knife to have his appendix removed. With the veteran on the shelf, Jones had a chance to show his worth to Navin and Jennings in the spring. He got himself into outstanding shape in the winter, according to *The Sporting News*, which wrote, "Jones looks good this winter and will be ready to jump in and take the place that Matty filled one year ago."[3]

Luckily, McIntyre recovered more quickly than what was originally thought, so it seemed likely he would be able to join the team for spring training. As he was getting ready to return, Matty was unhappy with the fact that Navin would not give him an advance for 1909, so did not sign his contract immediately. At question for the Tigers was his injured ankle that he had hurt the year before. McIntyre claimed that he had a good 1908 campaign that proved the ankle was in good shape. Navin contended that not only was his ankle still an issue, but also he now had a new condition (his appendectomy). Eventually Navin recanted, giving McIntyre the advance he requested thus ending the holdout, to give the Tigers their solid core of outfielders all under contract.

In the infield, the same could not be said. First baseman Claude Rossman and shortstop Germany Schaefer had decent seasons. Unlike Cobb, Schaefer was a player who was liked and respected by his teammates. He was humorous, a class clown, who did things such as wear a raincoat during several innings of a rainy game. He also was a very valuable, flexible member of the infield who covered a good amount of games at several positions, playing 58 contests at second, 68 at short and 29 at third, all the while hitting .259 in 1908. His flexibility was necessary since second baseman Red Downs and third baseman Bill Coughlin, who hit .221 and .215, respectively, struggled mightily during the season.

Rossman was coming off an up-and-down season. While he hit .294 and helped the club with his bat with 33 doubles, 13 triples and 71 RBIs, there were several times throughout the season that his fielding became a hindrance. This led to two rumors, one that the team was trying to pursue Hal Chase of the New York Highlanders, the other that Rossman was considering retiring from baseball to pursue a career as a teacher in Johnstown, New York. Both stories proved to be unfounded. Rossman returned to the club in 1909, although he did hold out for a short period of time looking for a small salary increase.

There were several conversations about potential moves in the infield. One had Schaefer taking over at second as his full-time position, while another had him moving to third. If third base was the move, then Downs and Red Killefer, a 23-year-old utility infielder who it .213, would be the favorites at second. If Germany stayed at second, Coughlin, the captain of the team who also struggled mightily in the Series with a paltry .125 average, and little-used Clay Perry would be the favorites to battle it out at third.

Another rumor making its rounds was that the club was aggressively pursuing George Moriarty, also of the Highlanders. This one seemed to have much more substance behind it, as it would allow Jennings to solve one of two issues. Either he could supplant Rossman at first, or more importantly give the club a huge plus at third. It was said that the club had to wait until New York found out whether or not Chase would be reinstated by the National Commission to play for the Highlanders. If so, New York would keep the star first baseman and send Moriarty to Detroit; if not, the plan was to keep Moriarty in New York.

When Coughlin decided leave the Tigers to become a minor-league manager and Downs was sold to the White Sox, it became even more of a priority to secure Moriarty. Eventually by the end of February, New York parted ways with Moriarty and sold him to Detroit. The signing of the feisty third baseman was not only important in turning what was a negative into a strength at third, but it also allowed Schaefer to have a permanent position, putting him at his natural position at second.

The tussle at shortstop was expected to be between veteran Charlie O'Leary, who was a .251 hitter in 211 at-bats in 1908, and twenty-year-old Donie Bush. Bush started the season in his native Indianapolis, playing for the city's entry in the American Association, and finished the year hitting .294 in 68 late season at-bats for the Tigers. The young shortstop wanted to secure the starting position so badly that he made the statement that he'd rather be a regular in the minors than a utility player with Detroit.[4] Bush, who eventually became a major league manager leading the Pirates to the 1927 National League title, did not have to worry about whether he needed to go to the minors to be a regular as he won the starting job at short over O'Leary. The move solidified the Tiger infield, which became one of the strongest in the league in 1909 after being a weakness the year before.

Behind the plate, things were also confused. Ira Thomas and Boss Schmidt had given up fifteen stolen bases to the Cubs in the five-game 1908 World Series, with Schmidt accounting for thirteen of the steals. He had played with pain over the previous couple seasons, even having to use three finger splints in 1907, but his arm was in question. Boss had spent the offseason hunting in the Arkansas mountains and out of communication with the team. Like his teammates Matty McIntyre and Claude Rossman, Schmidt hadn't signed his contract yet. Unlike their issues, his was one of recognition and not financial. The backstop did not think he was respected by the fans or the press and said he wanted to be traded to a team that would appreciate his hard work. While defensively he was sub-par, he was coming off his best offensive season hitting .265. Despite his request, Navin felt that Schmidt would eventually sign and take over his starting spot. Schmidt eventually did reconsider and ink his deal, so Navin began to look for catchers to back up Schmidt. Two such prospects were Oscar Stanage, a poor hitting catcher who played with Newark of the Eastern League in 1908, hitting only .197, and Heinie Beckendorf, who wasn't much better with Scranton of the New York State League with a .222 mark. Both rookie backstops eventually made the regular season roster, with Stanage taking over as the main backup.

The pitching staff, while not the strongest part of the Tiger championship club, was one that Navin decided to leave intact at this point. He committed to taking the whole staff south when they went to San Antonio for spring training. The lone one that was rumored to be cut was 30-year-old George Winter, who was supposedly to be sold to Indianapolis. Even with the reports of his departure, Navin insisted that Winter would join the club in spring training. Winter did in fact accompany the club to Texas, but he never made it back to Detroit as he was sold to Montreal, when spring training was about to conclude.

Navin and Jennings wanted all their pitchers to go to Hot Springs, Arkansas, before of the rest of the club reported to San Antonio to get some extra work. Only one hurler, Bill Donovan, showed up as the rest declined. George Mullin felt he overdid it in 1908 reporting early, thinking it was one of the reasons for his less than stellar campaign. The others just gave a polite no to the request.

Despite the fact that few showed up for the early work, Jennings felt he had a fine staff. He also had four young hurlers in San Antonio that he felt could help his team defend their crown. Ed Lafitte, Elijah Jones, Ralph Works and George Suggs all impressed their manager and would all spend time on the Tiger staff during the 1909 campaign.

With all the additions the team made and the youth the club portrayed, not to mention the two consecutive American League titles they had captured, it was surprising that Detroit didn't get the respect from the press that they most likely deserved. The Tigers were picked to finish third in the pre-season predictions by quite a few pundits, behind the St. Louis Browns and Cleveland.

On a cold day, the Tigers began the defense of their title by defeating

Leaving for spring training in San Antonio, Texas, in 1909 are the two-time defending American League champion Detroit Tigers. President Frank Navin wanted his pitchers to stop at Hot Springs, Arkansas, first for additional training but only Bill Donovan showed up (courtesy of Library of Congress, Bain Collection, Prints & Photographs Division, 3c35394u).

Chicago, 1–0, in front of 11,514 chilled fans. They went on to sweep the White Sox in their initial three-game series before capturing two straight from their rivals in Cleveland to start the season impressively with a 5–0 record. They also announced that first week of the season that the team had secured property in the city to finally replace antiquated Bennett Park and build a facility that would rival the new modern stadiums recently constructed in Philadelphia and Pittsburgh.

Detroit finished the first month with a four-game win streak and a 10–3 mark that found them in the spot where they were familiar with for much of the previous two years, first place. The remarkable thing about their record was they did it with their top two batters, Cobb and Crawford, mired in slumps. Rossman and McIntyre were hitting fine, but they didn't have the ability to takeover a game with their offensive abilities as did their Hall of Fame teammates. The fact that they sat in first place with their two biggest stars not playing to their full capabilities was indeed impressive, boding well for the team's pennant chances.

The pitching, led by Mullin who was 3–0, was in spectacular shape. The 28-year-old hurler seemed to be correct by not going to Hot Springs. Also dominant were Ed Willett and Ed Summers early on.

Their new acquisition, Moriarty, showed he that was well worth the money Navin paid for him, hitting around .300 early on while running the bases with abandon, stealing home twice. The issue with the new third basemen was his sore arm, which forced him to the bench for a while as he recovered.

With the Moriarty's injury, as well as that of McIntyre, who was down for a few days also during the month, the Tigers continued to lead the American League as May ended with the club sporting a 25–12 record, three games in front of Philadelphia. Despite the fine record, things were not as positive as they appeared in the standings.

Reports of the club's discontent surfaced again after a bit of a rough stretch towards the end of the month. The team asked waivers on 32-year-old veteran southpaw Ed Killian, who had a nice game in his first start of the season in mid–May, because reportedly Jennings was enamored with rookie lefty Kid Speer. In a game against the Athletics on May 22, which Speer started, *The Sporting News* reported that "certain Tigers apparently made no effort to play ball."[5] The players who apparently were at the root of this lack of effort were McIntyre, Schaefer and O'Leary. All liked Killian, but McIntyre was especially close to the hurler. The team and Speer was crushed by Philadelphia, 7–1, which put the Tigers temporarily in second.

Another source of discontent came with the apparent promotion of Stanage to be the number one catcher in place of Schmidt. Schmidt's friends on the team claimed the demotion was due to retribution by Jennings for the catcher's prolonged holdout in the spring.

In the infield O'Leary had moved out of his normal position at short to third base for the first time in his career, to cover for the injured Moriarty. After he spent a couple weeks on the bench recovering, Jennings inserted Moriarty at first, replacing Rossman, who was now mired in a bad slump. Worse than his cold hitting, Rossman had developed a mental block in regards to his throws. In practice he was fine throwing the ball around, but during the game, he became so fearful he'd make a bad throw, that he often did.

With all that was going on, this team of discontent was still winning, sweeping the White Sox to end May and taking two of three against Boston to begin June. After toying with the idea of releasing their first baseman the Tigers decided to keep Rossman after seeing how much interest there was out there for him. Even though they kept the big first baseman from Philmont, New York, he was now be relegated to late inning pinch-hitting roles. While for the time being, the club kept Rossman, but it did cut ties with Lafitte, as he went to Providence to work on his pitching.

Following the defeat of Boston in the first series of June, the club began to struggle, winning only four of their next ten games. The team stopped hitting during that time period, going 23 straight innings without a run and losing twice to the eighth-place Senators. The pitching also struggled as Mullin was out a few days due to illness and their other top hurler, Ed Summers, was not pitching his best. Moriarty and several others including Wild Bill Donovan were also sidelined with an illness. *The Sporting News* surmised it might have been from either bad water or something the team ate when they were in Washington playing their ill-fated series.[6] Whatever it was, with Moriarty out again, it gave Rossman a chance to reclaim his spot at first and he began to hit well.

Rossman wasn't the only one on a hot streak as Cobb also finally caught fire. With their superstar now hitting at a level Detroit fans had become accustomed to, things eventually turned around for Detroit as they reeled off ten wins in a row, eight victories coming against St. Louis and two versus Chicago to stretch their league lead to six games over Philadelphia. The Tigers ability to hit left-handed pitching was also on display as nine games were against southpaws during the streak. Mullin came back and continued to pitch exceptionally well, winning ten in a row himself on his way to a league-leading 29 victories. Moriarty was not part of the streak as his illness turned out to be more serious than expected.

Moriarty eventually returned to the lineup in the beginning of July, supplanting O'Leary at third, who had began to slump. While the team was happy the feisty third baseman returned, the pitching staff began to break down. Mullin, who had been the dominant pitcher not just for Detroit but in the entire circuit, showed the strain of his incredible amount of work and stayed home to rest when the team went to Cleveland to face the Naps. Donovan also stayed back in Detroit as he suffered from several maladies that ranged from a sore arm to a sore knee and even a reported kidney ailment. Mullin did eventually join his teammates against the Indians, losing 4–3 on July 7.

The pitching issues led to the first prolonged slump of the season for the defending champions losing five in a row and six of seven games to their nearest rivals in the Indians and Athletics. Shortly after the losing streak, Donovan returned to the club and Mullin began to pitch the way he had been. Wild Bill defeated the Senators in his return, 9–5, on July 15, and Mullin, after suffering his defeat in Cleveland and a 7–1 loss to Philadelphia, beat New York, 9–2, on July 18, lifting the Tigers to a 51–28 record. The month continued to be a roller coaster, winning five in a row and seven of eight in the middle before dropping five of six at the end. The final two of the losing streak, a doubleheader loss to Boston, saw what had been a 7½ game lead only seven days before over the Athletics drop to a mere two-game margin.

Jennings played around with the lineup looking for a spark, putting Red Killefer in at second for Schaefer, while sending Crawford to first and placing Davy Jones at center. The results did nothing to help the struggling Tigers. They went into Philadelphia and proceeded to lose three out of four to the Athletics, prompting a two-way tie for the AL crown. A few days later following two consecutive defeats at the hands of Chicago, the Tigers were looking up at Philadelphia in the standings, 1½ games back in second.

With the club reeling and the Athletics surging, Jennings looked for answers, putting O'Leary at second for Killefer. There were also rumors brewing that a trade between the Senators and Tigers would sent Schaefer to Washington in exchange for second baseman Jim Delahanty. The rumors turned out to be reality as the popular Tiger was sent packing to the nation's capital. Delahanty brought with him a reputation as a solid defensive player who was

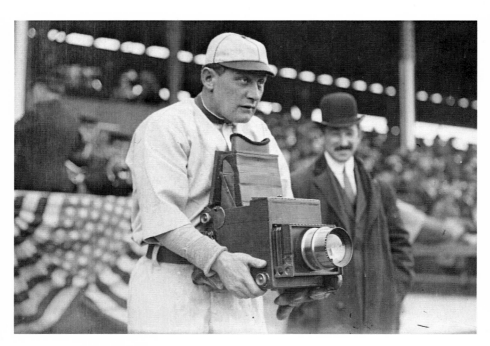

Second baseman William "Germany" Schaefer was with the Tigers for their first two American League championships. He did not remain for the third in 1909 as he was dealt to Washington in August for Jim Delahanty (courtesy of Library of Congress, Bain Collection, Prints & Photographs Division, 0931u).

a good right-handed hitter, finishing 1908 with a .317 average. He became expendable as he was in a prolonged slump with the Senators, hit hitting only .222. His new surroundings with a contending team sparked the .283 career hitter and gave Jennings, who had constant infield issues in his two years as the Tiger manager, a solid infield everywhere but first.

Navin and Jennings promptly took care of its hole in the infield by sending Rossman to St. Louis for their first baseman, Tom Jones. Jones was not considered a great player at the time, but he enjoyed his new surroundings. He got off to a great start with a single, double and sacrifice hit in his first game as a Tiger while hitting .281 in Detroit over the last month and a half of the season. As for their former first baseman, Rossman refused to report to the Browns, hoping that his holdout would prompt St. Louis to move him from first base, where he had become a very insufficient fielder, to the outfield. The Browns did give into his demands, for only two games, as he went one for eight in his very abbreviated St. Louis career, the last eight at-bats in his five-year major league career.

Finally the team was completely healthy except for McIntyre, who hurt his throwing hand, as the team was now set up for a strong September run. A fourteen-game winning streak at the end of August and early September saw the club take control of the pennant race, turning their 1½ game deficiency into a 4½ game advantage by September 2. Jones gave them consistent play defensively at first and Delahanty, who was not the best sportsman with umpires but had been a model citizen with the Tigers, played solid at second. Cobb continued his torrid pace and was having a fine season, but as usual found himself in the middle of controversy wherever he went. There was an episode where he horribly beat up an African-American house detective, causing a legal episode that would plague his efforts in the 1909 World Series. He was also loudly being criticized for spiking Athletics' third baseman Frank "Home Run" Baker, cutting his right arm while sliding into third. Despite all the troubles that constantly followed the Tiger superstar, he was well on his way to his third consecutive batting crown as he had a huge lead over Philadelphia's Eddie Collins.

Joining Cobb in the outfield in September was Davy Jones who also was on fire, hitting .429 with 27 hits in 17 games since he took over for McIntyre. Jones suffered a minor setback after his hot start, hurting his leg in early September, sitting out for a couple games. He came back immediately afterwards, taking over the starting spot in center hoping he could continue hitting at the torrid pace he was on before the injury.

The club continued to play well after their fourteen-game win streak and found themselves at 94–51 after defeating New York in a doubleheader on September 25. It gave them a 29–8 run over the five-week period. As well as they played, they could not shake the Athletics, who were still holding tough, trailing Detroit by only 2½ games at that point. Five days later following Philadelphia's doubleheader loss at the hands of the White Sox on September 30, the A's were eliminated, giving the Tigers their third straight American League pennant.

It was a banner year for the club. Cobb hit .377 to win the batting crown by thirty points over Collins, while leading the circuit in on-base percentage, slugging percentage, runs scored (over his teammate Donie Bush), total bases, hits, stolen bases, home runs and RBIs (which gave him the Triple Crown). Crawford had a league-high 35 doubles and Bush was tops in plate appearances and games played.

On the mound, Mullin and Willett both topped the 20-win plateau with 29 and 21, respectively (first and third in the AL). Mullin had the best winning percentage with an impressive .784 mark, a full 62 points ahead of Ed Cicotte of Boston.

The Tigers took their impressive statistics and put them against the best the National League had to offer, the Pittsburgh Pirates in the 1909 World Series. It afforded them an opportunity to finally put three years of frustration behind them and win the world championship. The matchup pitted Cobb against the man who was considered arguably the best the senior circuit had to offer, Honus Wagner. It was a matchup that turned out to be one for the ages.

1909 Detroit Tigers Players Stats

POS	Player	G	AB	R	H	2B	3B	HR	RBI	BB	HBP	SH	SB	AVG	OBP	SLG
C	Boss Schmidt	84	253	21	53	8	2	1	28	7	3	22	7	.209	.240	.269
1B	Claude Rossman	82	287	16	75	8	3	0	39	13	0	10	10	.261	.293	.310
2B	Germany Schaefer	87	280	26	70	12	0	0	22	14	0	14	12	.250	.286	.293
3B	George Moriarty	133	473	43	129	20	4	1	39	24	1	17	34	.273	.309	.338
SS	Donie Bush	157	532	114	145	18	2	0	33	88	4	52	53	.273	.380	.314
LF	Matty McIntyre	125	476	65	116	18	9	1	34	54	3	9	13	.244	.325	.326
CF	Sam Crawford	156	589	83	185	35	14	6	97	47	1	25	30	.314	.366	.452
RF	Ty Cobb	156	573	116	216	33	10	9	107	48	6	24	76	.377	.431	.517
IF	Charley O'Leary	76	261	29	53	10	0	0	13	6	1	10	9	.203	.224	.241
C	Oscar Stanage	77	252	17	66	8	6	0	21	11	2	4	2	.262	.298	.341
OF	Davy Jones	69	204	44	57	2	2	0	10	28	1	6	12	.279	.369	.309
1B	Tom Jones	44	153	13	43	9	0	0	18	5	3	11	9	.281	.317	.340
2B	Jim Delahanty	46	150	29	38	10	1	0	20	17	9	9	9	.253	.364	.333
2B	Red Killefer	23	61	6	17	2	2	1	4	3	3	1	2	.279	.343	.426
C	H. Beckendorf	15	27	1	7	1	0	0	1	2	0	1	0	.259	.310	.296
C	Joe Casey	3	5	1	0	0	0	0	0	1	0	0	0	.000	.167	.000
1B	Del Gainer	2	5	0	1	0	0	0	0	0	0	0	0	.200	.200	.200
1B	Hughie Jennings	2	4	1	2	0	0	0	2	0	0	0	0	.500	.500	.500
P	George Mullin	53	126	13	27	7	0	0	17	13	0	2	2	.214	.288	.270
P	Ed Willett	42	112	10	22	5	3	0	10	3	1	3	0	.196	.224	.295

POS	Player	G	AB	R	H	2B	3B	HR	RBI	BB	HBP	SH	SB	AVG	OBP	SLG
P	Ed Summers	35	94	4	10	1	0	0	3	4	0	3	0	.106	.143	.117
P	Ed Killian	25	62	4	10	0	0	0	0	2	0	3	0	.161	.188	.161
P	Bill Donovan	22	45	6	9	0	0	0	1	2	1	5	0	.200	.250	.200
P	Kid Speer	13	25	1	3	0	0	0	2	2	0	0	0	.120	.185	.160
P	Ralph Works	16	17	2	1	0	0	0	0	0	0	0	0	.059	.059	.059
P	George Suggs	9	15	0	1	1	0	0	0	1	0	1	0	.067	.125	.133
P	Bill Lelivelt	4	6	0	2	0	0	0	0	2	0	0	0	.333	.500	.333
P	Ed Lafitte	3	4	0	1	0	0	0	0	0	0	0	0	.250	.250	.250
P	Elijah Jones	2	4	1	1	0	0	0	0	0	0	0	0	.250	.250	.250
	Total	1561	5095	666	1360	209	58	19	521	397		39	232	280	.267	.325	.342

Player	G	GS	CG	SHO	GF	SV	IP	H	BFP	HR	R	ER	BB	SO	W	L	ERA
George Mullin	40	35	29	3	5	1	303.2	258	1189	1	96	75	78	124	29	8	2.22
Ed Willett	41	34	25	3	3	1	292.2	239	1173	5	112	76	76	89	21	10	2.34
Ed Summers	35	32	24	3	3	1	281.2	243	1132	4	91	70	52	107	19	9	2.24
Ed Killian	25	19	14	3	4	1	173.1	150	691	1	45	33	49	54	11	9	1.71
Bill Donovan	21	17	13	4	4	2	140.1	121	580	0	50	36	60	76	8	7	2.31
Kid Speer	12	8	4	0	3	1	76.1	88	317	2	39	24	13	12	4	4	2.83
Ralph Works	16	4	4	0	10	2	64	62	256	0	19	14	17	31	4	1	1.97
George Suggs	9	4	2	0	5	1	44.1	34	162	1	12	10	10	18	1	3	2.03
Bill Lelivelt	4	2	1	0	2	1	20	27	85	0	12	10	2	4	0	1	4.50
Ed Lafitte	3	1	1	0	2	1	14	22	67	2	14	6	2	11	0	1	3.86
Elijah Jones	2	2	0	0	0	0	10	10	36	0	3	3	0	2	1	1	2.70
Total	208	158	117	17	41	12	1420.1	1254	5688	16	493	357	359	528	98	54	2.26

◆ 3 ◆

GAME 1, OCTOBER 8

Forbes Field, Pittsburgh
Pittsburgh 4, Detroit 1

It had been six years since the Pirates legendary shortstop Honus Wagner had stumbled in his first World Series, hitting a miserable .222 with only 3 RBIs as heavily favored Pittsburgh fell in the best-of-nine Series, five games to three, to the upstart American League champions from Boston. Six long years intervened until he got his opportunity to make amends, an opportunity that finally came to be on a gorgeous fall day in the Bucs' sparkling new facility, Forbes Field.

For ten seasons since he came over from the Louisville Colonels in 1900, the Carnegie, Pennsylvania, native established himself as not only one of the greatest players of the decade, but arguably one of the top five in the history of the sport. Despite his seven batting titles to that point of his career (he would win his eighth and final crown two years later in 1911) and his five stolen base titles while sitting atop the senior circuit leader board in RBIs four times (a fifth would come his way in 1912), it was his less than stellar performance in the first fall classic that was an albatross around his neck.

The press and fans alike questioned his courage and ability as a clutch player after the Bucs' collapse in 1903. A Boston correspondent for *The Sporting News* claimed that while "Wagner is a fast, gingery player he is not a wonder as regards courage.... I am half inclined to think that old Honus has some yellow in him."[1] His hometown paper *The Pittsburgh Dispatch* concluded that if Wagner had played to his potential, the Bucs would have won ... but writer Frank McQuinston simply stated "But Wagner didn't."[2]

Wagner was a proud man and even though he continued his assault on baseball's record book in the ensuing six campaigns, it was still something that weighed heavily on him. As the quintessential team player, the Dutchman felt he left his teammates down in 1903, something that he had difficulty getting over. In baseball great Christy Matthewson's book, *Pitching in a Pinch*, the Hall of Fame pitcher tried to explain Wagner's dilemma. "This was the real tragedy in Wagner's career. Not-withstanding his stolid appearance, he is a sensitive player, and this hurt him more than anything else in his life ever has."[3]

Despite the fact this moment had such a lasting effect on Wagner, Honus was finally getting his opportunity to make up for it. The stocky, bowlegged shortstop was at the peak of his game and was taking the National League by storm in 1909. He not only captured his fourth consecutive batting crown with his .339 average, but he was at the top of the circuit in on-base percentage (.420), slugging percentage (.489), extra-base hits (54), total bases (242), doubles (39) and RBIs with 100 while finishing in the top 10 in homers, hits, runs and stolen bases. His impressive season was pivotal in the Bucs attaining what still remains a team record 110 wins, winning the NL pennant by six and a half games over the defending-champion Chicago Cubs.

Wagner now stood on the field this day with retribution on his mind. Winning his first World Series would not be an easy task, as he would have to face the American League's current juggernaught, the Detroit Tigers.

The Tigers were the Buffalo Bills of baseball in the twentieth century's first decade, winning consecutive junior circuit pennants in 1907 and 1908, but losing both fall classics to the Cubs in five games. Detroit captured its their third successive crown in 1909 as the Tigers hung on to beat Connie Mack and the A's by three and a half games.

Their leader and the other part of this titanic matchup, Ty Cobb, had several things weighing on his mind too. Unlike Wagner, it was not the fact he didn't lead his team to victory in the Series the previous two seasons. Cobb didn't play all that badly in his first two World Series experiences, though. While hitting a less than stellar .200 in the 1907 fall classic, Cobb did rebound with a .368 average in 1908 with a team-high four RBIs. It wasn't the two consecutive losses that had Cobb's attention before this game, it was how he was going to make the trip from Michigan to Pennsylvania. He had to figure out a way to avoid Ohio.

The reason Ohio was forbidden ground to Cobb had to do with an incident that occurred in Cleveland about a month before the fall classic began. Unlike his opponent in this World Series, Honus Wagner, who was considered the epitome of a sportsman, a great teammate and fine human being, Cobb was a violent, prejudiced, angry man who was above nothing if someone had incurred his ire ... and that night someone did. After a evening out following a game with the Naps, the Georgia native returned to the Euclid Hotel about 1:30 in the morning. Wanting to use the elevator to get to his room, Cobb was told by the elevator operator, an African-American, to use the steps, as there was no elevator service after midnight.[4]

Cobb was incensed, raising his fist and demanding that he be taken in the elevator to his room. After he yelled at and slapped the elevator operator, he returned to the lobby and was approached by an African-American house detective by the name of George Stansfield, who questioned the Hall of Famer about his late night uproar. Following a short argument, Stansfield pulled his nightstick. He began to hit Cobb as the Tiger great reached for his pocketknife and started slicing the detective's hand, shoulder and hands. As the fight ensued and became more violent, Stansfield pulled a gun on Ty. Cobb dropped him to the floor and kicked his gun across the lobby after it fell from the detective's hand. The Tigers' irascible outfielder continued to cut and kick the now prone Stansfield in the head. As author Al Stump stated in his classic biography on this baseball great, "Homicide wasn't far away when a desk clerk and janitor jumped in to pin a flailing Cobb to the floor."[5]

While severely injured,

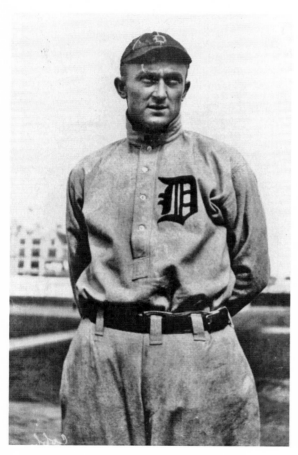

Ty Cobb came to Pittsburgh to begin the 1909 World Series in a roundabout way. He went through Buffalo down to the Smoky City instead of the more direct route through Ohio, trying to avoid Ohio authorities who were looking to arrest the Tiger superstar for beating a hotel house detective in Cleveland (courtesy of Library of Congress, Bain Collection, Prints & Photographs Division, 3b19123u).

the highly competitive Cobb did return to play the next day, playing both ends of a doubleheader and getting three hits in the first game. Despite his amazing return, Cobb was in legal trouble for the incident. Before the police could question Ty about the fight, the Tigers had left Cleveland on their way to play the Browns in St. Louis. Because Stansfield had filed a $5,000 civil law suit on top of the criminal complaint, Detroit owner Frank Navin was informed by an Ohio detective that next time the Tigers entered the state, the train would be stopped and Cobb would be "seized and brought to trial."[6]

This incident caused Cobb to have to concoct a way to get from Detroit to Pittsburgh without passing through Ohio. The method Cobb chose to avoid the state was a train ride taking him through Ontario to Buffalo then Erie and finally Pittsburgh.[7] Even by taking this roundabout way, the Hall of Famer was still worried about the authorities: "In case any cop bastards were on my train, I kept to my department and had my meals brought in by porters. My best bats were with me all the way."[8] First baseman Del Gainor found this humorous. "It was a laugh. You should have seen his coattails flying. Ty had to run for trains after games as soon as he'd had a bath. With his bats banging against his legs."[9] This method of travel increased the travel time incredibly, eventually tiring Cobb as the Series went on.

Fortunately for the rabid baseball fans looking forward to the titanic battle between Cobb and Wagner, Ty made it to the Steel City, taking his place on the field in the pristine new stadium that the Pirates now played in. These titans posed together on the field before this first game for pictures. There had been reports of a rift between the two greats, this supposed battle between good and evil, but later research has shown that while they may not have been the best of friends, there was a mutual respect between the two. Cobb said later on that he respected Wagner. The Tiger Hall of Famer even reportedly invited Wagner for a wild pig shoot in the off season.[10]

For his part, Wagner had the utmost respect for Cobb's baseball skills. When naming his all-time team years later, Honus picked his rival as the left fielder on his squad, stating that the Georgia native "comes mighty close to being the greatest ball player that ever lived ... Cobb is certainly a baseball wizard. He plays every game as if his life depended on it."[11]

Playing this Series as if each of their lives depended on it was in the cards. One would come away with his first world championship, while the other would be turned away with yet another frustration that would certainly be a black mark on what was otherwise a career for the ages.

With so much to play for, the fortunes of Wagner and the Bucs were placed in the hands of a little known hurler from Indiana by the name of Charles "Babe" Adams. Hall of Fame manager Fred Clarke had an impressive stable of pitchers at his command such as Howie Camnitz (25–6), Vic Willis (22–11), Lefty Leifield (19–8) and Nick Maddox (13–8). Add 1903 World Series star Deacon Phillippe and Bucs' great Sam Leever to the mix, both of whom were at the end of their careers yet sported 8–3 and 8–1 marks, respectively, and one could see why the selection of rookie Babe Adams was curious.

Adams was naturally left-handed and taught himself to throw right-handed "by throwing stones at tree stumps and rabbits after a childhood accident nearly severed the little finger of his left hand," according to writer Brian Stevens.[12] Babe had been taught to pitch by Walter Steckman, an opposing shortstop Adams played against in a league in Iowa, and then kept improving to the point where he became a major-league-quality hurler. After a couple fine minor league campaigns, he broke in with the Cardinals in 1906, pitching one very unsuccessful outing, and then was sold to the Bucs for $5,000. Making an appearance in only three games for Pittsburgh in 1907, the hurler was sent back to Louisville in 1908 where he had a highly respectable 22–12 mark.

Babe Adams returned to the Steel City in 1909 for his official rookie season and showed he was good enough to stay in the majors this time with a 12–3 mark and a miniscule 1.11 ERA. Despite his success, it was still a surprising decision that the Pirates legendary skipper made to start the 27-year-old rookie. According to one story, Clarke had made the call to start Adams when league president John Heydler suggested it to him after seeing Washington southpaw Dolly Gray shut down Detroit over 18 innings earlier that season. Heydler contended that Gray's style was very similar to the Bucs young hurler and thought Adams could be equally successful.[13] According to the Fred Lieb in his history of the Pittsburgh Pirates, Heydler told Clarke, "Fred, I don't know who you're going to pitch in your first game, but I saw Detroit play a late September game in Washington and they couldn't touch Gray. Dolly pitches very much like Adams; I think Babe is faster and he should give those fellows a lot of trouble."[14]

While it makes for a great story, there are historians who discount it. In the Honus Wagner biography by Dennis and Jeanne DeValeria, they point out that most likely it was the fact that Babe was the club's most consistent hurler in the last two months of the season with a 7–2 mark.[15] The DeValerias state that a local Pittsburgh newspaper even wrote before the Series began that Adams and Phillippe were the favorites to start for the Pirates in the first game.

Now whether or not it was Heydler suggesting to Clarke that Babe start the first contest or because Adams earned the spot with his performances,

Adams was thrilled at the prospects of being the Bucs opening game pitcher. Wagner would recall later on the thrill Babe got from the nod. "He asked me if I wasn't fooling and I told him I wasn't, and he hadn't better fool, either, when he got to the mound."[16]

Opposing Adams that day was a hurler who was anything but a surprise starter, veteran George Mullin. Unlike Adams, Mullin was the Tigers' unques-tioned top pitcher in 1909 who was having his best campaign in his 14-year major league career, going 29–8 with an impressive 2.22 ERA. His 29 wins and .784 winning percentage led the American League that season as he was getting ready to hopefully shut down the potent Pittsburgh bats.

Pirate manager Fred Clarke had a bevy of experienced starters to choose from to start Game 1 of the 1909 World Series, but instead tabbed rookie Babe Adams, who was 12–3 during the regular season (courtesy of Library of Congress, Bain Collection, Prints & Photographs Division, 08339u).

Entrenched in the middle of a battle between Detroit and Brooklyn, who were both vying for his services in 1901, Mullin signed with both teams, eventually choosing the Tigers because he had just married a girl from Wabash, Indiana, where he had played semi-pro ball, and Detroit was closer to Wabash. An intimidating, powerful pitcher who had a devastating fastball, Mullin was also very wild at times. A 20-game winner five times with the Tigers, Wabash George had almost as many walks as he had strikeouts, 1238 (45th on the all-time list) to 1482. The durable hurler, who is 25th all-time with 353 complete games, led the American League in free passes four consecutive seasons between 1903 and 1906 and finished in the top ten in eleven of his fourteen major league campaigns. To further illustrate Mullin's wildness, he is 20th in major league history with 131 hit batsmen.

Despite his penchant for the free pass, this was 1909 and George Mullin was at the top of his game. He only walked 78 batters in 303 innings, his sec-ond lowest total at that point of his career, while giving up but one long ball all season. Wabash George was more than a formidable challenger for the Pirates in this Series.

Watching Mullin and Adams go at each other in the first game was a huge throng of excited Pirate faithful, as 29,264 fans showed up, a World Series record at the time.[17] Bucs president Barney Dreyfuss had sold every reserve seat for the first two games. The team had planned a public sale of the reserve seats but had to cancel it, as all 18,514 seats had been sold by mail order. So popular were ticket sales that the team had to return over $100,000 worth of orders and eventually just didn't pick up their mail at the post office, instead having them send the letters back to the senders immediately. Dreyfuss had wooden stands erected in both left and right field to increase the capacity of the "largest baseball park in the world" by 8,000 in anticipation of the large crowds. There were 12,000 bleacher and standing-room-only seats that the team put on sale the day of each game. With the overwhelming antici-pation of excited Bucco fans looking to secure those 12,000 tickets, the city and team made sure that there was plenty of security to keep the swarm of Pirate faithful under control.[18]

The 29,000-plus all had their eyes on Babe Adams as the rookie pitcher took the mound to face the Tigers speedy left fielder Davy Jones. Jones had a unique purpose with Detroit, as the buffer between the fiery Cobb and his teammates. It was no secret that the Georgia Peach was not the most liked man in baseball, but as best he could, the Dixon College graduate, nicknamed Kangaroo because he jumped from team to team, tried to be his friend. "I used to stick up for him, sit and talk with him on long train trips, try and understand the man" Jones later confided.[19] Right now Jones had a seemingly less complicated job than trying to understand the fiery Hall of Famer, facing a rookie pitcher in the biggest game he ever hurled. Almost taking the first pitch of the game to his head, Jones walked on four pitches.

Donie Bush, the Tigers shortstop, came up next and laid down a bunt that was fielded by Pittsburgh first baseman Bill Abstein. Abstein tossed the ball to second baseman Dots Miller covering first, sending Jones into scoring position at second. Babe now faced Cobb with a man at second. Still unable to find his control, the man who eventually would become one of the games

Opposite, top: **Dolly Gray of the Washington Senators supposedly had the same style of pitching as Babe Adams, reportedly prompting NL president John Hey-dler to suggest to Pirate manager Fred Clarke that he start Adams. In reality, Gray was not exactly a stellar pitcher, finishing his three-year career in Wash-ington with a 15–51 mark (courtesy of Library of Congress, Bain Collection, Prints & Photographs Division, 09130).** *Opposite, bottom:* **National League pres-ident John Heydler, who took over from Harry Pulliam earlier in the year when Pulliam committed suicide, reportedly suggested that Clarke start Babe Adams, who reminded Heydler of a Washington pitcher that had success against the Tigers during the regular season (courtesy of Library of Congress, Bain Collec-tion, Prints & Photographs Division, 15266).**

greatest control pitchers of all time, with a WHIP (walks and hits given up per nine innings) of 1.092 over the course of his 19-year career (sixteenth best in major league history), walked his second man of the inning sending Cobb to first. Detroit's other future Hall of Famer, cleanup hitter Sam Crawford, who batted .314 during the season, smacked a shot back to Adams who was able to get the lead runner at third for the inning's second out.

With a chance to get out of the opening frame unscathed, Babe next faced Jim Delahanty. Not being able to take advantage of his good fortune, Babe gave up a clean single by Delahanty into left field scoring the speedy Cobb with the Series first run. Looking to add to the lead, George Moriarty hit the ball between first and second, unfortunately knocking Delahanty in the leg, making him the third and final out of the inning. While Babe Adams may have been very shaky in his first World Series stanza, he could be comforted by the fact that he kept the damage to a minimum as the Tigers were only able to score one run.

As the Pirates came up, they faced a veteran pitcher, one who had experience pitching in the last two World Series, who would not be nervous on the gorgeous Friday afternoon. Into the batter's box came third baseman Bobby Byrne. A slight man weighing all of 145 pounds, Byrne was traded from the Cardinals on August 19 for Jap Barbeau and Alan Storke. He batted only .226 for the season, .256 for Pittsburgh following the trade, but had a wonderful batting eye, walking 78 times giving him a .327 on-base percentage. This allowed Byrne to do something most .226 hitters don't do, score 92 runs, good enough for third in the senior circuit. Bobby's batting eye would not help him out this time as he hit a meaningless popup to Bush for the Pirates first out of the fall classic.

Center fielder Tommy Leach was the next victim for Mullin. A speedy centerfielder, Leach came to the Steel City along with such stalwarts as Wagner, Clarke, Phillippe and Claude Ritchey after Barney Dreyfuss ended his tenure of owner of the Louisville Colonels and purchased part of the Pirates Club in 1899. These players formed the nucleus of baseball's first dynasty of the twentieth century as the Pirates captured the NL crown for three consecutive seasons during the 1901–1903 period. Leach fared no batter against Mullin as he hit a groundball to Delahanty who tossed it over to first baseman Tom Jones for the second out. Manager Fred Clarke came up third with no better success that the first two, grounding out weakly to Mullin who tossed it to Jones completing the task of putting the Bucs down in order.

As the Bucs rookie pitcher sauntered up to the mound for the second inning, he knew a repeat of his wildness in the previous frame could put the Pirates in a hole for Game One that they might not be able to dig out from.

First baseman Tom Jones, who hit .281 for the men from the Motor City after coming to the Tigers via an August trade with the St. Louis Browns for Claude Rossman, was up first. Jones was retired on a grounder to Byrne who tossed it on to Abstein. Catcher Charles "Boss" Schmidt followed with an identical groundout to third giving the Tigers two easy outs with the pitcher coming to bat.

If Babe thought he was out of the woods with the pitcher coming to bat, he was mistaken. Mullin was a good hitter with a career .262 average (even though he hit, to that point, a career low .214 in 1909) and was not considered an easy out. Wabash George showed his hitting skills as he stroked a single to center field, bringing Davy Jones up to try and add to the Detroit lead. Jones, who walked the inning before, smacked an Adams pitch right on the button, but unfortunately hit it at Byrne, who caught the ball to retire Detroit.

Wagner came up to the plate to begin the bottom of the second for Pittsburgh in his first attempt to gain redemption for his poor 1903 Series performance. In that fall classic, things actually started off well for the all-time great as Wagner singled off Boston starter Cy Young in his initial at bat, scoring Tommy Leach for the first RBI in World Series history. This time the Flying Dutchman was not so lucky, grounding out to Delahanty. Second baseman Dots Miller who drove in 87 runs during the season flied out to Cobb in right for the second out, giving way to Abstein. In the midst of the finest season in his abbreviated three-year major league career hitting .260 with 70 RBIs, Abstein drew a bases on balls, giving the Bucs their first base runner of the game. He was eliminated moments later as he fell asleep at the wheel, getting picked off first base by Mullin, ending the frame.

By now the early game jitters were gone so the Pirates rookie hurler was pitching more like he did down the regular-season stretch when he was arguably the club's most effective pitcher. Bush started the third frame attempting to get aboard with a bunt, but he pushed it towards Adams who tossed it onto Abstein for the out. Cobb then was retired on a grounder to his rival Wagner, giving way to Crawford. A natural hitter, who had a .309 career average and set an all-time major league record that most likely will never be broken with 309 career triples, he was also a solid defensive center fielder. The three-time league RBI champion, who was second in 1909 with 97, singled off Adams for the team's fourth hit of the game. A Tiger baserunner was wasted once again, as Delahanty lifted a fly to Clarke for the third out.

As well as Adams was now doing, it was becoming apparent that it might all be for naught as Mullin continued his dominance over Pirate hitters in the bottom of the third. Right fielder John "Chief" Wilson grounded out to

Moriarity at third, defensive stalwart catcher George Gibson was retired on a ground ball to Delahanty, while Adams finished the frame by flying out to Davy Jones in left. Nine Pirates had come to the plate in the first three innings of Game 1 and all nine had been retired. Mullin was in a groove and it was becoming ever so apparent that the Tigers first-inning run might just hold up.

The fourth inning went eerily similar to the previous two for Detroit. In control by this point the young right hander once again retired the first two Tigers to face him. Moriarty grounded out to Byrne while Tom Jones flew out to Leach. With yet another chance to retire the American League champions in order, Adams gave up a baserunner, this time walking Schmidt, bringing up his mound opponent Mullin, who had singled his first time up. Unfortunately for the Tigers, George grounded out to Wagner, who tossed to ball to Miller at second, forcing out Schmidt as the frame came to an end with Detroit clinging to a 1–0 lead.

As the top of the inning had begun for Detroit in a similar manner to the second and third, so did the bottom of the fourth for the Pirates as the Tiger hurler continued to befuddle Pirate hitters. Byrne grounded out to Mullin and Leach became the Toledo, Ohio, native's first strikeout victim of the day as his dropped his bat while flailing at the third strike.

Eleven Pirates had come up and eleven Pirates gone down to begin this fall classic as the record 29,264 Pittsburgh faithful were wondering if they'd ever see the Pirate offense strike this day. The rabid Buc fans had come in record numbers. Approximately 20,000 fans had to be turned away without tickets as a huge number of city policemen had their hands filled trying to control the mayhem. Dreyfuss could have

Tommy Leach moved from third base to center field in 1909, helping the Bucs to strengthen their outfield weakness. The veteran took to his new position well, leading the league with 126 runs scored (courtesy of Library of Congress, Bain Collection, Prints & Photographs Division, 9309u).

brought in an additional 10,000 fans into the stadium, but he would have had to put them in the outfield. The problem at that point would be that every ball that was hit into the crowd would be ruled a double instead of a home run. The decision not to put fans on the field would prove to be a very fortuitous decision.[20]

Up to bat came the most successful manager the Pirates franchise has ever known, a man who also doubled as the club's Hall of Fame left fielder, Fred Clarke. The 5'10" field boss, who had a thin 165-pound frame, was a swift player as the .312 career hitter stole 506 bases and smacked 220 triples in his 21-year career. Even though his playing talent was the inspiration for his election to the Hall of Fame in 1945, Clarke's natural leadership ability helped propel this club to four National League crowns. At only 25 years old in 1897, Dreyfuss had tabbed Clarke to lead his Louisville Colonels as manager. Fred struggled the first three years, but came into his own when Dreyfuss brought his group of young stars to Pittsburgh in 1900.

One of the Hall of Famer's biggest attributes as a manager was his ability to help produce 20-game winners, a feat he did a major league record 25 times during his 19 years at the helm.[21] In the bottom of the fourth, though, it was Clarke's offensive abilities that were on display. The Pittsburgh skipper not only tallied the club's first hit of the game, but also their first run as he launched a deep shot over right field for a home run to tie the game, 1–1. Had the Bucco owner allowed the additional 10,000 fans into Forbes Field, the hit would have gone into the crowd that would have been lined up in the outfield, turning his home run into a ground-rule double. Luckily though there were no fans and the ball had sailed over the temporary fence for the first home run of the Series.

Standing at home following the blast was the great Honus Wagner. The Hall of Famer unfortunately had to face the wrath of an angry George Mullin and was plunked in the ribs, turning this respectful Series into a violent battle very quickly. Miller flew out to Cobb to end the inning but the damage had been done as the Tiger lead had been eliminated.

Trying to retake the advantage, the speedy Davy Jones led off the fifth with a solid single to right field. He was forced out at second when Bush hit a grounder to Wagner. Bush in turn was also afforded the same result as Cobb hit his second ball of the day to his nemesis at short. According to the DeValerias in their book about Wagner, this set up the single moment of the series that is most storied. According to the legend, Cobb looked down at Honus screaming, "I'm coming down on the next pitch, Krauthead!" Wagner replied, to which "I'll be ready, Rebel." The tale goes on that Cobb tried to steal second, slid hard with his spikes up, Wagner got the throw by Gibson, smashed

Cobb across the face with a tag, loosening some of Cobb teeth or even worse depending on what story you hear.[22] Good (Wagner) triumphing over Evil (Cobb) would be the moral of this tall tale.

Now in refuting this story, the DeValerias correctly pointed out that the term Kraut, a belittling term referring to people of German heritage, did not originate until World War I, which didn't start until 1914, five years later, while Krauthead was coined during World War II.[2] That and the fact that in reality, while the play was close and the Pirates argued the call, Cobb was in fact safe with his first stolen base of the Series.

While most historians consider this story nothing but legend, and the Tiger great himself even refuted it several times, including in a 1951 interview with Sportscaster Joe Clement, Wagner does make mention of such a situation in one of a series of articles he wrote for the *Los Angeles Times*. Never mentioning Cobb by name, the Flying Dutchman does say that it was common for a runner at first to yell down at Honus, "Hey, you big Dutchman, you better get out of the way down there or I'll cut your legs off. Watch out, I'm coming in a minute." Wagner said that he would yell back, "The old Dutchman I'll be down here waiting."[24] He also would embellish the story years later as he grew older.

Cobb, as stated above, would aggressively deny this version on several occasions throughout the rest of his life, calling it the "1909 Hans Wagner Hoax."[25] Arthur Hittner points out in his 2003 book on Wagner that while there had been an account claiming the Tiger trainer gave Cobb three stitches in his lip after the play, that he doubted a young star such as Ty Cobb would have slandered Wagner. Cobb in denying the story claimed that "no ballplayer had greater reverence for Wagner," and that he would have been run out of the league for making such a statement against a respected star as Wagner.[26] Regardless of what happened that day, Crawford popped up to Gibson, stranding Cobb in scoring position.

They say success in baseball is all about pitching and defense; for Detroit, the game began to unravel in the bottom of the fifth as they failed to adhere to that policy. Abstein led off the frame with a groundball to Delahanty at second. The Cleveland native, as the *New York Times* stated, made an "inexcusable fumble" and Abstein ended up on third when Cobb, backing up Delahanty, then kicked the ball.[27] Mullin followed this miscue by striking out Wilson, which brought up Gibson who precisely laced a double to center to give the Pirates their first lead of the day, 2–1. The Tiger fielding follies continued next when Adams hit an easy grounder to Bush, who booted yet another ball, putting Buccos at the corners with one out. The veteran Tiger pitcher then hit Byrne in the head, who walked to first on shaky legs, loading the bases for Leach. The Pirate center fielder lofted a fly to Davy Jones, whose throw home could not beat Gibson, allowing Pittsburgh to increase their advantage to 3–1. Clarke failed to extend the lead as he hit a ground ball to Delahanty, who did make the play this time by tossing to Jones for the third out.

Taking the mound for the first time that afternoon with the lead, Adams did something that he had failed to do the entire afternoon, set down in order the three-time American League champs in the top of the sixth. Looking as sharp as he had all day, Adams retired Delahanty, who could not make up for his error as he struck out looking, Moriarty, who grounded to Wagner, and Tom Jones, who hit a short fly to Leach in center.

As the rookie was now on a roll, the Motor City defense was definitely not. Honus came

Detroit's Sam Crawford was described once by writer F.C. Lane as the perfect model for a hitter. Crawford had a phenomenal career a .309 average in 19 major league seasons (courtesy of Library of Congress, Bain Collection, Prints & Photographs Division, 13534).

to the plate and unleashed a solid double to left. Leaning too far off second, Wagner was apparently caught leaning the wrong way, that is until Schmidt's throw sailed past Delahanty, sending the Hall of Famer to third. While Miller was unable to get the fourth run across, popping up to Schmidt, Abstein did, on a weak roller to Mullin as Wagner, running on the play, scored the Bucs fourth tally. Wilson followed with a single to center to get himself into scoring position when he then swiped second. Gibson stranded Wilson there with a harmless flyout to center, but once again the faltering Detroit defense let down Mullin.

The seventh inning for Detroit looked much like the previous five, though, as Adams got Schmidt to pop up to Miller and Mullin to ground out to Wagner. With two quick outs and Tiger hopes quickly fading, Davy Jones reached base for the third time with a single. Bush drew a walk, putting two men on and leaving the door open for great one himself, Ty Cobb, to rescue the Tigers.

Adams, who had been almost unhittable since the first inning, made one of his first mistakes since then, as Cobb lashed a shot deep to center. With the Hall of Famer's incredible speed, it looked like he would get at least a triple as two runs most certainly would score to put the American League champs within a run with a man on third. The only problem, though, was that Tommy Leach showed just how important defense is in baseball as he made a spectacular running grab of Cobb's majestic shot to end the Detroit inning and secure the Bucs three-run advantage.

After three rough innings thanks to the horrid defense behind him, Mullin finally settled down. Adams lashed a long fly ball to left which Davy Jones pulled in, Byrne struck out and Leach lined out to Crawford. But it was too little too late. Unfortunately for the Tigers, Babe Adams was in complete control and Detroit went down meekly in the eighth. The Indiana hurler retired Crawford on an unassisted grounder to Abstein, Delahanty on a popup to Miller, who ran it down behind first base, and Moriarty on a harmless fly ball to Gibson.

The Pirates threatened one more time in the bottom of the eight with a two-out single by Miller, who then stole second before being stranded in scoring position when Abstein struck out. But they had all the runs they needed. Adams put down Detroit in order one last time in the ninth as Matty McIntyre, batting for Tom Jones, and Boss Schmidt hit fly balls to Clarke and Leach, respectively, while Adams put it in the books for the Bucs by striking out his counter part, George Mullin.

It was a six-hit, one-run masterpiece that this record World Series crowd had the pleasure to witness. The great thing was that Clarke still had a stable of top quality pitchers, led by Camnitz and future Hall of Famer Willis, to send against the dangerous Tiger lineup in the next couple games in the Series. On this day, though, it was the young rookie that stole the headlines. If Heydler did in fact suggest to Clarke that he start Adams, then it was a tip with the vision of Nostradamus.

Game 1 Box Score

```
DET A    1 0 0    0 0 0    0 0 0—1 6 4
PIT N    0 0 0    1 2 1    0 0 x—4 5 0
```

BATTING

Detroit Tigers	AB	R	H	RBI	BB	SO	PO	A
D. Jones lf	3	0	2	0	1	0	5	0

Detroit Tigers	AB	R	H	RBI	BB	SO	PO	A
Bush ss	2	0	0	0	1	0	1	0
Cobb rf	3	1	0	0	1	0	2	0
Crawford cf	4	0	1	0	0	0	1	0
Delahanty 2b	4	0	1	1	0	1	0	4
Moriarty 3b	4	0	1	0	0	0	0	1
T. Jones 1b	3	0	0	0	0	0	10	0
McIntyre ph	1	0	0	0	0	0	0	0
Schmidt c	3	0	0	0	1	0	5	1
Mullin p	4	0	1	0	0	1	0	4
Totals	31	1	6	1	4	2	24	10

FIELDING—
E: Bush (1), Cobb (1), Delahanty (1), Schmidt (1).

BATTING—
SH: Bush (1,0ff Adams).
Team LOB: 8.

BASERUNNING—
SB: Cobb (1,2nd base off Adams/Gibson).

Pittsburgh Pirates	AB	R	H	RBI	BB	SO	PO	A
Byrne 3b	3	0	0	0	0	1	2	3
Leach cf	3	0	0	1	0	1	4	0
Clarke lf	4	1	1	1	0	0	2	0
Wagner ss	3	1	1	0	0	0	0	6
Miller 2b	4	0	1	0	0	0	7	0
Abstein 1b	3	1	0	1	1	1	8	1
Wilson rf	3	0	1	0	0	1	0	0
Gibson c	3	1	1	1	0	0	4	0
Adams p	3	0	0	0	0	0	0	2
Totals	29	4	5	4	1	4	27	12

BATTING—
2B: Gibson (1,0ff Mullin); Wagner (1,0ff Mullin).
HR: Clarke (1,4th inning off Mullin 0 on 2 out).
SF: Leach (1,0ff Mullin).
HBP: Wagner (1,by Mullin); Byrne (1,by Mullin).
Team LOB: 5.

BASERUNNING—
SB: Wilson (1,2nd base off Mullin/Schmidt); Miller (1,2nd base off Mullin/Schmidt).

PITCHING

Detroit Tigers	IP	H	R	ER	BB	SO	HR
Mullin L(0–1)	8	5	4	1	1	4	1

HBP: Mullin 2 (2,Wagner,Byrne).

Pittsburgh Pirates	IP	H	R	ER	BB	SO	HR
Adams W(1–0)	9	6	1	1	4	2	0

Umpires: HP — Jim Johnstone, 1B — Silk O'Loughlin
Time of Game: 1:55 Attendance: 29264

◆ 4 ◆

GAME 2, OCTOBER 9

Forbes Field, Pittsburgh
Detroit 7, Pittsburgh 2

Again the weather was spectacular, with sunny, blue skies trying to peak through the smoky air that Pittsburgh had been famous for most of the twentieth century due to the city's thriving steel factories, as both teams entered Forbes Field for the second contest of this fall classic. The night before, following their 4–1 win, many ecstatic Pirate fans descended on Pittsburgh to celebrate the Bucs' big win in a state of euphoria. As *The Sporting News* stated, "Everybody was on the street, you heard nothing, saw nothing, felt nothing, thought nothing but baseball."[1] Both teams spent their evenings at the Grand Opera House relaxing before the second contest; everyone, that is, but Wagner who spent his evening unwinding in his native Carnegie.

On the mound for the home team was a Center College alumnus by the name of Howie Camnitz. Camnitz was the Bucs best hurler during the 1909 campaign with a 25–6 mark and a National League high .806 winning percentage. The 1909 season proved to be the best campaign in the 11-year career of the Covington, Kentucky, native as he entered his third full season as a Pirate starter.

It would have been a natural move to start Camnitz in the first game, but the Pittsburgh starter suffered from quinsy, "an abscess in the tissue around a tonsil usually resulting from bacterial infection and often accompanied by pain and fever."[2] According to writer Fred Lieb, "The attack of quinsy had taken a severe toll on Howard, and he was far from his usual self."[3] While many reported that quinsy was the reason for Camnitz's issues in October 1909, others said that he simply fell off the wagon and started drinking heavily again.[4]

Whatever the issue, Camnitz had his opportunity to succeed in Game 2. During the 1909 campaign, while Camnitz utilized his powerful curveball to dominate National League hitters, he also always tried to be as well prepared for his opponents as he could. "I always inspect very closely the box score of the club we are about to meet next. My object is to ascertain what players are doing the hitting. If a player comes up who has been clouting the ball, it may be the safest plan to let him walk," Camnitz, who was nicknamed "Rosebud" due to his bright red hair, explained about his rudimentary scouting procedures.[5]

Facing the 28-year-old, 5'9" Pirate right-hander was a 190-pound New Englander from Lawrence, Massachusetts, "Wild Bill" Donovan. Donovan was dubbed "Wild Bill," not only for the fact that he had issues with control, as evidenced by the fact he lead the National League in walks with 152 for Brooklyn in 1901 as well as walking 69 in only 88 innings during his rookie campaign in 1898 for Washington, but also for his quick temper.[6] While giving up 152 free passes in 1901, Donovan also showed what a dominant pitcher he could be by winning a senior-circuit-high 25 games for the Superbas. He jumped to Detroit in the upstart American League two years later, winning 104 games for the Tigers over the next six seasons, including a remarkable 25–4 mark in 1907, topping AL hurlers with a .862 wining percentage. Wild Bill hurt his arm in 1909, causing him to drop to a sub par 8–7 record. Donovan, who had a reputation as a big game clutch pitcher, showed his mettle though in the last week and a half of the campaign by beating Washington, 8–1, and New York, 5–0, to help Detroit hold off the Senators for the Tigers' third consecutive AL Crown.

Choosing Bill Donovan to start the second contest wasn't a certain thing before the game began. While Tiger manager Hughie Jennings eventually did settle on his veteran hurler, he had to decide between his sore-armed right-hander or nineteen-game winner Ed Summers. The weather was the deciding factor as Jennings felt it would be best to start Donovan in the warmth of this October day for his sore arm as opposed to the cooler weather he might face in Detroit.[7]

Donovan took the hill in a packed Forbes Field. Pirate fans continued to show their love for their team as a then World Series record 31,114 tickets were sold for the second contest with 30,915 actually showing up to the Bucs' sparkling new facility. An estimated 15,000 other Pittsburgh faithful were

Opposite: Several of the Pirate faithful who didn't have tickets to the 1909 World Series climbed a pole to get a glimpse of the action inside Forbes Field (courtesy of Library of Congress, Bain Collection, Prints & Photographs Division, 18541).

turned away as the Pirates tried to beat their American League rivals once again to take a commanding 2–0 lead.

Left fielder Davy Jones came to the plate to start the second contest. Jones was coming off a solid opening game, where he went 2-for-3. He was able to maintain his hot streak in Game 2 by using his impressive speed to leg out a single on a bunt. Donie Bush came up next and sacrificed Jones to second, as Camnitz tossed the ball to first baseman Bill Abstein for the first out of the inning.

Batting third was the greatest player ever to don a Detroit Tiger uniform, Ty Cobb. Outplayed by his Hall of Fame counterpart Honus Wagner in Game 1, Cobb was determined to even the score. With Jones on second, Cobb had a chance to knock in the game's first run. Jones quickly took that opportunity out of the Georgia native's hands, however. Trying to pull within 90 feet of home plate, the Detroit left fielder challenged Pittsburgh's stalwart defensive catcher George Gibson as he took off for third. Gibson was an iron man for the Pirates catching in 150 of the club's 152 games in 1909, including a league-record 134 in a row. He was also a defensive catcher extraordinaire, leading the senior circuit three times between 1909 and 1912 in fielding percentage. Gibson also possessed a canon of an arm, one which had deadly accuracy for most opposing runners. That included Jones who was gunned down at third, leaving the Tigers with two outs. With the potential RBI situation now gone, Cobb grounded out routinely to Dots Miller to end the inning with no damage.

The Bucs now came up in the bottom of the first to begin their assault on taking a dominant 2–0 lead in the Series on this sparking fall afternoon. Donovan began the game with his legendary wildness as he walked Bobby Byrne, bringing up center fielder Tommy Leach. Leach, who made the defensive play of the game in the opening contest by robbing Ty Cobb of an extra-base hit in the seventh inning on a remarkable running catch to help the Pirates preserve their 4–1 win, was looking to use his offensive abilities to spark the club. The speedy Leach did just that. Byrne took off on a hit-and-run as the French Creek, New York, native lifted a blast into right field for a double, scoring Byrne on the play for a 1–0 Pittsburgh advantage.

The Hall of Fame left fielder and manager of the Pirates, Fred Clarke, strolled to the plate next. Clarke, who got the Bucs off to a great start the day before with a fourth-inning home run, went in a completely different direction on this day. The Pittsburgh skipper laid down a bunt, sending Leach to third, as he was tossed out by Donovan to first baseman Tom Jones.

With a man 90 feet away for the second run of the inning for the Bucs, up to the plate came the Pirates own legend, Honus Wagner. Wagner began

A career .236 hitter, catcher George Gibson nearly hit his career average in the 1909 World Series, going 6-for-25 for a .240 average (courtesy of Library of Congress, Bain Collection, Prints & Photographs Division, 14032u).

the process in Game 1 of removing the one blot on his legendary baseball resume, his sub-par performance in his only previous World Series experience in 1903. He now looked to add to his 1909 success. The sore-armed veteran Donovan was up to the challenge, though, as he struck out Wagner.

Now with two out, Donovan looked to get out of what could have been a devastating start with minimal damage as he faced "Dots" Miller. The Pittsburgh second baseman was coming off an outstanding rookie year in 1909, hitting .279 with 87 RBIs. As good as he was at the plate, he was equally impressive in the field topping all second baseman in assists, chances and fielding percentage after he took over the second base position from Ed Abbaticchio.

Miller became equally as adept defensively over his 12-year career at all infield positions to become the quintessential utility player. So good was Miller that journalist Ring Lardner named him to his all-time team in 1915 as the utility player stating, "The best utility player that I know anything about is Jack Miller. You can't call him a regular. He's in the game every day, but he don't never play the same place two days in succession. They're a'scared he might get thinkin' the game was monot'nous and quit."[8]

In this situation, the Tigers may have been "a'scared" of Miller as he smashed a Donovan offering into the lower right-field stands just inside the foul line for what appeared to be a home run, giving Pittsburgh a 3–0 lead. Working this contest were two of the greatest umpires in the history of the game, Billy Evans and Bill Klem, who were at the beginning of what would be sensational careers. They were confused about where the ball actually landed. They looked towards the stands trying to determine if the ball had gone into the stands, which would be a homer, or if it had bounced into the lower temporary stands, which would put Miler on second base with a ground-rule double, taking a run off the scoreboard for Pittsburgh.

According to Lieb, the umpires marched to the right-field stands to try and deduce where the ball landed. With rabid fans screaming that it was a home run, Evans asked the fans where the ball landed. They pointed to a spot in fair territory, that while a great hit, proved to the umpires that it must have bounced into the stands for a ground-rule double. When Clarke came out to argue the call asking why it wasn't a home run, Evans retorted, "Because your own fans out there showed me it was a ground rule double."[9]

Following the game, the National Commission sent for the two umpires to come to their room at the Schenley Hotel and explain the decision they made on the controversial ground-rule double. After American League president Ban Johnson asked what happened, the 25-year-old Evans made a suggestion. "You have two umpires in the game and two seated in the field boxes. Why do you not make use of the two extra men, by stationing them at the foul lines?"[10] The commission agreed and the left-field and right-field foul line umpires became a permanent fixture in the World Series the following year.

With the Pirates up, 2–0, first baseman Bill Abstein, who was embarking on a legendary Series for ineptitude, entered the game with a man in scoring position. Fouling off what would have been a third strike into Detroit catcher Boss Schmidt's glove, Schmidt dropped the ball giving Abstein a second chance to knock Miller in. Instead, Abstein looked helplessly as Donovan tossed a strike past him to end the frame with the Bucs ahead, 2–0.

The teams were at a crossroads now, the moment in a championship series or game that may define the outcome. With Pittsburgh up a game, having early success against the Tigers injured veteran hurler, and having their top pitcher on the mound, things could have gotten out of control very quickly if Detroit was unable to respond in rapid fashion. These were the defending three-time American League champions, though, a team with arguably the greatest player in the game, a team that knew how to win, one that in a matter of moments would show their National League counterparts that they were in fact not about to fall apart.

Following a relatively easy first frame, Camnitz strolled to the mound

With a capacity four times that of the Pirates prior playing facility, Exposition Park, Forbes Field enabled Pirate president Barney Dreyfuss to enjoy a financial boon. In the 1909 World Series, a record 59,459 filled the stadium for the first two games (courtesy of the Pittsburgh Pirates).

looking for similar results in the second. After mowing down future Hall of Famer Sam Crawford, who looked at a called third strike, then getting Jim Delahanty on a ground out from Wagner to Abstein, the nature of the game, and in fact the Series, took a dramatic turn. Third baseman George Moriarty came to bat and lifted a fly ball to Clarke. Instead of a third out, Clarke stumbled as the ball fell in for a single, giving the Tigers a new life.[11] Jones also enjoyed a little of the Tigers newfound luck, popping a Texas Leaguer right over third baseman Bobby Byrne's head to send Moriarty to third.

No longer another easy inning for Camnitz, Schmidt strolled to the plate to see if could continue Detroit's fortunate frame. Schmidt was not exactly the kind of hitter that would normally instill fear into a pitcher. A .243 lifetime hitter who hit only .209 during the Tigers third consecutive AL championship season, Schmidt's only notable offensive moments to this point was the fact he was the only hitter to make the last out of two World Series (1907 and

1908).[12] Defensively he also had less than stellar moments in the fall classic, giving up a record seven stolen bases to the Cubs in 1907 as well as dropping the third strike with two outs and a Detroit victory almost assured in the first game of the '07 series. The passed ball allowed Chicago to tie the game, which was suspended after 12 innings due to darkness.

The other thing Schmidt was known for at this point of his career was his ability as a boxer. The skilled pugilist fought an exhibition match against the great heavyweight champion Jack Johnson and bested his irascible team-mate Cobb several times when the two came to fisticuffs.[13] This would be Schmidt's day, though, as the brother of future Bucs catcher Walter Schmidt would have arguably the finest day of his career. Schmidt finally got the Tigers first solid hit of the day as his smashed a ball over Tommy Leach in center field to tie the game, 2–2. Camnitz struck out his counterpart Donovan to end the inning, but what looked like another easy frame for the Bucs top hurler ended up as anything but that.

Pittsburgh tried to answer back with Chief Wilson leading off the second, but Wilson hit a weak grounder to Donovan who tossed it over to first for the first out. Wild Bill lived up to his moniker once again by walking catcher George Gibson. He then faced Camnitz, considered one of the worst hitters in the Deadball Era with a .101 average, who popped up to Moriarty in foul territory for the second out of the inning. Wanting to get the Pirate offense in gear, Gibson took off for second base and was safe when Schmidt's throw was high. This set up Byrne with a man in scoring position and two outs. Whatever potential there was to take the lead again ended quickly as Donovan struck out Byrne for the last out.

After two innings, the game was looking like it would turn out to be a classic World Series struggle. That feeling lasted for only a short while longer as the Tigers came to the plate with a newfound confidence.

Jones led off, bunting once again. The ball went towards Byrne at third, who picked it up and tossed it to Abstein with what should have been the first out of the inning. Like the top of the second, Pittsburgh gave the Tigers yet another chance when Abstein muffed the throw and Jones was safe at first on the error. Donie Bush came up next and singled to left field, sending Jones to second. With the two Detroit legends coming to bat in Cobb and Crawford, Camnitz had to be at his best to avoid a troublesome situation. While he walked Cobb to load the bases, the 25-game winner was able to get Crawford to pop up to Clarke for the first out. While not in the same class as the two Tiger Hall of Famers, Delahanty came up and nevertheless had a legendary at-bat. He placed another ball over Leach's head, scoring Jones and Bush to give the Tigers a 4–2 lead.

With Camnitz reportedly ailing, Clarke had seen enough of his star and called in his 22-game winner, 33-year-old future Hall of Famer Vic Willis to see if he could end the Detroit onslaught in the third. Facing Moriarty with Cobb on third, Willis didn't even have to throw a pitch before Cobb tried to put a nail in Pittsburgh's coffin as he took off for home plate and slid across with a dramatic steal to give the Tigers a 5–2 advantage. The excited Cobb explained the play this way:

> The moment Willis took over, I decided to try for a steal. There were four angles to it. My reasoning was he would have his mind far more on stopping our rally than on me. But first I had to experiment. Willis was a 12-year veteran and smart. So far I was only guessing he'd be a bit careless watching me. As soon as he took his pose on the rubber, I walked off third a few times as a test and to disarm Willis, the catcher and third baseman Bob Byrne. Willis eyes were fixed on the signal from the catcher. I looked harmless. It was a great moment ... he'd left an opening. Just as Willis raised his arm to go into his windup, I broke for the plate with everything I had. Since a right handed hitter George Moriarity was at bat I had some protection — the screening effect of his body — for part way down the line. Gibson didn't see me at first. Willis did see and reacted like his pants were on fire. He had to check his stance in order to throw home.[14]

Willis' throw, of course, was not be in time as Cobb slid cleanly past Gibson for the tally. A shaken Willis walked Moriarty, but then was able to get Tom Jones to ground out to himself, forcing Moriarty at second, and then Schmidt to fly out to Clarke in left. It was too little too late, though, as the damage was done and the Tigers were now firmly in control of the game.

Down by three runs, Leach began the bottom of the third with a stinging double into left field, his second two-bagger of the game. The Bucs were facing one of the best clutch pitchers of the era, though, a hurler that despite his arm issues during the season had been incredible down the stretch in September when the Tigers needed him most. Donovan was about to show the Pirates that as he was just getting into a groove. Clarke came up and lifted a harmless fly ball to Davy Jones for the first out. Wagner followed with a pop out to Schmidt before Miller flailed aimlessly at Donovan's three masterful pitches for an inning-ending strikeout.

On the mound strolled Willis for his first full inning of work in his first World Series. A University of Delaware alumnus, Willis had begun his career before the turn of the century in fine fashion by going 52–21 in his first two campaigns with the National League's franchise in Boston in 1898 and 1899. By the time he was dealt to the Pirates in 1905 for Dave Brain, Del Howard and Vive Lindaman, he looked to be at the end of his career, fashioning three consecutive losing seasons, including the low point of 12–29 in his last campaign in Boston. Luckily for Pittsburgh, Willis resurrected his career in the

Smoky City by rolling off four consecutive 20-win seasons, including his 22–
11 mark in this championship season. It was his four years with the Pirates
that turned the Cecil County, Maryland, native from a very good pitcher into
one that would eventually be given baseball's highest honor with his election
to the Hall of Fame by the Veterans Committee in 1995.

Willis looked every bit like a Hall of Fame pitcher in his first full inning
of a World Series. The top half of the fourth began with controversy as Willis
faced Donovan. Wild Bill hit a slow roller to Byrne at third base, who threw
to Abstein apparently too late as Donovan appeared to beat the throw for a
single. To Detroit's dismay, Klem called the Tiger hurler out. Davy Jones was
retired in similar fashion, Byrne to Abstein, before Bush fanned for a quick
1-2-3 inning.

Once again the Bucs got off to a solid start in the bottom of the fourth.
For the third time in four innings, the Bucs leadoff hitter reached first base
as Abstein stroked a single to right field. Donovan bore down to get Chief
Wilson to pop up to Schmidt in foul territory and then Gibson on a fly ball
to Davy Jones for two quick outs. Willis came up and smashed a Donovan
offering up the middle. Unfortunately the hard liner came to rest in second
baseman Jim Delahanty's mitt for the inning-ending out.

Willis had retired five consecutive batters in his inning and two thirds
of relief when he faced Cobb to begin the fifth, who made it six on what the
New York Times referred to as a "remarkable one handed stop of Cobb's
bounder over first base."[15] Unfortunately the streak ended there. If the record
Pittsburgh throng was disappointed to this point of the game, they were now
about to be devastated. Crawford laced a shot past Byrne at third, down the
left-field line for a double. Delahanty then walked before Moriarity popped
up to Abstein for the second out of the inning. With Tom Jones up next,
Willis was looking to end the potential Tiger rally before it ever started. They
say walks kill a pitcher and Willis was about to find that out as he gave Jones
a free pass, loading the bases.

Up to the plate strolled the Tigers' .209 hitting catcher who had enjoyed
one of his best World Series moments in his three fall classics with a second-
inning two-run double earlier in the day. While listed as a switch-hitter in
baseball's official records, Bill James made the following observation about
Schmidt, claiming he was actually more of a left-handed platoon player.
"Schmidt was, obviously, a left handed hitter who couldn't hit left-handed
pitching and tried to switch hit in desperation."[16] Despite James' assertions,
it was very fortuitous for Detroit that Schmidt would be at his best this day.
Facing a future Hall of Fame pitcher, Schmidt laced a clean single to center
field, plating Crawford and Delahanty to put the proverbial nail in the coffin

of Pittsburgh, stretching the Detroit lead to 7–2. If not for a fine throw from Leach to Byrne to toss out Jones at third, as he was trying to advance on Schmidt's clutch single, the damage could have been worse.

Schmidt's two hits and four RBIs show just how close this game could have been. Twice the poor-hitting catcher came to the plate with two outs, facing two of the game's best pitchers of the era. Getting Schmidt to strike out, hit a meaningless popout or ground ball were certainly things not out of the question in the situation. In fact, odds dictated that's exactly what should have happened and in a worst-case scenario, Pittsburgh should have only been down by a single run. In this case, though, Schmidt laced two incredibly clutch hits to put this game out of reach.

In the bottom of the fifth, Donovan retired the Bucs in order as Byrne flied out to Crawford, Leach was thrown out by Moriarty and Clarke ended the easy inning with harmless grounder to The Tiger hurler.

With the game seemingly out of reach, Detroit came up in the sixth looking to turn this contest from a rout into an absolute embarrassment. Willis, though, was able to shake off the poor last inning, getting Donovan on a slow grounder to Miller and Davy Jones who tagged a ball that was run down by Leach in deep center. Bush reached first on four wayward pitches, but was gunned down by the strong arm of George Gibson.

Donovan was in a groove so the Bucs were unable to chip away at the Tiger lead. Wagner hit an easy shot to the Detroit hurler, but an errant throw put the Pirate legend on first. Miller sent Wagner to second with a roller to Bush, but the Pirates soon-to-be 1909 World Series goat, first baseman Bill Abstein, struck out as he looked overmatched by the Tiger veteran. Wagner tried to take matters into his own hands by attempting to steal third on the questionable arm of Schmidt. This was a day when the baseball gods were smiling on Detroit, though. Schmidt's throw was off line, but Moriarty made a spectacular snag of the errant toss and tagged out Wagner before he reached third base safely, ending the frame with the Tigers still up by five runs.

Cobb broke his hitless streak to begin the seventh inning when he smacked a ball past Wagner into left field. While Abstein would soon make himself known in Pirate lore for his less than questionable play in this fall classic, he made a phenomenal defensive play. The Pirate shortstop snagged a hot shot off the bat of Crawford who tossed the future Hall of Famer out at first. Abstein took the throw and ripped a toss to Byrne at third to try and catch the speedy Cobb. Byrne slapped a tag on the Georgia native for the Series first double play. Willis finished the job in the top of the seventh by striking out Delahanty.

Donovan, who began his career in 1898 with Washington as a poor-hitting outfielder as well as a pitcher of questionable talent, showed those days were long past as he continued his mastery of the potent Pirate lineup. Wilson did reach first to start the frame off, thanks to a poor throw by Delahanty. Gibson then hit a ball to Bush, who threw it to first for one and then off to Moriarty at third to catch the major's all-time single-season triples record holder for a double play. Donovan ended the Pirate inning once again with a strikeout, this time retiring his mound opponent, Willis.

With the game out of hand, offenses were rendered useless over the last two innings. Willis set down the remaining Detroit Tigers he faced, retiring Moriarity, Tom Jones, Schmidt, Donovan, Davy Jones and Bush, in order. Bush's shot was the potentially most damaging as he crushed a shot to deep center field that Leach tracked down to conclude the Tiger ninth.

Donovan did his part in the eighth as Byrne, Leach and Clarke were unable to reach first. Wagner, though, would not go down quietly as he opened the Pirates last chance in the bottom of the ninth with a stinging hit to right field. Up came Dots Miller to the plate. He now had a chance to bat with a man in scoring position as the Pirates bow legged shortstop swiped second base. Miller, whom the *Connellsville Daily Courier* noted "had a pair of bow legs just like Honus, only worse," sent Wagner to third on a groundball to second.[17] The Pittsburgh threat ended there when Donovan struck out Abstein before retiring Wilson on a fly ball to center to finish a clutch five-hit, complete-game performance.

The Tigers returned to the Colony Hotel, the place when they were lodging in Pittsburgh, in a celebratory mood as they were able to take a huge advantage in this fall classic. By splitting the two games at Forbes Field, they now traveled to the friendly confines of Bennett Park, home of the Tigers, for the next two games hoping to take control of the Series. The Bucs, on the other end, had flashbacks to their first failed attempt to wrest a World Series championship in 1903. A heavy favorite before both Series began, Pittsburgh was now in a position where the club would have to win at least once, if not twice, in enemy territory (the venue for the seventh game had yet to be decided) to give the club its inaugural fall classic crown. It was a task its leader, Honus Wagner, and the rest of the Pirates were more than capable of accomplishing.

Game 2 Box Score

```
DET A    0 2 3    0 2 0    0 0 0—7 9 2
PIT N    2 0 0    0 0 0    0 0 0—2 5 1
```

BATTING

Detroit Tigers	AB	R	H	RBI	BB	SO	PO	A
D. Jones lf	5	1	1	0	0	0	1	0

Detroit Tigers	AB	R	H	RBI	BB	SO	PO	A
Bush ss	3	1	1	0	1	1	0	2
Cobb rf	3	1	1	0	1	0	0	0
Crawford cf	4	1	1	0	0	1	3	0
Delahanty 2b	3	1	1	2	1	1	3	1
Moriarty 3b	3	1	1	0	1	0	3	1
T. Jones 1b	3	1	1	0	1	0	8	1
Schmidt c	4	0	2	4	0	0	9	1
Donovan p	4	0	0	0	0	1	0	4
Totals	32	7	9	6	5	4	27	10

FIELDING—
DP: 1. Bush-T. Jones-Moriarty.
E: Delahanty (2), Donovan (1).

BATTING—
2B: Schmidt (1,0ff Camnitz); Delahanty (1,0ff Camnitz); Crawford (1,0ff Willis).
SH: Bush (2,0ff Camnitz).
Team LOB: 4.

BASERUNNING—
SB: Cobb (2,Home off Willis/Gibson).
CS: D. Jones (1,3rd base by Camnitz/Gibson); Bush (1,2nd base by Willis/Gibson).

Pittsburgh Pirates	AB	R	H	RBI	BB	SO	PO	A
Byrne 3b	3	1	0	0	1	1	4	2
Leach cf	4	1	2	1	0	0	2	1
Clarke lf	3	0	0	0	0	0	3	0
Wagner ss	4	0	1	0	0	1	1	2
Miller 2b	4	0	1	1	0	1	0	5
Abstein 1b	4	0	1	0	0	3	12	1
Wilson rf	4	0	0	0	0	0	0	0
Gibson c	2	0	0	0	1	0	4	2
Camnitz p	1	0	0	0	0	0	0	1
Willis p	2	0	0	0	0	1	1	2
Totals	31	2	5	2	2	7	27	16

FIELDING—
DP: 1. Miller-Abstein-Byrne.
E: Abstein (1).

BATTING—
2B: Leach 2 (2,0ff Donovan 2); Miller (1,0ff Donovan).
SH: Clarke (1,0ff Donovan).
Team LOB: 5.

BASERUNNING—
SB: Gibson (1,2nd base off Donovan/Schmidt); Wagner (1,2nd base off Donovan/Schmidt).
CS: Wagner (1,3rd base by Donovan/Schmidt).

PITCHING

Detroit Tigers	IP	H	R	ER	BB	SO	HR	BFP
Donovan W(1–0)	9	5	2	2	2	7	0	34

Pittsburgh Pirates	IP	H	R	ER	BB	SO	HR	BFP
Camnitz L(0–1)	2.1	6	5	4	1	2	0	14
Willis	6.2	3	2	2	4	2	0	24
Totals	9	9	7	6	5	4	0	38

Umpires: HP — Billy Evans, 1B — Bill Klem
Time of Game: 1:45 **Attendance:** 30915

◆ 5 ◆

GAME 3, OCTOBER 11
Bennett Park, Detroit
Pittsburgh 8, Detroit 6

A much needed day off was in store for both teams as Sunday baseball was illegal in both Michigan (although tolerated at Bennett Park during the 1909 regular season) and Pennsylvania. Pirate owner Barney Dreyfuss and manager Fred Clarke were still both concerned after the dominant Detroit victory, although Clarke was still confident in his championship club. According to Lieb, Dreyfuss lamented, "I guess Detroit will give us more trouble then they made for the Cubs the last two years," to which Clarke replied, "Yes, they're stronger; Cobb is a better player, but we'll beat them."[1]

Clarke was correct, Cobb was becoming better, as scary as that seemed, but he was also a man who continued to run from the law. Once again not wanting to face the powers that be in Ohio who were looking to arrest the irascible Georgia native, Cobb bypassed the state once again, causing him to be delayed in his arrival to his hometown ballpark. He showed up just in time for batting practice prior to Game 3.

For Wagner and his teammates, the trip to Detroit would be more conventional, yet just as eventful. The Bucs shortstop had planned to stop for a quick fishing trip to unwind after the second game debacle but decided to forego those plans once he found out the rest of the Pirates were chartering a touring car to take them to the Motor City in class. The trip went smoothly until the club was about 10 miles from its final destination, when it began to rain hard. Since the touring car had no roof, the pleasant trip to Detroit ended with the Pirates team getting soaked.[2]

The rain continued for this third clash, a stark difference from the unseasonably warm weather the two clubs had enjoyed in Pittsburgh. It not only was rainy, but cold, as the showers that pounded down on Bennett Park were very icy and uncomfortable for the standing-room-only crowd of 18,277. The throng included 3,000 of Pittsburgh's loyal fans who had also made the trip up to Detroit to see if their heroes could erase the poor memories of two days earlier in this rickety old venue that was described as an "Allegheny County League ball field" by one Pittsburgh pundit.[3]

Those 18,277 were only a portion of the immense crowd that lined up in front of the facility waiting to enter to see this contest. According to the *New York Times*, "The street in front of the principle entrance was thronged before 10 o'clock in the morning, and the rush for seats when at last the gates were flung wide was so furious that it was a wonder that hundreds of the women among the spectators were not hurt."[4]

While seating was limited on the inside of the stadium, many rabid baseball fans climbed to the top of roofs and bleachers that fans had erected right outside the outfield fence to peer inside Bennett Park and catch the action, a move that infuriated Tiger president Frank Navin. In an attempt to dissuade fans from doing this, Navin had a canvas pulled along the area above the fence that did little to stop the fans from seeing the contest free of charge.[5]

Poor weather had also hit the Steel City as many freezing Bucco faithful were gathered to see the progress of Game 3 on huge boards erected at the offices of the major newspapers around the city.[6]

The impressive throng saw the Tigers 19-game winner Oron Edgar Summers stroll to the mound to pitch for the hometown team. Summers came into this game after a convincing campaign for Detroit. The Wabash College alumnus was in his second year with the Tigers, finishing with a 19–9 mark and an impressive 2.24 ERA. Summers had an even better rookie campaign, where the Indianapolis native finished second in the American League in victories with 24 and fourth in ERA, giving up a miniscule 1.65 earned runs per nine innings.

A practitioner of the knuckleball, Summers had been passed over for the Game 2 start in favor of Wild Bill Donovan, because Jennings felt Donovan would be better off starting in the warm Pittsburgh weather. Summers now got the opportunity to pitch in a vastly different weather setting. It was also an opportunity for Summers to forget about his World Series experience from a year ago, when he lost both Games 1 and 4 to the eventual world champion Chicago Cubs.

Facing Summers was 23-year-old Nick Maddox. Maddox was known in Pirate lore for tossing the first no-hitter in franchise history, when he beat the Brooklyn Superbas, 2–1, in 1907, a game which turned out to be the only no-hitter thrown at a Pittsburgh venue by a Pirate until John Candelaria turned

Pitcher Ed Summers (sitting), with trainer Harry Tuthill and first baseman Del Gainer, won 19 games for Detroit in 1909. Unfortunately, he could not match that success in the World Series, losing twice to the Pirates (courtesy of Library of Congress, Bain Collection, Prints & Photographs Division, 10297u).

the feat 69 years later in 1976 at Three Rivers Stadium. Maddox's gem came one game after his major league debut on September 13, 1907, when he blanked the Cardinals, 4–0. The Pirate right-hander went on to go 5–1 in his first major league month before winning 23 games the following campaign. While enjoying decent success his first 2 two and a half major league seasons, this Game 3 was without a doubt his marquee moment in what would be a very short career. In fact, for the Govanstown, Maryland, native this would be his first and last World Series performance.

Wagner, though, was certainly more experienced than his young pitcher when it came to experience in the fall classic. While he played well in Game 1, he still had yet to have a signature game, one that would completely erase the stink from his inaugural venture into the World Series six years before. If he was to have his big moment, it would be done in weather that the forefathers of baseball really didn't have in mind for the national pastime. The wind was blowing with a fury and the intermittent showers pelted the packed crowd with an icy fierceness.

The rain had been consistent over the previous day as well as on game day, putting into doubt whether or not Game 3 could be played at its schedule time. Despite the questionable weather, the huge tarpaulin that lay over the Bennett Park infield saved the day as the umpires deemed the field dry enough to play.

The umpire crew of Jim Johnstone and Silk O'Loughlin also made another momentous decision this day. They asked umpire Bill Klem, who was in the crowd but not working the third game, to stand next to the right-field foul line where the crowd met the field and, as the *New York Times* reported that day, "to watch hits into the crowd and act in an advisory capacity to the two other umpires."[7] Thus the World Series foul-line umpires were born, just like Klem had suggested to the National Commission only 48 hours earlier following the Game 2 controversy. With the chilly fans dressed in their warmest winter garb in their seats and the three umpires at their stations ready to go, all that was left was for the game to begin. That is exactly what happened when Pirates third baseman Bobby Byrne came to the plate at approximately 1:30 P.M.

Described by Alfred Spink as "cool, nervy and smart," Byrne was the epitome of a leadoff hitter.[8] In a short biography of Byrne by Irv Goldfarb, the author tells of a play that happened in 1911 against the Dodgers that illustrates this point very nicely. At first with his manager Fred Clarke at third, the duo tried to pull off a double steal. Clarke was safe on a close play at home. Brooklyn catcher Bill Bergen argued with Klem, who was umpiring the contest. Seeing that Bergen was incensed and not paying attention, Byrne swiped third. Miller came up and walked putting men on first and third once again. The two tried another double steal for the club that the inning, as Byrne slid past the throw thus stealing second, third and home in the same inning.[9] An avid bowler, who once threw 19 consecutive strikes that included a perfect 300 game, Byrne started off this chilly contest being the quintessential Bobby Byrne. He laid a bunt down the third base line, barely beating Summers' throw to Moriarty for a single.

Speedy center fielder Tommy Leach drove a pitch to his counter part in center for the Tigers, Sam Crawford, dropping in for a single. Byrne, taking off on a hit-and-run, strolled into third with no problem. The 37-year-old manager of the Bucs came to the plate next. Leading the senior circuit with 80 walks in 1909, Clarke wasn't as patient in this at-bat. He immediately topped the ball to Summers, who tossed it to Moriarty at third trying to catch

The Pirates solidified their issues at third base when they traded for Bobby Byrne in August 1909. Byrne hit .256 during the final month of the season, before leading the league in hits and doubles a year later in 1910 (courtesy of Library of Congress, Bain Collection, Prints & Photographs Division, 08244u).

Byrne off base. Getting caught in a rundown, the Pirates cunning leadoff hitter remained in it long enough before he was tagged out to allow Leach and Clarke to get to third and second, respectively.

This set up a great opportunity for Pittsburgh's Hall of Fame shortstop. With two men in scoring position and a baseball legend looking for his World Series redemption, Wagner began to shed his tag of fall classic disappointment with a monster game. The Carnegie native slashed a ball through Tiger shortstop Donie Bush, scoring Leach with the game's first run. So hard was the ball hit that several papers, including the *Daily Courier* of Connellsville, Pennsylvania, and the *New York Times* were certain it was a single and reported it that way in their early editions. The official scorer saw it differently, though, crediting Bush with an error instead. Regardless, the stroke gave the Bucs an early lead.

Moments later Pittsburgh stretched its lead to two when Wagner took off for second base, sliding in safe for his first theft of the day. Boss Schmidt's throw sailed into center field instead of hitting its intending target at second base, sending Clarke home with a second unearned run. Wagner went to third on the miscue. As this first inning was unfolding, it seemed to be more apt to be called the Tiger follies. Pitcher Ed Summers contributed to the sea of miscues when he uncorked a wild pitch to Dots Miller that plated Wagner.

Now with his concentration seemingly broken, the Tigers knuckleballer gave a free pass to Miller and then faced first baseman Bill Abstein, who responded with a solid hit to center field, sending Miller to third. Crawford uncorked a throw to Moriarty at third trying to catch Miller, but the throw was anything but accurate as it flew past Moriarty, scoring Miller with the fourth unearned run of the inning. Abstein went to third on Detroit's third error of the inning.

Jennings had seen enough and pulled the knuckleballer in favor of Tiger 21-game winner Robert Edgar "Ed" Willett. In his fourth season in Detroit, Willett was just coming into his own with his finest season to date in 1909, finishing third in the junior circuit in victories and sixth with a .677 winning percentage. It would end up being Willett's finest campaign of his 10-year, 102-win career. Right now he was responsible for keeping the Tigers ship from completely falling into the sea as he faced Owen "Chief" Wilson. Wilson gave Willett a rude introduction to World Series play as he laced a shot into left field for the fifth and final unearned run of the inning for Pittsburgh. Willett proceeded to retire Gibson on a grounder to second baseman Jim Delahanty and then Maddox on a pop up in foul territory to Schmidt, finally ending the inning on this dreary cold debacle of a game with the Bucs up, 5–0.

In Game 2, the Pirates gave a two-run lead to starter Howie Camnitz. He was unable to maintain it, immediately surrendering two runs to Detroit the inning after Pittsburgh gave him a 2–0 lead. The Pirates would now see if Nick Maddox could do a better job than Camnitz as he faced Detroit with an even bigger advantage.

Davy Jones led off for the Tigers with a harmless fly ball to Leach, who cradled it in his glove for the first out of the inning. Looking to make up for his blunder off the bat of Wagner, Bush also sent Maddox's offering to center, with different results though as it fell to the ground in front of Leach's glove for a single. Cobb came to the plate next to try and chip away at the Pirate advantage. After arriving at the park only moments before batting practice, Cobb was complaining about feeling "gas pain."[10] He did nothing to help the Tigers cause in this at-bat, looking at a third strike after working Maddox to a full count. Crawford ended the fruitless inning with a ground ball to Miller, who tossed it to Wagner forcing Bush out at second.

Although Ed Willett won 21 games for the Tigers in 1909, he didn't start a game in the fall classic. Nevertheless, Willett pitched well in relief, giving up only three hits and no runs in seven and two-thirds innings (courtesy of Library of Congress, Bain Collection, Prints & Photographs Division, 13806u).

If the Tiger faithful thought that their hometown club got their share of muffs and miscues out if their system in the first inning, they were extremely disappointed as the second frigid inning began. It started out good enough when Byrne, leading off for the second inning in a row, laced a solid shot down the third baseline that Moriarty made a spectacular leaping snag of. The Detroit third baseman tossed it over to Tom Jones for the first out of the frame, barely beating the speedy Byrne to the bag.

It was at that point Detroit felt very generous once again. Willett struggled with a sudden bout of wildness as he hit Tommy Leach on the hand. Up came the Bucs manager Fred Clarke who, like Leach, was about to experience a wayward Willett pitch. This one hit Clarke in the knee, sending the Hall of Fame left fielder to the ground writhing in pain. Eventually the Pirate manager got to his feet and strolled down to first base, putting two men on with Honus Wagner coming to the plate. Willett fortuitously had the only Tiger success on this day against the Pirate shortstop as Wagner hit a harmless grounder to Bush, who tossed it on to Delahanty for the second out of the inning.

Finally things looked to be going the Tigers way when Pittsburgh tried a double steal, with Leach taking off for home. Detroit seemingly had Leach for the final out when the Pittsburgh center fielder was caught in a rundown. Amazingly, Willett made his third costly miscue of the second inning by dropping the ball, which allowed Leach to score the Bucs sixth run of the contest as Wagner went into second. Miller popped up to Delahanty to end the threat. But once again what could have been a meaningless venture for the Pirates turned into a critical run that they would sorely need by the end of the game. The box score read six runs for the Pirates in two innings — none earned.

As inept as the Tigers were in the field, they were equally as futile at the plate. After Tiger second baseman Delahanty smoked a shot down the third base line for a double to begin the frame, Moriarty came to the plate to try and get Detroit on the board. Maddox completely dominated the Tiger third baseman by befuddling him as he swung wildly three times for the first out. First baseman Tom Jones then attempted to plate Detroit's initial run, but managed just a pop up to Byrne. Schmidt did no better, stranding Delahanty in scoring position when he hit a harmless grounder to Dots Miller, who tossed it to Abstein for the final Tiger out in the second.

As the third inning began the pitchers began to take control of this contest, at least control of the middle innings. Maddox continued to keep the Detroit offense at bay while Willett and his defense behind him finally showed the talent that led them to three consecutive World Series appearances. The Tiger hurler retired Abstein and Wilson on fly balls to Delahanty and Crawford, respectively. Gibson could do no better as he hit a slow roller to Moriarty at third, who charged towards home, grabbing the ball and tossing it to Jones at first, rendering the Pirates scoreless for the first time in this contest.

Maddox relied on the Pirate manager to keep his shutout in tact. Playing Willett shallow in left field, the Tigers 19-game winner surprised Clarke with a long shot into left center. Clarke took off and ran down the ball until it fell into his glove for a fine catch to retiring the Detroit pitcher. Davy Jones then lined a hit into short left field. Once again Clarke took off after the ball, catching it in what was described as a "sweet capture" by United Press Telegram.[11] Bush tapped a ball to Byrne for the third out; it was the only time in the game that Maddox would be successful against Detroit's fine fielding shortstop.

The fourth inning was just as dominant as the third was for both hurlers. Willett set down Maddox on an easy grounder back to the mound and Byrne on a roller to Bush, retiring his seventh consecutive Pirate. Leach then launched one into the deepest part of center field. With the Tigers' Hall of Fame centerfielder running right up against the grandstand where the crowd met the field, he was able to capture the long hit for the final out.

In the bottom of the fourth, the Pirates 13-game winner befuddled Cobb, who hit a soft grounder to the Pirates young pitcher for the first out. Crawford tried to get to Maddox next, and almost did, sending a long fly to deep left field. Unfortunately, that's where fly balls went to die on this day as Clarke ran it down for the long out. Delahanty singled to left, giving the large frozen throng at Bennett Park a moment of hope. Moriarty came to the plate next and he too hit a solid shot off Maddox. Unfortunately, this was not the Tigers day, as it belonged to Wagner, the day he truly began his retribution for the 1903 debacle. Wagner made a phenomenal stop of Moriarty's smash, throwing a strike to Abstein to retire the amazed Detroit third baseman.

With the Tigers still down, 6–0, they at least had been able to cease their untimely miscues that would have allowed the game to get further out of hand than it already was, that is, until the top of the fifth. Clarke, whose play in the field had been sparkling this afternoon, started things off with a weak grounder to Bush, who fumbled the ball allowing Clarke to reach first on Detroit's fifth error of the contest. Wagner followed Clarke with a lazy fly right over first baseman Tom Jones into right field, putting men on first and second with no outs.

Dots Miller came up with a genuine opportunity to increase the Pittsburgh advantage. The Pirates star rookie had a very unique nickname that he picked up in spring training when a reporter asked Wagner who Miller was, which the Pirate shortstop answered, "That's Miller." Thinking Wagner said

Dots, the reporter listed his name as Dots Miller. It was a mistake, but the name stuck as the second baseman would now forever be known by the moniker.[12] The man with the memorable nickname came to the plate looking for a huge moment. This at-bat, unfortunately, wouldn't be one of those situations as Miller blew his opportunity by popping up to Willett. Abstein hit a long fly to Crawford that moved Clarke to third. Wagner proceeded to swipe second and was stranded along with Clarke when Wilson hit a hard liner right at Bush to end the frame with the Pirates unable to extend their lead.

The Pirate threat was the only serious one over the next inning and a half. Maddox continued to rule the Tiger offense, getting Tom Jones, Schmidt and Willett on a popup and two groundouts, respectively, in the fifth and doing the same to Davy Jones, Cobb and Crawford in the sixth, with Donie Bush the only one to break his domination with a harmless one-out single. For his part Willett was just as strong, thanks to his defense. Crawford made a nice play in center snagging a deep smash from Gibson. Maddox then hit a fly ball to right for the second out, bringing Byrne up to the plate. The Bucco third baseman hit a grounder back to Willett, which deflected off his glove as Bush ran in towards it to make a tremendous play, throwing to Tom Jones to turn what could have been yet another Detroit miscue into an exciting last out of the frame.

Six innings were now in the books and there were two things very evident on this cold fall day. Maddox was completely dominating the Tigers, holding them to only four non-productive hits, and the Detroit defense was nonexistent, booting five balls and surrendering six unearned runs. The Pirates were comfortably ahead, a comfort zone they would soon relinquish with their young pitcher tiring as the Tigers were about to turn this rout into a nail-biter.

In his last inning of work, Willett shut out the Pirates for the fifth consecutive inning. Leach started out the frame with a innocent fly to Crawford in center. Clarke did even worse as he hit what was referred to as a "puny roller" by the United Press Telegram game description.[13] Willett picked up the weak ground ball, sending to it Tom Jones to retire the Pirate manager. Wagner kept the inning alive with his second hit of the day, a single to left center. With the Pittsburgh rookie second baseman coming to bat, Wagner wanted to get into scoring position and he took off for second base. One of the best basestealers in the game against a catcher with a questionable arm who held the all-time World Series record for stolen bases against, odds dictated Wagner would pull into second easily with the steal. Reality said otherwise, as Schmidt threw a strike to Bush, who put the tag on the Bucs great shortstop to end the inning.

With a shutout in hand and the Tigers coming up in the last half of the seventh, the Pittsburgh right-handed starter, who had been efficient at silencing the Detroit offense, was told by his manager, "Nice going Nick, you've got them eating out of your hand."[14] If he could only have those words back, Clarke would have taken them back moments later. Delahanty led off the frame with his second double of the day, this one a long shot over Leach's head in center. With a man on second to start the inning, Moriarty came to the plate with the hope of giving the Tigers a spark with a hit. What he provided was a full-fledged fireworks show.

The play began innocently enough as the Detroit third baseman hit a grounder to Miller who threw it on to Abstein, who dropped the ball, putting Moriarity at first with Delahanty moving to third. First base umpire Jim Johnstone inexplicably called Moriarity out, beginning one of the longest rhubarbs in the history of the fall classic. Moriarity, Detroit manager Hughie Jennings, as well as a good portion of the Tiger bench ran after Johnstone wondering why he had called Moriarty out. Upon further review, Johnstone said he had thought he had seen his partner Silk O'Loughlin signal that Moriarty had interfered with Abstein and was out. O'Loughlin had said he made no such signal, so Johnstone then reversed his decision, putting men on first and third with no outs.[15]

This reversed incensed Clarke and the Pirates, who then took their turn trying to plead their case to the umpire. The Pittsburgh manager sprinted in from left field, claiming Moriarty had knocked into Abstein causing the ball to fall from his glove. Clarke became more incensed when it was becoming apparent that his argument was falling on deaf ears. He even was claiming that the Pirates were not getting the calls in this game from the American League umpire staff that was calling this game. Those statements cost the Bucs skipper as well as Gibson, Camnitz, and Tommy Leach a $25 fine after the game.[16]

The long delay did not have a good effect on Maddox afterwards as he quickly gave up a single to Tom Jones, who put a pitch into right field, scoring Delahanty with the Tigers first run. Maddox then came back, forcing Schmidt to hit a pop up in foul territory, which was snagged by Byrne for the first out.

Jennings then sent up outfielder Matty McIntyre to bat for Willett. McIntyre had been a clutch hitter for Detroit in the past, helping to propel the Tigers to the 1908 American League championship by leading the league in at-bats, runs and singles while hitting .298. He did not enjoy similar success in Detroit's third consecutive AL championship campaign. After a bout of appendicitis at the beginning of the year, he hit only .244 and appeared in limited action in this Series, batting only three times. What McIntyre was more known for than his fine play in the field was the fact he was not a fan of his teammate, the great Ty Cobb. His feud with Cobb would cause several issues over his seven-year career in the Motor City. There were several alleged instances where he didn't help out Cobb in the field, causing balls to fall in between the two for hits. When seeing this in a game on two consecutive occasions, then Detroit manager Bill Armour asked McIntyre, "How is it you don't make plays that are yours and never bear down when Cobb is on base." McIntyre, who was more interested in making Cobb look bad than helping the Tigers win, retorted, "Why should I help that no good son of a bitch."[17] In this at-bat, McIntyre gave the Pirates some hope that they could get out

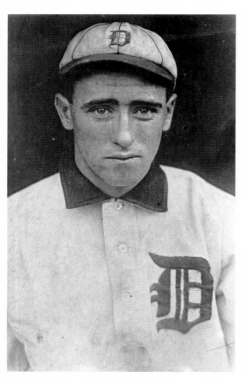

Even though the Tigers lost Game 3, 8–6, shortstop Donie Bush had an outstanding game going 4-for-5 with two RBIs. Bush went on to hit .318 in his only World Series as a player (courtesy of Library of Congress, Bain Collection, Prints & Photographs Division, 10670u).

of the seventh with minimal damage when he struck out.

Leadoff hitter Davy Jones came to bat and beat a bunt down the third base line to load the bases with two out. This brought up shortstop Donie Bush. Bush, who already had two hits in the game, certainly knew that if he didn't come through now, the game was most likely over. A shortstop who was more known for his soft hands and defensive ability, Bush led the league in putouts three times while heading the circuit on seven occasions. Offensively Bush was the quintessential number two man in the lineup. He knew how to work a count and sacrifice hitters. A league leader in walks five times, Bush finished his 16-year career fifth on the all-time list with 337 sacrifices. In 1909, the Indianapolis native was at his best in these two disciplines, leading the junior circuit with 88 free passes and 52 sacrifice hits. With two outs, this situation called for anything but a sacrifice. Bush responded with a line drive in front of Clarke that plated two runs with his third hit of the day.

His nemesis Marty McIntyre

failing miserably earlier in the inning, Ty Cobb came up next and showed exactly how a player is supposed to be in the clutch when he hit a solid single to center scoring Davy Jones. This cut the once seemingly invincible Pirate six-run advantage to a mere two, 6–4.

Abstein, whose controversial miscue led to the big Detroit inning, finally put an end to things in the seventh when he did hold on to a Sam Crawford pop up. Even though the inning was over, Detroit gave Pittsburgh a little of their own medicine as three of the four runs they scored in the seventh were unearned, all courtesy of Abstein's blunder.

Now desperate to make sure their once safe lead didn't evaporate, the Bucs faced a rookie right-handed reliever that Hughie Jennings summoned from the bullpen by the name of Ralph Works. Following a 21–17 campaign in 1908 pitching for Syracuse of the New York State League, Works enjoyed a fine rookie campaign for Detroit with a 4–1 mark in 16 games with a 1.97 ERA. In the eighth inning, Works continued the control over the Pittsburgh offense that Willett had for the previous five innings. The first batter he faced in his initial World Series appearance was fellow rookie Dots Miller. Works won this war of rookies as he struck out Miller.

Trying to make up for his error that cost the Bucs at least three runs the previous frame, Abstein cracked a shot to right center for a double. At this point the rain once again began falling. A wet Chief Wilson moved the Pirate first baseman to third as he grounded out to the pitcher. Abstein moved no further as Gibson was retired, ending the inning with a pop up in foul territory to his counterpart, Boss Schmidt.

Luckily for Pittsburgh, Maddox was able to gain some composure in the eighth after his rocky performance an inning before. Delahanty began the frame with a grounder to Dots Miller, who tossed it to Abstein, getting the Detroit second baseman in time. He walked the next batter, Moriarty, who immediately was thrown out stealing on a strike from Gibson to Wagner. A tiring Maddox then issued a free pass to Tom Jones, but Maddox got Schmidt to fly out harmlessly to Clarke, sending this now exciting contest to its final chapter, the ninth inning.

Works, who became a writer after his career ended, started the top of the ninth by striking out Maddox, who was caught looking at the third strike.[18] Byrne followed with a solid strike to center field for his second hit of the game. Leach followed by putting a ball into the crowd in left field for a double, with Byrne going to third. After six innings of futility, Pittsburgh finally broke back into the scoring column when Clarke sent a long fly to Cobb in right, scoring Byrne as Leach advanced 90 feet to third. Up to bat with two outs came Honus Wagner. Wagner continued to dominant Detroit pitchers, slicing a hit past Bush's head, bringing Leach home with Pittsburgh's eighth score of the day, giving the Pirates a much more comfortable four-run lead. Trying to make it five, Wagner stole his third base of the game. It looked like he would, in fact, come home with a ninth run as Miller ripped a Works offering into right. Cobb came hustling in, making a spectacular catch that United Press Telegraph described as the Detroit right fielder sliding forward 10 feet on his face following the inning-ending, breath-taking grab.[19]

Now leading comfortably again by four, the only question for the Bucs was could a tiring Maddox have enough left in the tank to hold off the fast charging American League champs. He did ... barely.

Batting for Works was pitcher George Mullin to start the final frame. A fine hitter in his career, Mullin was nonetheless overmatched by Maddox as he struck out. Davy Jones looked to be the second out when Wagner made a fabulous play, picking up his grounder and throwing on to Abstein. Unfortunately for the Pirate faithful, the bumbling Pittsburgh first baseman dropped yet another throw at first base so Jones was safe at first.

The fumble seemed to open the door for the Tigers as Bush collected his fourth hit of the day, a slow hopper to Byrne at third that Bush beat to the bag, sending Jones to second. Cobb was up next, looking to take the thunder away from his rival Wagner. The Bucs shortstop was the star of the game so far with three hits, three stolen bases, two runs batted in and several stunning plays in the field that writer Hugh Fullerton claimed he ran 37 and 40 feet to turn Tiger hits into outs.[20] Cobb came as close as you can to wrest that title away, hitting a very long shot to right field that in most cases would have been a three-run homer, cutting the lead to one. Unfortunately, the ball landed into the overflow throng that was standing there, rendering it a ground-rule double instead, scoring only Davy Jones to cut the Pirate advantage to 8–5. Crawford ended his unspectacular 0-for-5 day with a ground ball to Wagner, who tossed it on to Abstein for the second out. The play did advance both runners as Bush scored with the Tigers' sixth run, the fifth unearned, mostly given to them by the untimely errors of the Pittsburgh first baseman.

With two out, a man on third and the tying run at the plate in Delahanty, the tiring Maddox faced Delahanty who hit the ball solidly, lining the ball into the left field area where Clarke had made one phenomenal play after another. This one would be no different as the Bucs Hall of Fame left fielder slid on his knees on the wet outfield to catch what would be the final out of the game to give Pittsburgh a two to one lead in the World Series. As if it wasn't bad enough for the cold disappointed Detroit fans, the rain began to fall once again just as the ball entered Clarke's glove, this time in a much more aggressive manner.[21]

For the Pirates Hall of Fame shortstop, it was his day of retribution, one that according to Fullerton erased his yellow reputation that had followed him since the inaugural fall classic.[22] Wagner could breath a sigh of relief, he was yellow no more.

Game 3 Box Score

```
PIT N    5  1  0    0  0  0    0  0  2 — 8 10 2
DET A    0  0  0    0  0  0    4  0  2 — 6 11 5
```

BATTING

Pittsburgh Pirates	AB	R	H	RBI	BB	SO	PO	A
Byrne 3b	5	1	2	0	0	0	2	2
Leach cf	4	3	2	0	0	0	1	0
Clarke lf	3	1	0	1	0	0	5	0
Wagner ss	5	1	3	2	0	0	3	4
Miller 2b	4	1	0	0	1	1	3	6
Abstein 1b	4	1	2	0	0	0	8	0
Wilson rf	4	0	1	1	0	0	0	0
Gibson c	4	0	0	0	0	0	5	1
Maddox p	4	0	0	0	0	1	0	1
Totals	37	8	10	4	1	2	27	14

FIELDING—
E: Abstein 2 (3).

BATTING—
2B: Abstein (1,0ff Works); Leach (3,0ff Works).
SF: Clarke (1,0ff Works).
HBP: Leach (1,by Willett); Clarke (1,by Willett).
Team LOB: 6.

BASERUNNING—
SB: Wagner 3 (4,2nd base off Summers/Schmidt,2nd base off Willett/Schmidt,2nd base off Works/Schmidt).
CS: Leach (1,Home by Willett/Schmidt); Wagner (2,2nd base by Willett/Schmidt).

Detroit Tigers	AB	R	H	RBI	BB	SO	PO	A
D. Jones lf	5	2	1	0	0	0	0	0
Bush ss	5	1	4	2	0	0	3	3
Cobb rf	5	0	2	2	0	1	3	0
Crawford cf	5	0	0	1	0	0	5	0
Delahanty 2b	5	1	3	0	0	0	3	2
Moriarty 3b	3	1	0	0	1	1	0	4
T. Jones 1b	3	1	1	1	1	0	8	0
Schmidt c	4	0	0	0	0	0	4	2
Summers p	0	0	0	0	0	0	0	1
Willett p	2	0	0	0	0	0	1	3
McIntyre ph	1	0	0	0	0	1	0	0

Detroit Tigers	AB	R	H	RBI		BB	SO		PO	A
Works p	0	0	0	0		0	0		0	1
Mullin ph	1	0	0	0		0	1		0	0
Totals	39	6	11	6		2	4		27	16

FIELDING—
E: Bush 2 (3), Crawford (1), Schmidt (2), Willett (1).

BATTING—
2B: Delahanty 2 (3,0ff Maddox 2); Cobb (1,0ff Maddox).
Team LOB: 8.

BASERUNNING—
CS: Moriarty (1,2nd base by Maddox/Gibson).

PITCHING

Pittsburgh Pirates	IP	H	R	ER	BB	SO	HR	BFP
Maddox W(1–0)	9	11	6	1	2	4	0	41

Detroit Tigers	IP	H	R	ER	BB	SO	HR	BFP
Summers L(0–1)	0.1	3	5	0	1	0	0	6
Willett	6.2	3	1	0	0	0	0	25
Works	2	4	2	2	0	2	0	10
Totals	9	10	8	2	1	2	0	41

WP: Summers (1).
HBP: Willett 2 (2,Leach,Clarke).
Umpires: HP—Jim Johnstone, 1B—Silk O'Loughlin
Time of Game: 1:56 **Attendance:** 18277

◆ 6 ◆

GAME 4, OCTOBER 12

Bennett Park, Detroit
Detroit 5, Pittsburgh 0

If Tiger fans thought the weather for Game 3 was intolerable, they were in for a rude awakening on this blustery day when Detroit and Pittsburgh squared off in the fourth game of the 1909 World Series. Winter had come to Detroit, with temperatures falling to 34 degrees, as yet another big crowd was in their heaviest winter garb, battling the frigid winds that blew through Bennett Park.

Despite the horrendous conditions, 17,036 filled just about every space in the small rickety facility to see if the Tigers could battle back to tie this fall classic at two games apiece. It was yet another showing of just how incredibly popular the game was at the end of the twentieth century's first decade. In the regular season, 7,370,000 fans had filled major league stadiums. In this fall classic, there was such a demand for tickets to see the two grand titans of baseball battle for the world championship that the teams probably couldn't have satisfied all those who wanted tickets even if they doubled the capacity in their respective parks. For Game 4, the chilled throng showed up to root for their club's attempt to make it a respectable series. If Detroit was able to beat their National League rivals, it would mark the first time in their futile three years as American League champions that they would win a second game in a fall classic.

This contest also had a historic tone to it, as the National Commission, so pleased with the utilization of a third umpire in the World Series stationed at the left-field foul line, for the first time decided to do one better and have a fourth umpire to patrol the right-field line. It was a decision that would be in use for the remaining games in this fall classic.[1]

Detroit's Hughie Jennings had done everything he could as a manager, except guide the Tigers to a world championship. His tremendous leadership ability was evident in the fact that in his first season at the helm of the Tigers he took a substandard team that was 71–78 in 1906, finishing in sixth place in the eight-team American League, and improved them 21 games to capture the junior circuit championship in 1907. He won a record three pennants in his first three seasons as a manager, but had yet to achieve his ultimate goal, a World Series title. With a loss in Game 4, the chances that he would emerge victorious in this fall classic were very slim.

To try and accomplish this feat, Jennings turned to his 29-game winner, George Mullin. Mullin was phenomenal in his first start in the initial game, although in a losing effort. He held the Pirate offense to only five hits, but with the help of four Tiger errors, he gave up three unearned runs in the 4–1 loss. While blessed with an outstanding array of pitches, Mullin was also a practitioner of several mental strategies that kept opposing hitters off balance. He would wonder off the mound, playing with his cap, belt and the laces on his shoes, stalling as much as he could. He would also talk to himself, like a future Tiger pitcher 67 years later by the name of Mark Fidrych. He would also talk to batters and heckle opposing fans that got on him for his antics.[2]

Most thought Pirate manager Fred Clarke would send out his rookie hurler Babe Adams to face the colorful Tiger pitcher. After all it was Adams who was the surprise starter in the first game where he completely shut down Detroit for the victory. As he did in the first contest, Clarke once again surprised scribes and fans alike with his World Series pitching decision. This time, instead of choosing the right-handed Game 1 star, he went for veteran southpaw Albert "Lefty" Leifield.[3] It's not as if it was a shock that Leifield was chosen as the starter. After all he had won 19 times during the Pirates' championship campaign of 1909, seventh best in the National League, while only losing eight games, good enough for a .704 winning percentage, fifth best in the league.

Leifield was not a pitcher that possessed devastating stuff. He did not have a 90 mile per hour fastball, nor did he a curveball that would break at incredible angles like the great Sandy Koufax. He did, like another pitching great Greg Maddox, rely on outstanding control and guile, often throwing his curve when the count didn't dictate such a pitch. *The Sporting News* described Lefty Leifield as "one of those ain't-got-a-thing pitchers who never threw a ball where a batter wanted it."[4] His phenomenal control led him to a career 2.47 ERA, the 39th lowest figure in the history of the game, while his WHIP (walks plus hits per innings pitched) was at 1.21 per nine innings, the 153rd fewest in baseballs annals.

Time would tell if Clarke's decision to start Leifield would be as successful as the one that led him to put Adams on the mound in the opening game. No matter who took the rubber for Pittsburgh, he would have a tough time going against Detroit's veteran starter.

Mullin gave leadoff hitter Bobby Byrne a sign of things to come when he threw a laser past the Pirate third baseman for a strike in the first pitch of the game. The second was equally as effective, prompting Byrne to hit a harmless ball to Jim Delahanty who threw it to first baseman Tom Jones for the first out. Up next was the Pirates' speedy center fielder Tommy Leach. Mullin was just as tough on him as Leach managed an equally ineffective grounder, this one to Donie Bush. Manager Fred Clarke, who doubled as the club's Hall of Fame left fielder, completed the futile frame with a hopper to Delahanty.

Leifield took the hill and appeared as if would match Mullin pitch for pitch, just like Adams did in the first contest. Leach was playing in for the Tigers leadoff hitter Davy Jones. It looked like he had the perfect position when Jones lined the ball right to his direction. Leach slipped, almost falling down, but he was able to regain his balance and caught Jones' liner for the first out. Bush was unable to handle Leifield's offering with a dribbler to the Pittsburgh southpaw, who tossed it onto first baseman Bill Abstein retiring Bush easily.

Strolling to the plate next was Detroit's legendary right fielder, Ty Cobb. Cobb, who had some stomach issues in Game 3, was in no better shape in this contest as Leifield plunked the Tiger superstar in the ribs that according to his biography by Al Stump, "did not help his nausea."[5] Despite the fact he was not up to par, the scrappy Cobb nonetheless was aggressive in his lead at first. When the Bucs veteran starter saw Cobb was leaning, he threw over to first base in a pickoff attempt. Having seemingly caught Cobb for the inning's final out, Abstein bumbled once again, inexplicably dropping Leifield's throw for his fourth error of the Series to date, allowing Cobb to saunter into second.[6] Abstein's folly would not hurt the Bucs in this inning, though, as Sam Crawford stranded his fellow Tiger legend in scoring position with a fly to Leach ending the threat.

As easy as the first inning was for both hurlers, the second was a little more challenging. For Mullin and the Tigers, they came perilously close to having the game forfeited in favor of the Pirates before the second inning was minutes old.

The other titan in this 1909 World Series, Honus Wagner, led off the frame and worked Mullin for a walk. Jennings, who was coaching at third, was joined there by Game 2 winner "Wild" Bill Donovan. Donovan's sole purpose for being next to Jennings was to ride umpire Bill Klem. Klem ordered

Donovan to the bench but he refused to leave the field. According to writer Fred Lieb, Donovan shouted at Klem, "I'm taking this to the man; you go on and do your umpiring." Still refusing to exit the field after a second warning from Klem, Donovan added, "What are you doing, trying to make yourself look important?"[7]

Klem had enough and threw the Tiger hurler out of the game at this point. With Donovan still screaming at him, Klem turned to Jennings, pushing him to get Donovan off the field to the locker room by threatening to forfeit the game to Pittsburgh if he didn't leave in "thirty seconds." The umpire further warned Jennings by saying, "If I've got to forfeit, I wouldn't like to be standing in your shoes when you're standing before Ban Johnson."[8] Getting his point across, Jennings finally got the angered Detroit hurler off the field to allow the game to continue after the lengthy delay.

If Mullin's concentration wasn't altered after the melee, it certainly might have affected the Pirate shortstop at first. Concerned he may take off for second at any given moment, Mullin constantly threw to first, trying to keep Wagner in place. Of course, you don't become a 29-game winner by losing your concentration, so the Indiana native was able to compose himself long enough to not only keep Wagner at first, but strike out Dots Miller.

Hoping to make up for his first inning error, Abstein hit a grounder to Delahanty, who did not make the play cleanly, and failed to get Abstein at first. Chief Wilson was unable to take advantage of the situation as he hit a roller back to the Tiger hurler who threw to third forcing Wagner for the second out. On his way to the bench, the Pirate great was presented with large bunch of yellow chrysanthemums.[9] With two on and two out, Bucs catcher George Gibson could not do any damage either, hitting a hard shot to the mound. Mullin made a great stop, tossing it to Tom Jones to complete this long and strange inning by rendering the Pirates scoreless again.

Leifield did not have as much luck as Mullin did in his part of the second frame. Once again the Pirate southpaw gave up a baserunner via the hit batsman, this time Delahanty. Third baseman George Moriarty then placed a fly ball into short left field in front of Clarke for a single, sending Delahanty into third.

With men at the corners and no one out, Leifield had to bear down if he had any hope of keeping this game scoreless. He began his quest in a positive mode getting Tom Jones on a grounder back to the mound. When Delahanty took off for home on the slow roller, Leifield threw the ball to Gibson for the supposedly easy out. Delahanty smartly got himself caught in a rundown, which allowed Moriarty to get to third and Jones to pull into second before Gibson tagged him out.

Up to plate with men in scoring position was Oscar Stanage, the rookie catcher out of Tulare, California, who got the nod in this game over Boss Schmidt against the Pirate lefty. Purchased by the Tigers from his minor league club in Newark of the Eastern League, Stanage hit .262 in 1909, compared to Schmidt's .209. Stanage eventually grew into one of the most durable, intelligent backstops in his era. Between 1911 and 1915, he played in 125 more games at catcher than any other junior circuit backstop. Writer H.G. Salsinger said of Stanage, "No backstop ever had the ability to outguess the opposition on the hit and run and squeeze play than Stanage had." Salsinger further went on to say, "He never moved faster than he had to but he always got there. His lack of wasted motion made him a favorite of pitchers, he was an easy man to pitch to and he had the ability to steady the twirlers."[10]

While eventually becoming so successful defensively behind the plate, on this day Stanage had one of his greatest moments offensively in his fourteen-year career in this at-bat. The California native slashed a single into right, scoring the first two runs of the game.

The Detroit veteran pitcher tried to keep the rally going, but hit into a tailor-made double play to Wagner, who threw it to Miller at second for one out. Miller then tossed the relay throw into the crowd behind Abstein at first, allowing Mullin to get into scoring position at second. Davy Jones ended the frame with a ground out to Leifield, but the excited chilled overflow throng at Bennett Park was thrilled as they saw their American League champions hold a 2–0 lead.

Trying to even up the score, Pittsburgh sent up the top of its impressive lineup in the top of the third after Leifield struck out for the first out. Byrne followed by slicing a long shot that fell inside the left-field foul line for a double. Tommy Leach worked a walk off Mullin, putting men on first and second with one out, with Pittsburgh's Hall of Fame duo coming to the plate. It was at this point Mullin showed what kind of toughness he possessed. The *New York Times* put it best when it wrote, "Mullin performed a feat in the third inning that will live long in the annuls of baseball and was frozen in the minds of those who saw it."[11]

The Toledo, Ohio, native set down Fred Clarke on strikes for the second out. Byrne and Leach took off on a double steal at that point, putting men at second and third with the great Honus Wagner coming to the plate. These were moments that were meant for the great Pirate shortstop, moments that made him the legend he is today. Moments that he had already taken advantage of in this Series. It was Mullin, though, that was about to have his moment at the expense of the Carnegie, Pennsylvania, great. Wagner, after going down two strikes to start this potentially clutch at-bat, worked the count to 3–2

In hopes of slowing the aggressive Pirate running game, Detroit manager Hughie Jennings started catcher Oscar Stanage (left) in Game 4. While the Bucs kept running, swiping two bases, Stanage came through offensively with two RBIs in the Tigers' 5–0 victory (courtesy of Library of Congress, Bain Collection, Prints & Photographs Division, 10527u).

and thought that Mullin missed the strike zone on the final pitch. He started to jog to first, loading the bases for Dots Miller. Klem rung up Wagner for a third strike, though, causing the Pittsburgh Hall of Famer to question the young umpire's ability. As the angry Wagner squawked at Klem, his argumentative words fell on deaf ears as the umpire turned his back to him and the Bucs threat was rendered useless once again.[12]

Detroit shortstop Donie Bush tried to continue the Tigers good fortune when he smashed a ball into deep left field that Clarke was able to corral for the first out. Trying a different strategy, Cobb laid down a bunt in front of the plate between Gibson and Leifield. The Pittsburgh pitcher picked up the bunt and tossed out the legendary Tiger right fielder. What was looking like a quick breather for the Pirates all of the sudden got interesting. Crawford, who was not having a great Series, hitting only .186 to this point, laced a single to center.

The horrendous fielding of Bill Abstein reared its ugly head again on the following play. Delahanty struck a ball that bounced off the fumbling Pittsburgh first baseman and veered towards Miller at second. Miller picked up the ball but was unable to toss out Delahanty at first. Regrettably for the Tigers, Moriarty sent a ball to Wagner, who tossed it to Miller at second for the final out.

Making the last put out of the inning, Miller came up to see if he could ignite the feeble Bucco offense. He sent a high bounding ground ball to Moriarty at third, who made a phenomenal play to toss him out at first. Showing the lack of respect that was garnering for the Pirate first baseman, the United Press Telegram described Abstein's at-bat, who came up after Miller, the following way: "Abstein did his usual World Series stunt of fanning."[13]

Following Mullin's fifth strikeout of the day, Wilson ripped a strong single into left field. He was stranded at first when Moriarty hustled over to the pitcher's mound, grabbed Gibson's slow roller, and tossed it over to Tom Jones to retire the Bucs veteran catcher, ending their half of the fourth.

Twice Pittsburgh had threatened against Mullin in the first four innings to cut the Tiger advantage, and twice Mullin rebuked their challenge. The Bucs now hoped that their tough southpaw could keep the game under control so they could continue their quest to take a commanding three to one lead in this fall classic, which would all but end the three-time American League champions attempt to win their first world championship. The Tigers had other ideas, though.

Tom Jones led off the bottom of the fourth with a beautiful bunt down the third base line for a single. Stanage, who had knocked in the first two runs of the game, could not repeat his heroics as he hit a shot to Wagner at short. Almost blowing the play, the Pirate shortstop fumbled the grounder, but got control of it to tag second and then throw on to Abstein for the double play.

Two out, no one on base, and the pitcher coming up, things looked good for Pittsburgh. While Mullin was a good hitting pitcher, the odds were definitely in Leifield's favor of getting out of this inning unscathed. Unfortunately for the Bucs hurler, he committed the ultimate sin and walked the opposing pitcher, giving the Tigers new life.

Leadoff hitter Davy Jones laced a single to left field, sending Mullin to second. Bush came up and poked a long shot into the overflow crowd in left field for a double, scoring the Detroit pitcher, giving the home team a 3–0 lead with one of the greatest hitters the game of baseball has ever known, Ty Cobb, coming to the plate. Cobb followed Bush's lead and put a ball into the overflow crowd in left for another double, increasing the Tiger advantage to 5–0 and just about putting an end to the first World Series start for Pittsburgh's 19-game winner. Crawford was retired on a harmless groundball to Leifield for the inning's final out, but it was too late, as what was once a close game was now much more in Tiger control.

Crawford turned out to be Leifield's final batter of the game, as Clarke had seen enough, choosing to replace him with seldom-used catcher Paddy O'Connor in the top of the fifth frame. While a solid backstop with Bristol and Springfield in the Connecticut League before coming to the Steel City in 1908, O'Connor had only 32 at-bats in his two seasons with the Pirates to that point after being picked up in the rule 5 draft in December 1907. Even though he was used very sparingly in the Pirates pennant-winning season, he did have some success with five hits that included a double and three RBIs in 16 at-bats for a .313 average. On this occasion, though, he was no match for the superior Mullin, as he struck out for the first out.

Byrne, who was hitting a substandard .200 to this point of the Series, did no better, becoming Mullin's seventh strikeout victim of the game. Tommy Leach, who had substantially more success against Tiger pitchers than Byrne so far with a .286 average and a team high .853 OPS after four games, could only say he prevented the tough Detroit hurler from striking out the side as he hit a hot grounder that was scooped up by Tom Jones, who beat Leach to the base, retiring the side.

Trying to stop the bleeding, Clarke turned to an old warrior, Deacon Phillippe. While Honus Wagner's performance in the 1903 World Series was so substandard that it scarred him for the six years prior to this fall classic, Phillippe's was just the opposite. A right-hander out of Rural Retreat, Virginia, Phillippe completed five of the nine games in that Series, winning all three Bucs victories in the disappointing upset to the Boston Americans. It was a gutsy performance as Pittsburgh's pitching staff was depleted. Sam Leever, who won 25 games for the National League champs in 1903, was injured and starter Ed Doheny was gone, suffering a nervous breakdown which eventually had him committed to an insane asylum.

Phillippe was the Pirates' preeminent pitcher during their dynasty run in the early part of the decade, winning twenty or more games in five of his first six seasons in a Pittsburgh uniform (six of his first seven major league campaigns if you include his 21–17 mark for the Louisville Colonels in his rookie season of 1899). By 1909, though, Phillippe was 37 years old and coming to the end of his career. His arm was wearing down. In the season prior to the Bucs' championship run, he missed almost the entire year with a sore shoulder and then a broken finger on his pitching hand. In 1909, he was reduced to a relief pitcher, starting only 12 of the 22 games he entered, but Clarke was hoping that the World Series magic he had performed in 1903 would be reproduced six years later. He was not disappointed.

He started off by getting Delahanty to pop up in foul territory to Gibson. Moriarty did no better with a lazy fly to Leach in center. Phillippe then forced

Tom Jones into a grounder to Byrne at third to set down the Tigers in order for the first time on this miserable October day.

To completely stop the onslaught, Clarke would need more than his grizzled veteran hurler to get back into this game, he'd need his offense to finally crack the puzzle that was George Mullin. To begin the comeback he would depend on his star left fielder who was leading off the inning ... himself. Unfortunately, he would not be the one to figure out Mullin, as he struck out for the second time against the 29-game winner.

Wagner thought he was able to start a rally as he moved into a Mullin off-speed pitch. Thinking he'd get first base via the hit batsman, the Pirate great started down the line, but Klem didn't see it that way, so Wagner came back to continue the at-bat. He did get hold of a Mullin pitch, sending a liner down the first base that Tom Jones snagged for the out.

The Tigers crafty right-hander finished the Bucs in the sixth by ringing up Dots Miller for his ninth strike-out of this cold contest. He did so with controversy as Miller thought the last strike was off the plate. The Bucs second baseman got into a heated argument with Klem and slammed his bat into the ground, prompting yet another fine for a Pirate player in this Series.[14]

While not being able to score, at least Phillippe kept the game from being a complete embarrassment. Stanage was retired by the 37-year-old Pittsburgh pitcher on a harmless slow roller to Wagner. His mound opponent came to the plate next and received a rousing ovation from the hometown fans. He rewarded them with line drive to Miller that the frustrated Pirate second baseman couldn't handle, allowing Mullin to get to first on the Pirates fourth error of the day. Miller did have a moment of reprise next as he took a throw from Wagner, retiring

A star in the first ever World Series in 1903, when he beat Boston three times, pitcher Deacon Phillippe was at the end of his career in 1909. He still managed to pitch effectively from the bullpen in the fall classic, giving up no runs and two hits in six innings of work (courtesy of the Pittsburgh Pirates).

Mullin on a grounder from Davy Jones. The good moment for Miller would be temporary as Jones took off in an attempt to steal second. Gibson's throw hit Miller's glove, who tagged out the Tiger left fielder for the last out. In the process, Jones' slid high and his spikes met Miller's arm on the play, adding yet another chapter to what was becoming a day that the Bucs rookie would most likely want to forget.

Whether or not Phillippe was sharp, the damage had already been done and Mullin was impenetrable this day. In the seventh and eighth innings, only Gibson was able to make it to the basepaths with a two-out, seventh-inning single. Other than that, the rest went down without a struggle as Abstein flew out to Crawford, Wilson hit a grounder back to the mound and Phillippe became strikeout victim number ten in the seventh. In the eighth Mullin got Byrne, Leach and Clarke all on fly balls.

The only positive for the Pirates on this day was the Virginian who stood on the Pittsburgh mound. Detroit tried to unsuccessfully bunt their way on in the seventh as Bush and Cobb were both retired in their attempts. Crawford did reach first as he grounded a ball to Abstein, who tossed it on to Phillippe for the apparent out. Deacon dropped the throw for an error, but then retired Delahanty on a roller to the mound to strand Crawford with the third out.

The eighth inning proved to be the only time in his four sterling innings of relief that Phillippe got into trouble. Moriarty got the only hit of the day against the then eleven-year veteran. Tom Jones tried to move into scoring position with a sacrifice bunt. He was able to do that and more when Gibson committed the Bucs' sixth error of the day, putting two men on and no one out.

Stanage successfully sacrificed Jones and Moriaty into scoring position, with Mullin coming to the plate trying to add to the team's advantage. It was at this point Phillippe showed his mettle by striking out his opponent for the second out. He walked leadoff hitter Dave Jones to load the bases, but Bush could not take advantage, grounding out to Byrne to retire the side.

Despite the fact Mullin blew an opportunity at the plate, he remained incredible on the mound and put on the finishing pieces to his masterpiece in the top of the ninth. Honus Wagner led off grounding out to Moriarty, completing what would be his most fruitless day of the Series. So important was he to the Pirate cause that the *New York Times* gave him almost complete blame for the inevitable Pittsburgh defeat. The paper made the claim after his disastrous strikeout in the third inning that "the downfall of Wagner apparently disheartened his teammates, for they were as clay in the hands of the pitcher Mullin during the remainder of this chilly battle."[15]

It was more than just Wagner, of course, as no one, except for Phillippe, came to the forefront to pick the team up. Although Miller got to first following Wagner's ground out on a bunt single, he certainly was frustrated by the Tiger hurler on more than one occasion, as was Abstein who followed Miller with a ground out to Mullin. Wilson, whose average dropped to .200 for the fall classic, ended this miserable day for the Pirate faithful with a harmless grounder to Tom Jones at first, tying the Series at two games a piece.

The Tigers had new life as they departed to Pittsburgh to try and take the Series advantage from the Bucs. The Pirates returned to their accommodations in the Motor City, at the Pontchartrain Hotel, as they picked up their belongings amid the heckles and good natured taunts of the Tiger fans who rode the team, Wagner specifically. One sign said, "Hans Wagner — Punkin-Head."[16]

Pittsburgh now headed for the friendlier confines of Forbes Field, as their once dominant stance was diminished. A heavy favorite at the beginning of the World Series, it was now an even bet between the Tigers and Pirates as to which club would emerge victorious to lay the claim to the title of 1909 World Champions.

Game 4 Box Score

```
PIT N     0 0 0    0 0 0    0 0 0 — 0  5  6
DET A     0 2 0    3 0 0    0 0 x — 5  8  0
```

BATTING

Pittsburgh Pirates	AB	R	H	RBI	BB	SO	PO	A
Byrne 3b	4	0	1	0	0	1	0	2
Leach cf	3	0	0	0	1	0	3	0
Clarke lf	4	0	0	0	0	2	1	0
Wagner ss	3	0	0	0	1	1	2	4
Miller 2b	4	0	1	0	0	2	3	1
Abstein 1b	4	0	1	0	0	1	12	1
Wilson rf	4	0	1	0	0	0	0	0
Gibson c	3	0	1	0	0	0	3	4
Leifield p	1	0	0	0	0	1	0	5
O'Connor ph	1	0	0	0	0	1	0	0
Phillippe p	1	0	0	0	0	1	0	2
Totals	32	0	5	0	2	10	24	19

FIELDING—
DP: 1. Wagner-Abstein.
E: Wagner (1), Miller (1), Abstein 2 (5), Phillippe 2 (2).

BATTING—
2B: Byrne (1,0ff Mullin).
Team LOB: 7.

BASERUNNING—
SB: Byrne (1,3rd base off Mullin/Stanage); Leach (1,2nd base off Mullin/Stanage).

Detroit Tigers	AB	R	H	RBI	BB	SO	PO	A
D. Jones lf	4	1	1	0	1	0	0	0
Bush ss	5	1	1	1	0	0	0	1
Cobb rf	3	0	1	2	0	0	1	0
Crawford cf	4	0	1	0	0	0	2	0
Delahanty 2b	3	0	0	0	0	0	1	2
Moriarty 3b	4	1	2	0	0	0	1	3
T. Jones 1b	3	1	1	0	0	0	13	0
Stanage c	3	0	1	2	0	0	9	1
Mullin p	3	1	0	0	1	1	0	4
Totals	32	5	8	5	2	1	27	11

BATTING—
2B: Bush (1,0ff Leifield); Cobb (2,0ff Leifield).
SH: T. Jones (1,0ff Phillippe); Stanage (1,0ff Phillippe).
HBP: Cobb (1,by Leifield); Delahanty (1,by Leifield).
Team LOB: 9.

BASERUNNING—
CS: Cobb (1,2nd base by Leifield/Gibson); D. Jones (2,2nd base by Phillippe/Gibson).

PITCHING

Pittsburgh Pirates	IP	H	R	ER	BB	SO	HR	BFP
Leifield L(0–1)	4	7	5	5	1	0	0	22
Phillippe	4	1	0	0	1	1	0	16
Totals	8	8	5	5	2	1	0	38

HBP: Leifield 2 (2,Cobb,Delahanty).

Detroit Tigers	IP	H	R	ER	BB	SO	HR	BFP
Mullin W(1–1)	9	5	0	0	2	10	0	34

Umpires: HP — Bill Klem, 1B — Billy Evans, LF — Silk O'Loughlin, RF — Jim Johnstone
Time of Game: 1:57 **Attendance:** 17036

♦ 7 ♦

GAME 5, OCTOBER 13

Forbes Field, Pittsburgh
Pittsburgh 8, Detroit 4

With the pivotal fifth game on the horizon in the Smoky City, Detroit had to be feeling good as they took the Lake Shore Railroad to Pittsburgh. There was one Tiger, of course, who once again was conspicuous by his absence, Ty Cobb. As he had before Games 1 and 3, he chose once again to avoid Ohio, where he feared the police were still waiting to arrest him, by taking the much longer Detroit through Canada to Buffalo to Pittsburgh route, a practice that was starting to wear down the Tiger superstar.

What was wearing down the fans the last three games was the weather. When the two participants in this fall classic last stepped on the diamond in Forbes Field, it was an unseasonably warm, sunny fall day. As the combatants returned four days later, all tied up at two games each, they brought the cold weather from Detroit with them.

The temperature had fallen to the upper 30s with a strong wind that kept the expected overflow crowd down to 21,706 chilled patrons. The *Pittsburgh Gazette* felt that the weather was the overriding factor in the less-than-capacity attendance, stating that "had the weather been more propitious no doubt another record breaking crowd would have attended." The *Gazette* further went on to point out that despite the smaller crowd "it was larger than the attendances at Detroit (and) was large enough to speak well of Pittsburgh as a baseball center."[1]

What baseball's center saw this day was a battle between the young Pirate hurler who was the surprise starter and winner in Game 1, Babe Adams, and the Tigers 21-game winner Ed Summers, who didn't make it out of the first inning of Game 3, surrendering five unearned runs in one-third of an inning of work. Both hurlers were well rested for this encounter, with Adams some-what surprisingly being held out of Game 4, and Summers barely breaking a sweat in his abbreviated World Series disaster.

Picking up his nickname while pitching in the minors for Louisville the prior year, Adams was presumably considered to be the first baseball player in the history of the game to be given the moniker "Babe," which he was dubbed due to his good looks.[2] The handsome right-hander was a welcome sight to the Forbes Field throng, who were not only thrilled by his fine rookie campaign that included a 5–2 mark down the stretch in September, winning his last five starts, but also his dominance over the Tigers earlier in the fall classic.

The knuckleballer Ed Summers, nicknamed Kickapoo Ed due to his her-itage with the Kickapoo Indian tribe, was also effective in September as Detroit emerged victorious in four of his six starts during the season's last month. Jennings chose Summers to start this game over the injured Bill Donovan, presumably not wanting to start his sore-armed veteran in cold weather. He was looking to finally get in the win column in World Series play, as he had a less than stellar 0–3 mark to this point that included giving up a fall classic record six consecutive hits to the Cubs in the ninth inning of a 10–6 Game 1 loss. It was a game where Summers blew a 6–5 ninth inning lead that took whatever momentum the Tigers had in the Series and turned it into a five-game Cubs victory.

Adams hope of continuing his domination of Detroit hitters was put on hold at the beginning of the game when leadoff hitter Davy Jones parked a home run into the temporary center field stands that had been erected for this Series, yet stood empty today due to the cold weather. The run stunned the now-silent crowd, as did the free pass that Adams gave to Donie Bush.

Now somewhat rattled, Adams faced Ty Cobb and missed the plate on his first three pitches. Trying to further intimidate the young Pirate pitcher, Cobb made faces towards him. He then took off for first on what he thought was ball four. Umpire Jim Johnstone thought otherwise, as he called a strike on the pitch. An incensed Cobb argued his point, slammed his bat on the plate and settled once again into the batter's box. Instead of flustering the pitcher, Cobb seemingly frustrated himself as he lofted a harmless fly to Tommy Leach in center for the first out.

Sam Crawford now came to the plate. Despite the fact he was not having a great World Series to this point, hitting only .176 coming into this game, he was still widely respected as one of the best players in the game by most experts. Writer F.C. Lane wrote an article for *Baseball Magazine*, claiming that "while we are no sculptor, we believe if we were and were looking for a

The only bright spot for the Tigers in a disappointing 8–4 loss to the Pirates in Game 5 of the World Series was Sam Crawford. The Hall of Fame outfielder had three hits, including a home run and double and two RBIs (courtesy of Library of Congress, Bain Collection, Prints & Photographs Division, 3c3539).

model for a statue of a slugger we would choose Sam Crawford for that role."[3] A natural hitter, he stated his philosophy as: "My idea of batting is a thing that should be done unconsciously. If you get to studying too much, to see what a fraction of a second you must swing to meet a curved ball, the chances are you will miss it all together."[4] Described as a "typical broad shouldered slugger" by Lane, Crawford was in the top ten in slugging fourteen times in his career, and homers thirteen times including leading both leagues in long balls (for Cincinnati in the National League in 1901 and for Detroit in 1908).[5] The Detroit slugger finally started to show the patrons of the 1909 World Series just how good he was as he laced a single into left that sent Bush to third.

Adams then bore down, striking out Jim Delahanty looking. The Tigers second baseman seemed just as irritated towards Johnstone as Cobb was, questioning the umpire's eye for calling balls and strikes. Crawford then took off for second, stealing the base and setting up George Moriarty with men in scoring position. Moriarty was unable to inflict any further damage on the Pirates, popping up between first and second, where Pirate first baseman Bill Abstein ran in front of a surprised second baseman Dots Miller to secure the final out.

With a run on the board and the momentum in the Series, Summers took the hill to face a Pirate offense coming off one of its most inept performances of the campaign. Bobby Byrne came up to try and spark the Bucs, hitting a hot grounder to short that nipped Bush's glove and rolled to Crawford for a single. Tommy Leach strolled to the plate next looking to move Byrne into scoring position. A diminutive figure on the diamond, standing a mere 5'6" and weighing 135 pounds, Leach was one of the most prodigious home run hitters of the Deadball Era, finishing in the top ten five times in the twentieth century's first decade, including a league-leading six in 1902. It wasn't that Leach had a powerful stroke; it was his speed that put him among the best home run hitters of his era. Forty-nine of his 61 career homers came via the inside-the-park variety, second in the history of the game behind Sam Crawford's 51. "Every so often I'd manage to drive a ball between the outfielders and it would roll to the fence. I was pretty fast, and by the time they ran the ball down and got it back to the infield, I'd be home," Leach recalled.[6] Leach was also close to increasing those inside-the-park totals as his speed led him to an impressive 172 triples, the 23rd best career mark in the history of the game.

This particular situation called for a sacrifice, though, something Leach had done 240 times in his successful 19-year career, another outstanding mark as only 45 other major leaguers had bested his career total. This time, though,

Leach was unsuccessful in his attempt, which ironically would be unfortunate for the Tigers. Leach hustled down first, beating Oscar Stanage's throw for a single.

Manager Fred Clarke himself tried to bunt, and did an outstanding job putting the ball perfectly between Summers and Stanage, with the Detroit catcher throwing Clarke out at first and putting men in scoring position. The sacrifice set up the great Honus Wagner perfectly, the man that the Bucs effective southpaw starter Lefty Leifield once remembered was "the grandest player that I ever looked at. He could hit anything, field anything and steal bases on any catcher or pitcher in the business. And he never made a mistake."[7] As Forbes Field was now alive with cowbells ringing and cheers at a feverish pitch, Summers wanted no part of Wagner, intentionally walking the Pirate shortstop to load the bases. Dots Miller looked like he would clear the bases with his liner to right field. Luckily for Detroit the ball dropped in foul territory, sending everyone back to their bases. Miller was unable to take advantage of the situation, striking out for the inning's second out.

Two outs, the bases loaded and the poor-fielding Pirate first baseman Bill Abstein coming to the plate, the Tigers hoped they had weathered the storm and would be able to get out of the inning with no damage. It looked like Summers World Series faults would continue as he put three consecutive pitches outside of the strike zone. It was at that point Wagner began to do what was described as a cannibal dance by the *Pittsburgh Gazette*, to try and destroy the concentration of the Detroit hurler.[8] It did not work immediately as Abstein looked at the next two pitches for strikes, leaving the count full at 3–2. The sixth pitch went by the Pirate first baseman also, this one for a ball and Abstein went to first on the free pass, sending Byrne across the plate with the tying run. Chief Wilson struck out for the final out, but the Pirates finally were able to break their futile streak, scoring for the first time since Game 3.

With the Bucs now on the scoreboard, Adams shook off his shaky first inning and thoroughly dominated the Tigers in the second inning. Tom Jones flew out to Wilson in right, Stanage struck out as did the pitcher Summers, who Adams blew away on three straight pitches. Following the Summers strikeout, a Pirate fan took out his horn and played "hail, hail the gang's all here."

While Adams was able to get over his less than desirable first inning, the Detroit hurler was not. George Gibson cracked a shot to Bush at short and was able to leg out a hit, beating the throw by Bush. Adams came to bat and did his job, laying down a perfect bunt between Summers and Tom Jones. Summers picked up the grounder and threw it to Delahanty, who was covering first, as Gibson took second.

Bobby Byrne came as close as he could to getting his second hit in two innings, sending a grounder towards Delahanty at second. However, he was denied an infield single when Delahanty made a great bare-handed stop and threw it to first hurriedly and accurately, just beating the speedy Byrne at first.

Once again Summers was within one solid pitch of getting through an inning scoreless. For the second time in two frames he hurt his own cause with an unfathomable mistake. This time the Tiger hurler uncorked a wild pitch that got past Stanage to the backstop. Gibson, who went to third on Delahanty's remarkable play, scored easily, giving the Bucs a 2–1 lead. Leach concluded the second with a fly ball to Crawford.

Davy Jones, who hit the leadoff home run in the first to give the Tigers their lone tally, began the Tigers part of the third inning. He tried once again to get his club on the board, smacking yet another shot to center field. Luckily

After a subpar first three games in the 1909 fall classic, Fred Clarke broke loose in Game 5, homering with two hits and three RBIs in the Pirates' 8–4 victory (courtesy of the Pittsburgh Pirates).

for Pittsburgh, Leach was able to settle under this one to retire the Detroit left fielder. Bush stayed alive with Adams, fouling off several pitches, but he wasn't able to get to the Bucs rookie pitcher either, becoming Adams' fourth strikeout victim in three innings. A now dominant Adams also fooled Cobb, who swung mightily, but could only muster up a harmless grounder to Byrne for the Tigers eighth consecutive out after their fast start in the first inning.

Clarke led off the bottom of the third crushing a ball into the left-field bleachers for what he thought was his second homer of the series. However, the umpires deemed the ball foul, putting the Pirate manager back in the batter's box. He eventually was able to work a walk off Summers.

Not wanting to let Clarke steal second and put himself in scoring position for Wagner, Bush gambled and broke for second to anticipate the throw, hopefully getting the Bucs Hall of Fame left fielder. Stanage called for an outside pitch to which Wagner reached out and poked a single to left as Clarke, who did take off for second, ended up on third. The clutch hitting set up Pittsburgh's third run of the game when Miller's grounder to Bush scored Clarke and sent Wagner to second. Abstein and Wilson were retired on hoppers to Moriarty and Bush, respectively, putting a cap on the third inning, but not before Summers surrendered his eighth run in three and one-third innings of work in this fall classic.

With Pittsburgh up, 3–1, the Pirate rookie hurler continued to baffle Tiger hitters in the fourth and fifth inning. Except for a leadoff hit in the fifth by Tom Jones, who sliced a hit over the third base bag and down the left-field line for a double, the Detroit offense was rendered useless. In the fourth, Adams got Crawford to bounce into a ground out to Wagner. Delahanty popped a high shot in foul territory behind the plate that Gibson missed when he slipped and fell down. Unable to take advantage of his second chance, he struck out for the second time. Moriarty then hit a harmless bounder to Miller to extend Adam's streak of eleven consecutive Tigers up and eleven consecutive Tigers retired.

In the fifth, after Jones broke the team's hitless streak with his double, Stanage struck out once again. It looked like the irritated catcher was going to throw his bat in frustration, but decided to just carry it back to the bench with him. Summers became strikeout victim number seven before Davy Jones sent a third consecutive long fly into the outfield, this time Clarke catching it before it reached the fence.

Summers himself also finally had some success in the fourth and fifth innings, keeping the Pirates at bay and holding the deficit to 3–1. He retired the Bucs in order for the first time in the fourth with Gibson hitting a roller to Moriarty at third, Adams fouling out to Stanage and Byrne flying out to Davy Jones.

Leach almost extended the Pittsburgh lead the following inning with a long fly to the left-field bleachers that went foul. He tried to put it back into the bleachers a second time, but didn't quite get enough of the ball and was retired by Davy Jones. Clarke was then fooled on a pitch as the bat flew out of his hands towards first base. The Pirate skipper looked liked more of a force on the next pitch as he legged out an infield single. Clarke then swiped second and went to third when Wagner grounded out to Bush.

With two outs and a man in scoring position, it was a situation that seemed eerily similar to the first two innings when the Pirates scored on mistakes by Summers with two outs. This time the Detroit righty was up to the challenge and retired the side when he forced Miller in to a ground out to Moriarty.

With the Tigers down to their last twelve outs and looking like their Game 5 chances of victory were fading quickly, Jennings sent up the meat of his lineup to try to solve Adams. After Bush struck out and slammed the bat into the plate, things finally began to turn in the right direction for the Tigers. Cobb, whom writer F.C. Lane called "the wisest batter who ever lived," singled to left with Crawford coming to the plate.[9] The Detroit center fielder, who had been having a subpar World Series to this point, ripped a ball to the left-center field wall for a double, scoring Cobb and cutting the Pittsburgh advantage to a single run.

Adams seemed to get the game back under control when Delahanty hit a roller to Wagner at short. Considered one of the greatest defensive players in the annals of the game, the Hall of Famer was not at his best here, sending his throw to first past Abstein, which scored Crawford with the tying run and put Delahanty in scoring position with the potential go-ahead tally.

Jennings, whom the inning before must have been wondering how his club would ever find its way back into this game, was now very thrilled. "That's the break; were back in the game," said the joyous manager following Wagner's error. "From here on we ought to go places."[10] Unfortunately, that was as far as the Tigers would go as Moriarty hit a fly to Clarke and Jones popped up to Abstein to keep the damage from getting worse.

It was a new game now, one that saw Summers now in control of the Pirate offense. He was able to put the Bucs down 1-2-3 for the second time in three innings as Abstein hit an easy fly to Bush at short, Wilson grounded to Tom Jones at first and Gibson rolled one to short.

The Pirates rookie pitcher was able to shake off the sixth inning and once again retire the Tigers in order as he had done in three of the first six frames. Matty McIntyre, who pinch-hit for Stanage, and Summers both were retired by Abstein unassisted. Davy Jones, who seemed very unlucky following his leadoff long ball, tagged another hard hit off the Indiana native. For the third straight time his solid shot want for naught when Wagner snatched it and threw onto Abstein for the final out.

In the bottom of the seventh, the crowd got excited and the horn was blowing loudly as the Pirate faithful hoped their hometown team could find away to surge ahead again. Like the Tigers in the top of the sixth, the Pirates had the strength of their lineup coming to the plate. Well almost the strength of their lineup, as Adams came up first before the Bucs big hitters. Adams struck out after a couple foul balls for the first out. Byrne then tagged Summers by slapping his second hit of the game to left. Leach followed suit with a similar shot to left. Davy Jones stumbled and fell, allowing Byrne to make it to third with the go-ahead run.

Up came the veteran Pirates left fielder Fred Clarke, who except for his first-game home run, was having a miserable fall classic, batting a mere .071 coming into the all-important fifth contest. The 37-year-old Pirate manager was in the twilight of his great career, as 1909 represented the 16th season of his remarkable 21-year career. It was a fabulous career that saw the Winterset, Iowa, native hit .312 and garner 2,672 hits, 1,619 runs, an all-time seventh best 220 triples and 506 stolen bases, the 34th best mark in the history of the game.

A line-drive hitter who began his professional baseball career by answering an ad in *The Sporting News* by a team in Hastings, Nebraska, Clarke was as efficient defensively as he was at bat. He had made several clutch defensive plays in this fall classic to prove that point. Despite the fact the left-field area in the sparkling new Forbes Field was expansive, Clarke led the senior circuit in fielding percentage in this championship campaign for the Bucs, an impressive feat for an aging player. What Clarke was most of all as a player, was dependable and consistent in the clutch. Despite the fact he never had more than 82 RBIs in a season, he still managed to crack the 1,000 RBI barrier for his career, with 1015. That ability in the clutch was about to be on display in this game. With two on and the score tied, the Pirate manager hit a long fly to center that bounced over Crawford's head into the temporary stands that had been erected for this Series for a three-run homer, giving his club a 6–3 lead.

Summers followed the home run by plunking Wagner in the kidneys, sending the Bucs shortstop to the ground writhing in pain. The concerned Pirate bench rushed to the field to see if their leader was hurt. After several minutes, Wagner emerged from his pack of teammates and ran to first base.

Dots Miller sauntered up to bat and was very close to making this contest an 8–3 affair by lifting a long shot towards the left-field stands. Luckily for Summers, Davy Jones caught up to it and caught the ball for the second out of the frame. At that point Wagner seemed recovered and decided to challenge the Tigers new catcher, Boss Schmidt, who replaced Stanage in the top of the seventh.

With Abstein at the plate, Wagner took off swipe second. Wanting to challenge Schmidt's questionable arm once again, he then took off for third. The throw from the Detroit backstop flew into left field and Wagner strolled home with what would prove to be the nail in the proverbial coffin for the Tigers in Game 5. Abstein struck out to end the inning, but the Pirates duo of Clarke and Wagner had put this game seemingly out of reach as Detroit entered the top of the eighth down, 7–3.

While the odds were against a Tiger comeback, Donie Bush nonetheless came up in the top of the eighth with the intention of bringing his team back. Bush hit a stinging liner to center field where Leach, playing Bush correctly, moved in for the catch. Cobb, whose Series average dropped to .278 following his mediocre 1-for-4 performance in Game 5, hit a grounder back to Adams for the second out, leaving it to fellow Hall of Famer Sam Crawford to try and inspire the Tigers potent offense.

After not being much of a factor in the first four contests of this fall classic, Crawford was at his best today with two hits in his three previous at-bats; at-bat number four would be his best, though. Crawford took the Babe Adams offering and sent it towards the temporary stands in center field. Tommy Leach gave chase and dove towards the wall in a vain attempt to catch Crawford's drive. Both the ball and Leach disappeared, with the Pirate center fielder taking the top part of wall with him as he went crashing into it.

The crowd was silenced and the worried Pirates ran out to center to see if their diminutive veteran was badly injured. Even Crawford was concerned as he trotted around the bases after his magnificent home run looking towards the situation. Moments later a cheer from the crowd erupted as Leach reappeared on the field and took his position appearing fine. Once things settled down, Adams returned to the mound and finished Detroit in the eighth, getting Delahanty to ground out to Byrne.

In the bottom half of the frame, the Pirates quickly reclaimed their four-run cushion when Chief Wilson met Summers with a leadoff fly ball to left. Davy Jones appeared to lose the ball in the sun and Crawford tried to make up for the miscue, hustling to the ball to no avail. Wilson trotted into second for a double. Gibson came up next and smacked a shot to Cobb in right for an RBI single, as Wilson scored the final run of the game making it 8–4.

Jennings had seen enough of Summers and promptly replaced him with Ed Willett.

Willett, who had cleaned up Summers' mess in Game 3 with six and two-thirds innings of three-hit ball allowing only one unearned run, tried to finish the Pirates with a man on first and no one out. He promptly got Adams to pop up to first baseman Tom Jones, then after Gibson stole second, struck out Bobby Byrne. With Tommy Leach up, Gibson took off for third and was pegged down by Schmidt for the Bucs final out.

With Willett stopping the Bucs in the eighth, the Tigers had only three outs left to try and reverse their bad fortune on this day. Moriarty started the frame off for Detroit by popping up in foul territory to Byrne for the first out. Tom Jones then popped up to Wagner at short, who inexplicably dropped it, allowing Jones to reach first. The fans seemed to enjoy the miscue, laughing at the Pirates shortstop as the game was out of hand. Wagner appeared not to be amused. He got his chance for retribution, retiring Schmidt on a grounder after Jones stole second unabated. George Mullin walked to the plate, batting for Willett, and popped up to Wagner, who was able to firmly hold on to this one for the Tigers' final out. Pittsburgh had the advantage in the Series with a three games to two lead as the two clubs headed for Detroit now.

As the teams left, the National Commission stayed in Pittsburgh temporarily. With a good possibility that the Series would go seven games, they first had to determine where the final game would be hosted should it need to be played. There was a sentiment to play it at a neutral site, one which American League president Ban Johnson quickly put to rest, pushing instead for either Pittsburgh or Detroit to host the contest. It was decided by the powers that be to flip a coin. National League president John Heydler called heads; to his dismay it came up tails, which meant Bennett Park would host the seventh and deciding game if the Detroit somehow could find away to overcome this loss and emerge victorious in Game 6.

For the Pirates, they had now played the final game at their brand new facility in 1909, a stadium that had seen them through one of the greatest seasons in the franchise's history. Ironically if the final game needed to be played, it would fall on October 13, the same day that 51 years later the Pirate faithful at Forbes Field would see the Bucs end the 1960 World Series on Bill Mazeroski's dramatic Game 7 home run. Because of the unfortunate flip of a coin, Pittsburgh would now have to defeat their American League rivals in one of the final two games in Detroit if they hoped to emerge victorious in this World Series.

Game 5 Box Score

```
DET A    1 0 0    0 0 2    0 1 0— 4  6 1
PIT N    1 1 1    0 0 0    4 1 x— 8 10 2
```

BATTING

Detroit Tigers	AB	R	H	RBI	BB	SO	PO	A
D. Jones lf	4	1	1	1	0	0	3	0
Bush ss	3	0	0	0	1	2	1	4
Cobb rf	4	1	1	0	0	0	0	0
Crawford cf	4	2	3	2	0	0	1	0
Delahanty 2b	4	0	0	0	0	2	0	1
Moriarty 3b	4	0	0	0	0	0	1	3
T. Jones 1b	4	0	1	0	0	0	12	0
Stanage c	2	0	0	0	0	2	3	1
McIntyre ph	1	0	0	0	0	0	0	0
Schmidt c	1	0	0	0	0	0	3	1
Summers p	3	0	0	0	0	2	0	1
Willett p	0	0	0	0	0	0	0	0
Mullin ph	1	0	0	0	0	0	0	0
Totals	35	4	6	3	1	8	24	11

FIELDING—
E: Schmidt (3).

BATTING—
2B: T. Jones (1,0ff Adams); Crawford (2,0ff Adams).
HR: D. Jones (1,1st inning off Adams 0 on 0 out); Crawford (1,8th inning off Adams 0 on 2 out).
Team LOB: 5.

BASERUNNING—
SB: Crawford (1,2nd base off Adams/Gibson); T. Jones (1,2nd base off Adams/Gibson).

Pittsburgh Pirates	AB	R	H	RBI	BB	SO	PO	A
Byrne 3b	5	2	2	0	0	1	1	2
Leach cf	4	1	2	0	0	0	3	0
Clarke lf	2	2	2	3	1	0	2	0
Wagner ss	2	1	1	0	1	0	1	3
Miller 2b	4	0	0	1	0	1	0	1
Abstein 1b	3	0	0	1	1	1	11	0
Wilson rf	4	1	1	0	0	1	1	0
Gibson c	4	1	2	1	0	0	8	0
Adams p	3	0	0	0	0	1	0	1
Totals	31	8	10	6	3	5	27	7

FIELDING—
E: Wagner 2 (3).

BATTING—
2B: Wilson (1,0ff Summers).
HR: Clarke (2,7th inning off Summers 2 on 1 out).
SH: Clarke (2,0ff Summers); Adams (1,0ff Summers).
HBP: Wagner (2,by Summers).
Team LOB: 5.

BASERUNNING—
SB: Clarke (1,2nd base off Summers/Stanage); Wagner 2 (6,2nd base off Summers/Schmidt,3rd base off Summers/Schmidt); Gibson (2,2nd base off Willett/Schmidt).
CS: Gibson (1,3rd base by Willett/Schmidt).

PITCHING

Detroit Tigers	*IP*	*H*	*R*	*ER*	*BB*	*SO*	*HR*	*BFP*
Summers L(0–2)	7	10	8	7	3	4	1	35
Willett	1	0	0	0	0	1	0	2
Totals	8	10	8	7	3	5	1	37

Summers faced 2 batters in the 8th inning
WP: Summers (2).
HBP: Summers (1,Wagner).

Pittsburgh Pirates	*IP*	*H*	*R*	*ER*	*BB*	*SO*	*HR*	*BFP*
Adams W(2–0)	9	6	4	3	1	8	2	36

Umpires: HP — Jim Johnstone, 1B — Silk O'Loughlin, LF — Bill Klem, RF — Billy Evans
Time of Game: 1:46 **Attendance:** 21706

◆ 8 ◆

GAME 6, OCTOBER 14
Bennett Park, Detroit
Detroit 5, Pittsburgh 4

It was a different atmosphere in Detroit than when these two combatants had met in Game 3. The ecstatic Tiger faithful that jammed every nook and cranny of archaic Bennett Park following Detroit's 7–2 Game 2 thrashing of the Pirates that knotted up the series at one a piece was replaced by a less than stellar crowd of 10,535. The small crowd was there despite the fact this would be the first contest in the Motor City that didn't feel like it was being played in a freezer. The temperature was around 40 degrees, and while there was still a feisty wind blowing, the sun had finally made an appearance.

The lack of nasty weather aside, the enthusiasm for the Tigers was beginning to waver after the Bucs took a three games to two advantage in this fall classic. After all, this is exactly where the Tigers were in the previous two World Series, on the brink of elimination, and certainly Tiger fans thought it was only a matter of time before their hometown team would falter once again. While early on it seemed like the fans' attitude was passive, this game would turn into a classic, one that the *Pittsburgh Gazette* would claim "was far and away the most exciting game of the World Series, and one of the most exciting ever played on any diamond."[1]

The mound opponents for this thrilling contest were two of the era's greatest hurlers. For Detroit, it was their 29-game winner, George Mullin. Except for a three-inning period between the fourth and sixth innings of Game 1, Mullin had completely perplexed the Bucs in this fall classic. Because the Toledo native had shut down the potent Pirate bats, 5–0, in Game 4, manager Hughie Jennings had to wonder if the 29-year-old pitcher had enough steam to keep the Tigers' championship hopes alive. According to sportswriter Fred Lieb, Jennings said to his pitcher, "I want to start you if you are right, but if you're not I want you to tell me. In that case I'll pitch Willett."[2] To the joy of his teammates and Jennings, Mullin reportedly shot back, "The arm feels fine; I think I can tie that series up for you."[3]

On the Pittsburgh hill was veteran Vic Willis. Thirty-three years old from Cecil County, Maryland, Willis was a power pitcher who had a dominant curveball. According to the *Boston Sunday Journal*, "Willis has speed and the most elusive curves. His 'drop' is so wonderful that, if anyone hits it, it is generally considered a fluke."[4] Willis broke in with Boston in 1898 and won twenty games or more in four of his first five seasons, leading the circuit in ERA and with a 2.50 in 1899. Coming to the Pirates in 1906, Willis told owner Barney Dreyfuss that he was happy to be in Pittsburgh and would "do my best to bring another pennant to the Smoky City."[5] Willis kept his promise to Dreyfuss, winning 22 games in 1909 with a miniscule 2.24 ERA. Despite the fact he had won the second-most games on the team next to Howie Camnitz's 25 victories, Willis had only appeared in a relief role in the fall classic to this point. He pitched fine in his six and two-thirds innings of work during Game 2 after Camnitz surrendered five runs by the third inning.

It was Willis' first chance to start a World Series game after 12 years and 240 career victories, and what an opportunity it would be. Not only getting the ball for this clutch game, but having the opportunity to be on the mound when his team won its first world championship. According to Lieb, Pirate manager Fred Clarke looked at his veteran and told him, "I've been holding you back just for this one, Vic; you can wind it up for us."[6]

While it was Willis' initial post-season start, the pressure in this contest stood firmly on the shoulders of Mullin and his Tiger teammates. There was no room for error against their powerful Pirate foes. Any mistake would mean Detroit's third consecutive championship campaign would end in futility. They didn't have to be perfect, just damn close to it.

Pittsburgh wanted to take any guesswork out of this game early on as they quickly solved the puzzle that was George Mullin. Mullin got the best of leadoff hitter Bobby Byrne early, getting two strikes on the speedy third baseman. In the end, Byrne won the battle, striking a single to left field. The confrontation between Mullin and Byrne wasn't over, it was just heating up. Several times Byrne leaned off first, drawing a throw from Mullin. Finally the Detroit veteran hurler threw home to Pittsburgh center fielder Tommy Leach. Leach laced a hit right at first baseman Tom Jones. The ball shot off Jones and bounced into right field for a single. Byrne, who took off on contact, made it easily into third base.

Clarke was up next and made it three for three by the Bucs, sending the ball to Ty Cobb in right, scoring Byrne. On the play, Leach hustled into third with an attentive Clarke getting into scoring position by making it to second when the throw went to third trying to retire the Pirate diminutive center fielder. Frustrated, third baseman George Moriarty, who was irascible to begin with, tried to take matters into his own hands by disrupting Leach at third. Moriarty first went to Leach and kicked him in the shins. After the 32-year-old Pirate veteran protested, Moriarty took it to the next level, taking Leach's hat, which hit a nerve given the New York native's sensitivity towards his baldness, which was compounded by the fact he had shaved his head after being told it would stop his hair loss. An irritated Leach explained his reaction, "I turned around and grabbed my cap, and at the same time, gave him a good healthy kick in the shins."[7]

Once things calmed down, Honus Wagner came to the plate and proceeded to launch a long fly to left field. In his attempt to flag down the shot, Detroit left fielder Davy Jones fell down as Wagner rolled into second, plating both Clarke and Leach, extending the Bucs lead to 3–0. The Tigers were now down by three with Wagner at second and no outs. If the Tigers had damn little room for error at the beginning of the contest, it was now down to absolutely no room. One more hit at this point would likely end whatever championship hopes Detroit had.

What few fans were in the stands from Pittsburgh were making quite a ruckus now as their club was threatening to make this sixth contest a blowout. Dots Miller came up next and hit a grounder to Jim Delahanty at second. Wagner moved over to third as Miller was tossed out at first. Bill Abstein, who was struggling defensively throughout the Series, showed he could have issues offensively too as he struck out once again with a man in scoring position. Mullin finally ended this less than stellar opening frame by inducing Chief Wilson to ground out back to the mound for the Bucs' third out. While at the time Pittsburgh was feeling good, by the end of the game, stranding Wagner on third and causing no more damage after the first four batters got on base would prove to be catastrophic for the Bucs.

Willis stepped on the mound with a three-run lead. Since he was one of the best pitchers of the era, Detroit certainly had their work cut out for them. They began to chip away in the bottom of the first when the veteran Pirate hurler gave shortstop Donie Bush a free pass after Davy Jones lined out to Dots Miller to start the frame. Cobb came to the plate next in hopes of yet another legendary effort that marked his Hall of Fame career. On this day the Tiger great was not at his best. Even though he had aborted taking his roundabout way between Pittsburgh and Detroit for the fourth time to avoid a certain arrest in Ohio in favor of a more direct route (he hid wrapped in a blanket in the back seat of a car driven by his uncle A.C. Ginn going straight through Ohio), the whole episode, as well as the previous travel escapades, were taking its toll on Cobb. Willis was able to win this battle, striking out the irascible Detroit right fielder for the second out, before facing another Hall of Famer by the name of Sam Crawford.

Where Cobb could not deliver the clutch hit, Crawford did, smacking a rocket to right field. Chief Wilson picked up the ball and rifled a throw to his cutoff man Miller, who sent the relay to George Gibson behind the plate. The throw was off the mark as Bush scored with Crawford moving to third. Detroit was unable to cut into the Pirate lead any further as Jim Delahanty flew out harmlessly to Leach, ending the first inning with Pittsburgh still hanging on to a 3–1 advantage.

The double by Crawford was just the beginning of a turnaround for the Tigers. George Mullin was about to take it to the next level. Following his rocky start in the first, when he gave up four straight hits, Mullin calmed down and got tough. He retired the last three Bucs to end the opening frame and kept the streak going in the second. Gibson opened the inning by striking out. Tiger catcher Boss Schmidt dropped the third strike, but tossed out Gibson at first to complete the play. Willis then grounded out to his counterpart, bringing Byrne to the plate. Like he did to begin the game, Byrne caught hold of the Mullin offering, this time lacing it down the third-base line. Moriarty made a fabulous play, robbing the Pirate leadoff hitter of a hit, tossing him out at first to the delight of the Tiger faithful.

Willis was able to control the Detroit offense in the bottom of the second, getting Moriarty and Tom Jones to bounce out to Byrne and Wagner, respectively, before facing Boss Schmidt. Schmidt had been given the starting nod following a controversy in Game 5. The *Pittsburgh Gazette* reported that American League president Ban Johnson, who was not impressed at all with Schmidt and was desperate to wrestle away the world championship from the hated National League, wanted Oscar Stanage behind the plate instead of Schmidt.[8] Johnson insisted and pleaded with Hughie Jennings to have Stanage start the contest, which he finally reportedly gave in to. After Stanage went 0-for-2, Jennings pulled the catcher, pinch-hitting Matty McIntyre before inserting Schmidt. Regardless of who was behind the plate, Jennings was less than complementary towards either backstop, stating, "Neither Stanage or Schmidt were sure of themselves. I think it helped to keep Summers unsteady."[9] In this sixth game, Jennings went with Schmidt, who continued the Tigers woes behind the plate with a harmless flyout to Leach in center.

As Leach came strolling in from the outfield following the putout, he proceeded to head directly to the plate as he was leading off the top half of the third. Mullin tossed the first two pitches by the Pirate centerfielder for strikes before Leach sent the third offering to Bush at short, who bobbled the ball allowing Leach to reach first. Clarke put Leach into scoring position with a sacrifice bunt, bringing up Wagner. Trying to return the Pittsburgh advantage to three, Wagner lashed a hard shot to Delahanty at second. The ball came fast to Delahanty and temporarily shook him up. He was able to recover in time to get Wagner in time at first. Leach advanced to third on the play. Mullin then walked Miller, bringing up Abstein with two on and two out. Once again with men in scoring position and an opportunity to add to the Pittsburgh run total, the Pirate first baseman struck out as he had in the first inning, keeping the game at 3–1.

Trying to slice into the Bucs lead, the Tigers started off quickly with Mullin showing off his offensive prowess by striking a single into left field, sending the Detroit faithful into a frenzy. The fans were quieted quickly when Davy Jones lined out to Miller at second, who quickly tossed the ball to Abstein at first to catch Mullin off base for the double play.

While seemingly in control, there were signs that Willis was, in fact, about to be just the opposite. The Pirate Hall of Fame hurler, who was elected by the Veterans Committee 86 years after his lone World Series start, threw one above Donie Bush's head, then hit him on the foot as the Detroit shortstop ran quickly to first with the free pass. He then took off, beating the throw by Gibson to steal second base. Looking to turn around what was a disappointing fall classic to this point, Cobb came up and once again was unable to come through in the clutch, popping to Miller to end the threat.

For the Tigers, George Mullin on the mound had found his groove. He sent the Bucs down in order in the fourth, all on ground balls with Wilson, Gibson and Willis distributing the ball equally around the infield, grounding out to Bush, Moriarty and Delahanty, respectively. For the Pirates, Willis was about to lose his groove.

Willis walked Crawford to start the bottom of the fourth inning. He was so off the mark with his pitches that the *Pittsburgh Gazette* described the sequence as it "looked like a deliberate gift."[10] Delahanty then tried to send Crawford to second with a sacrifice. He failed twice before giving up on the strategy. Unfortunately for the Bucs, he sent the next pitch to center field sending Crawford to third. Moriarty then plated Crawford with a stinging single to right. Chief Wilson showed off his arm with a perfect throw to third, in time to retire Delahanty who was trying to advance an extra base on the hit.

Tom Jones came up next in an attempt to tie the game. A first baseman out of Danville, Pennsylvania, Jones came to the Tigers only a little over a month before the Series began, as the St. Louis Browns sent him to the Motor City in exchange for Claude Rossman. Starting with the Baltimore Orioles in 1902 before being sent to the Browns two years later, Jones had been an average hitter who excelled in the art of the sacrifice hit, leading the junior circuit in 1906 with 40, accumulating 205 in his career, the 80th best mark in the history of the game. A .251 career hitter, Jones was at his best following the August 29 trade, hitting .281 in the final month and a half of the season. While the situation he was in at this point in the game may have called for his specialty, the sacrifice, he instead continued the scoringfest by lacing a liner past Byrne to Clarke in left. The ball went between Clarke's legs, sending Jones to second and Moriarty home with the game-tying run. Willis continued his struggles by walking Schmidt before finally settling down by retiring Mullin and Davy Jones on fly balls to Clarke.

What had looked like at rout leading to the Bucs' coronation as world champions earlier in the day was now anything but. The Tigers had all the momentum and a pitcher who seemed unbeatable. In the top of the fifth, Mullin once again dominated Pirate hitters, forcing Byrne and Clarke to ground out to Bush, sandwiched in between a fly ball out by Leach.

The Detroit offense continued to do their part in the bottom half of the fifth. Bush led off the frame, getting the pro–Tiger crowd into an uproar with a single to center field. The inning almost ended before the American League champions had a chance to take the lead. Cobb once again failed to come through with a man on base in this game by hitting a ground ball to Abstein at first. The Bucs first baseman stepped on the bag and turned to throw a strike to Wagner at second, but Bush got to the base in time to avoid what could have been a game-changing double play.

Crawford came up next and gave Pittsburgh a golden opportunity to once again end this inning with the score tied. The Tiger center fielder lash a liner to Wagner at short. Bush was leaning off second and would have been an easy out for a double play. Fortunately for Detroit, Wagner, who was one of the greatest fielders of his era, dropped the ball, allowing Bush to get to third as Wagner regained his composure, picked up the ball and got Crawford at first for the second out.

Two outs yet two opportunities to retire Bush on the basepaths for the third out failed. The question now was could the Pirates' blown opportunities hurt them or could they get out of this inning unscathed. The answer was the former as the Tigers took advantage of the missed Pirate opportunities. Delahanty drove a Willis pitch down the left-field foul line for a double, scoring Bush with the go-ahead run. Moriarty followed with a walk before Willis finally ended the fifth as Tom Jones popped up to Byrne at third.

As they saw their once-dominant lead completely whittled away, the Bucs offense continued to be thoroughly ineffective against Mullin. Wagner, looking to make up for his miscue in the bottom half of the fifth, immediately went after Mullin's first offering in the sixth. He was only able to connect with a lazy fly ball to Davy Jones in left for the first out.

Miller finally broke Mullin's hitless streak over the previous five frames as he laced a single to center for the first Pittsburgh hit since the three-run first inning, a frame that must have seemed so long ago for the Bucs faithful. The single was for naught when Abstein came to the plate for the third time in this game with a man on base. While the Pittsburgh first baseman did not strike out as he had done in the first and third, he nonetheless could manage only a foul popup to Schmidt. During the popup, the Detroit catcher ran down to the grandstand to catch the foul ball. In an attempt to get some someone in scoring position, Miller took off for second after Schmidt snagged the ball. The Tiger backstop turned around and threw a strike to Bush at second to get Miller for the inning-ending double play.

Fred Clarke had seen enough of Willis and turned to 25-game winner Howie Camnitz, who was unproductive himself in the 7–2 Game 2 defeat, to try and keep the Bucs in the game. Schmidt, who made a great throw to end the top of the sixth, showed his offensive prowess in the bottom half of the frame by striking a solid shot to Wilson. The Pirate right fielder misplayed the ball, which went behind him into the crowd for a ground-rule double.

Mullin failed to advance Schmidt with a grounder to Camnitz, who tossed the ball to Byrne getting the lead runner at third. Davy Jones also could not move the runner into scoring position when he hit the ball to Abstein, who tossed it on to Wagner to retire Mullin at second. Trying to put a Detroit runner in scoring position, Jones took off for second, successfully swiping the base on Gibson's less than stellar throw. Camnitz walked Bush and then faced Cobb. To this point in the contest, Cobb had not been at his best, leaving men on base in the first, third and fifth innings. Camnitz was not able to extend that streak to four when Cobb slammed a ball to right field, which bounded into the crowd for a double, plating Jones with the Tigers' fifth run, extending the lead to 5–3.

While the crowd may not have been large, it nonetheless erupted into a deafening roar. Even though Camnitz was able to retire Crawford on a fly to Leach to end the sixth inning without the game getting out of hand, the enthusiastic crowd was starting to feel confident that their hometown team would be able to extend this Series to a seventh and deciding game.

The Pirates, on the other hand, were not feeling confident as their bats continued to be rendered useless against Mullin. John Gruber of the *Pittsburgh*

Gazette said about Mullin that he "pitched so hard it made the dust fly out of Schmidt's glove."[11] Wilson was his first victim as he lifted a lazy fly to Cobb in right. Gibson gave Pittsburgh a momentary glimpse of hope as he grounded one up the middle for a single. At that point Clarke sent up rookie Robert Hamilton "Ham" Hyatt to bat for Camnitz. Hyatt had a decent rookie season for the Bucs, batting .299 in limited play after being purchased from Vancouver of the Northwestern League a year earlier. The native of Buncombe County, North Carolina, hit .318 in eleven minor league seasons. At this moment, though he would try and etch his name in Pirate lore. However, Mullin was able to get the best of the Bucs rookie, forcing him into a grounder to Delahanty for the second out of the seventh, with Gibson moving into scoring position on the play. Unlike his teammates Bobby Byrne was able to get hold of a Mullin offering and drove a liner towards left. Before it got out of the infield though, Bush jumped up to snag the ball to end the top of the seventh. On his way to the bench, Cobb stopped by Wagner. The two baseball giants engaged in light conversation, both with a smile, fanning the air as they appeared to shoo away a bee.

Into the game came the 1903 Pirate World Series hero Deacon Phillippe to face the Tigers offense. After Clarke's big-game pitchers Willis and Camnitz failed in their attempts to tame the vaunted Detroit offense, Phillippe was successful. In his two innings of work, he gave up only one hit, an eighth-inning double to Mullin. Other than that, he easily retired Delahanty, Moriarty and Tom Jones on a strikeout, grounder to third and pop up on a bunt attempt to himself in the seventh. Schmidt, Davy Jones and Bush were sent down just as smoothly in the eighth as none of the Tigers hitters were able to get the ball out of the infield following the one-out double to center by Mullin.

It didn't matter that Phillippe was unhittable, Pittsburgh just couldn't break Mullin. A frustrated Tommy Leach walked angrily to the bench after Schmidt caught his foul ball pop up for the first out in the eighth inning. The 10,000-plus Tiger faithful were ecstatic when Clarke struck out and were at a more elevated fever pitch when Wagner was set down on a fly ball to Crawford in center to end their half of the frame.

With only three outs left in this contest, the Pirates came up in the ninth to begin their monumental task to try to tie the game. First batter Dots Miller had more success against Mullin than any of his teammates on this afternoon, with a third inning walk and a single in the sixth. Miller tried to get aboard via the bunt, twice, failing each time. Aborting the strategy, Miller laced a single into right. Bill Abstein, who had little success against Mullin stranding three runners, finally came through with a single to center, sending Miller to second.

Two up and two aboard with the Pirates matching their output of the previous seven innings in the top of the ninth with two hits, Chief Wilson came to the plate. The Pirate right fielder tried to sacrifice his teammates into scoring position. Wilson placed the bunt in front of Schmidt and "shot to first like a steam engine."[12] The hustling right fielder rammed into Tiger first baseman Tom Jones, who collapsed to the ground unconscious. The ball rolled out of the glove of the motionless Jones, sending Miller home with the Pirates' fourth run and Abstein to third. Detroit carried their fallen teammate into the locker room, where he would regain consciousness before the Tigers called for an ambulance to transport him home. On the field, Detroit was angry at the aggressive play, which cost them their first baseman, eventually calming down so that play could continue. Sam Crawford came in from centerfield to take Jones place at first, with Davy Jones moving to center and Matty McIntyre coming in to play left.

With men at the corners and no one out, Gibson smashed a ball to Crawford at first. At that point Abstein decided to take matters into his own hands, taking off for home with the potential tying run. Abstein had anything but a great World Series in 1909. With five critical errors in the first four games and hitting a mere .227 at this point in time of the fall classic while leaving several men on base in the process, Abstein was dangerously close to being one of the biggest World Series goats in the history of the game. This wasn't how this Series was supposed to go for the Pirate first baseman. In his only season as a regular in his three-year major league career, Abstein had a fine year for the National League champs, hitting .260, while finishing 10th in the senior circuit in sacrifices with 27 and 6th in RBIs with 70. Purchased from Shreveport from the Southern Association in 1906, Abstein was having a miserable Series, and was trying to change it in one fleeting moment to become a Pirate hero.

Crawford threw the ball to the plate immediately, as Schmidt put his right leg in front of the dish in an attempt to block Abstein from scoring the tying run. If he got there before Schmidt tagged him, the game would be tied, no one would be out and there would be men on first and second with the Pirates very close to turning certain defeat into a world championship. Abstein went in hard, spiking Schmidt's right leg to open up a nasty gash. Unfortunately for the Pirates, the Detroit backstop got the tag on Abstein in time for the out. This added yet another chapter to the Pittsburgh first baseman's horrific World Series, getting tagged out at home plate in what would be described as a questionable lapse of judgement on the basepath.

Despite the injury, Schmidt stayed in the game as Clarke called on Ed Abbaticchio to see if the veteran utility player could tie the score. Abbaticchio had manned the starting spot at second for the two previous seasons before Dots Miller took over the position in this championship campaign. Before that, the Latrobe, Pennsylvania, native had been a solid player, hitting .262 and .250 in 1907 and 1908, respectively. More important than being a solid second baseman, Abbaticchio broke barriers, in not just one sport, but two. Given the strange moniker of "Awful Name," Abbaticchio is not only regarded as the first player of Italian decent to play major league baseball, but football too. One of the finest players ever produced at the turn of the nineteenth century in the football hotbed of Latrobe, the hometown hero was not only a member of the 1897 All Western Pennsylvania Team, but also on what is considered the first football club that was composed completely of professional players. To take it one step further, that would make Abbaticchio the first player of Italian decent to play professional football also.[13] On this day, though, he was a professional baseball player, looking to overcome a disappointing season that saw him with a mere 87 at-bats. It was his first and only at-bat in World Series play in his career, hopefully one that would make him a hero in the city of Pittsburgh. Mullin had other ideas as the Detroit pitcher was too overwhelming for Abbaticchio, striking him out as he swung aimlessly at the last pitch.

If that wasn't bad enough, Gibson and Wilson took off for second and third, respectively. Schmidt chose to try and get Wilson out at third, tossing a strike to Moriarty. Wilson came in hard, hurting Moriarty's right knee as he came in. It appeared that Wilson was safe, but the umpire thought otherwise, calling him out with the game's final play. It was over. The Tigers not only overcame an early 3–0 deficit, but also hung on late to a precarious one-run lead to force a seventh and deciding game that would be played right there in Bennett Park.

The Detroit fans, who were placid at the beginning of this contest, were now euphoric. They rushed the field, some surrounding Moriarty to see the condition of their fallen third baseman while others attempted to pick up the victorious pitcher on their shoulders in victory. Mullin successfully avoided his enthusiastic fans, running into the clubhouse to see his teammates. Detroit, which seemed at one point certain of a third consecutive World Series debacle, now had a second chance, a second chance that would occur on their home turf 48 hours later, one win away from finally tasting the sweet joy of a world championship.

Game 6 Box Score

```
PIT N    3 0 0    0 0 0    0 0 1—4  8  1
DET A    1 0 0    2 1 1    0 0 x—5 10  2
```

BATTING

Pittsburgh Pirates	AB	R	H	RBI	BB	SO	PO	A
Byrne 3b	4	1	1	0	0	0	2	4
Leach cf	4	1	1	0	0	0	3	0
Clarke lf	3	1	1	1	0	1	2	0
Wagner ss	4	0	1	2	0	0	3	2
Miller 2b	3	1	2	0	1	0	2	1
Abstein 1b	4	0	1	0	0	2	9	1
Wilson rf	3	0	0	0	0	0	0	1
Gibson c	4	0	1	0	0	1	2	0
Willis p	2	0	0	0	0	0	0	0
Camnitz p	0	0	0	0	0	0	0	1
Hyatt ph	1	0	0	0	0	0	0	0
Phillippe p	0	0	0	0	0	0	1	0
Abbaticchio ph	1	0	0	0	0	1	0	0
Totals	33	4	8	3	1	5	24	10

FIELDING—
DP: 1. Byrne-Abstein.
E: Clarke (1).

BATTING—
2B: Wagner (2,0ff Mullin).
SH: Clarke (3,0ff Mullin); Wilson (1,0ff Mullin).
Team LOB: 5.

BASERUNNING—
SB: Miller (2,2nd base off Mullin/Schmidt).
CS: Wilson (1,3rd base by Mullin/Schmidt).

Detroit Tigers	AB	R	H	RBI	BB	SO	PO	A
D. Jones lf,cf	5	1	0	0	0	0	2	0
Bush ss	2	2	1	0	2	0	2	3
Cobb rf	4	0	1	1	0	1	1	0
Crawford cf,1b	3	1	1	1	1	0	1	1
Delahanty 2b	4	0	2	1	0	1	0	4
Moriarty 3b	3	1	1	1	1	0	1	3
T. Jones 1b	4	0	1	1	0	0	13	0
McIntyre lf	0	0	0	0	0	0	0	0
Schmidt c	3	0	1	0	1	0	7	3
Mullin p	4	0	2	0	0	0	0	2
Totals	32	5	10	5	5	2	27	16

FIELDING—
DP: 2. Schmidt-Bush, Schmidt-Moriarty.
E: Bush (4), T. Jones (1).

BATTING—
2B: Crawford (3,0ff Willis); Delahanty (4,0ff Willis); Schmidt (2,0ff Camnitz); Cobb (3,0ff Camnitz); Mullin (1,0ff Phillippe).

HBP: Bush (1,by Willis).
Team LOB: 9.

BASERUNNING—
SB: Bush (1,2nd base off Willis/Gibson); D. Jones (1,2nd base off Camnitz/Gibson).

PITCHING

Pittsburgh Pirates	IP	H	R	ER	BB	SO	HR	BFP
Willis L(0–1)	5	7	4	4	4	1	0	25
Camnitz	1	2	1	1	1	0	0	6
Phillippe	2	1	0	0	0	1	0	7
Totals	8	10	5	5	5	2	0	38

HBP: Willis (1,Bush).

Detroit Tigers	IP	H	R	ER	BB	SO	HR	BFP
Mullin W(2–1)	9	8	4	3	1	5	0	36

Umpires: HP — Billy Evans, 1B — Bill Klem, LF — Jim Johnstone, RF — Silk O'Loughlin

Time of Game: 2:00 **Attendance:** 10535

♦ 9 ♦

GAME 7, OCTOBER 16

Bennett Park, Detroit
Pittsburgh 8, Detroit 0

In the short six-year history of the World Series, there had never been one that extended to the maximum, until now. Game seven. Win and you're the world champions; lose and you go home empty-handed. There had been one other Game 7, the inaugural fall classic when these same Pittsburgh Pirates took on the Boston Americans. But that was a best-of-nine, which ended with Boston defeating Pittsburgh five games to three, not best-of-seven during the current World Series.

The finality of the upcoming contest piqued the interest of the rabid Detroit baseball fans. The National Commission gave the Tigers an extra day between Game 6 and 7 in order to sell tickets. It worked beyond their wildest dreams. The *New York Times* declared that the game "will be witnessed by the largest crowd that ever saw a game in this city. The reserved seats were out on sale today and a wild rush ensued."[1]

Other than time to sell tickets, the other reason the day off was fortuitous was the thing that had plagued this exciting Series from the outset — the weather. On the day before the scheduled contest it was doing everything possible to prevent the teams from playing at their peak. It rained heavily, then it mixed with snow, high winds and temperatures that fell around the freezing mark.

An other positive aspect of the extra time off for the Tigers was a chance to rest their three injured starters. In a period of just a few plays in the top of the ninth in Game 6, Chief Wilson injured two Tigers, knocking Tom Jones unconscious in a collision at first before hurting George Moriarty's knee in a steal attempt at third. Bill Abstein injured the third Tiger of the inning by putting a huge gash in Boss Schmidt's leg.

While it was expected that no matter what Schmidt and Moriarty would find their way into the starting lineup, things were not so certain for Jones. The time off increased the odds he'd play, as he was back on the field for practice the day before the contest, even though he didn't participate. The Pirates also practiced at Bennett Park the morning before, luckily with no apparent injuries. After the clubs finished practicing, both the Tigers and most of the Bucs went to relax and unwind as they took in the races at Windsor in the afternoon. Some of the Pirate players chose to stay at the Pontchartrain Hotel while others went with their Hall of Fame shortstop Honus Wagner to ride in a Regal automobile that he got with his connections.[2]

Once the two teams finished their relaxation, it was back to business, and decisions had to be made. This was to be arguably the most important game ever played in the national pastime to this point. While each manager was not commenting to the press about the contest, both needed to focus on which pitcher would give them the best chance to emerge victorious.

The Pirates' starting picture scene was pretty clear, even though Clarke warmed up three starters: Babe Adams, the surprise of the Series who won two of the three Pittsburgh victories to this point, Nick Maddox, who emerged victorious in the other game the Bucs won, and Deacon Phillippe, who had been effective in a relief role in this fall classic. But it was apparent who his selection had to be. Despite battling a cold, Adams had been the one constant in this Series on the mound for Pittsburgh. The rookie would get what would prove to be the most important start of what was the beginning of a fabulous career. According to writer Fred Lieb, Clarke told Adams, "You are the only pitcher I have who had tied up Jennings hitters. Don't think it's the deciding game of a World Series. Just think you are out there to pitch tomorrow's game, and that you have eight men in back of you."[3]

For Hughie Jennings, the selection was a bit more muddled. Would he go with George Mullin, the hurler who had befuddled the Bucs for the most part in this fall classic, yet had pitched a complete game two days ago or Wild Bill Donovan, the wily veteran whom had battled arm injuries during the season yet pitched an outstanding complete game victory in Game 2. One of the major aspects of the Detroit manager's decision was the weather. In Game 2 at Pittsburgh, it was unseasonably warm, the perfect condition for a pitcher with a sore arm. Game 7 was not as pleasant. While not as bad as the off day, it was still 40 degrees with a cold wind blowing off Lake Huron. Regardless of the less than stellar conditions, Jennings decided to give the ball to Donovan, feeling that Mullin might not be properly recovered from his Game 6 start. If Donovan failed, Mullin would be the one given the opportunity to keep the Tigers' world championship hopes alive.

Despite the fact Detroit had several issues in front of them, three injured players, a fragile arm on the mound in cold weather and a tired arm as the first out of the bullpen, Tiger fans were betting on their hometown team in huge numbers, making the Tigers the new betting favorite in the Series. The enthusiastic Detroit faithful, who were putting their earnings on the table in record numbers betting on their team, filled up every corner of Bennett Park as a sold-out crowd of 17,562 showed up. The game was played an hour earlier than the other contests had started in order to give the newspapers in the East a better opportunity to tell the tale of this magnificent contest in a more timely manner.

It was a wonderful day for sportswriters in Michigan. They not only had the first final and deciding game in World Series history, but they also had the chance to report on the world heavyweight championship between the champion Jack Johnson and Hall of Famer Stanley Ketchel. Named the "Michigan Assassin" from Grand Rapids, Ketchel was one of the greatest middleweight champions in the history of the sport and would give this state one of the most memorable days it would ever enjoy if he could combine with the Tigers to emerge victorious. Michigan's favorite team on the diamond got the first opportunity to attempt to win a championship this day when at 1:00 P.M. central time Donovan took the mound to face Pirates third baseman Bobby Byrne.

Two pitches into the game, Jennings looked like a genius in tabbing Donovan to start this contest as he got Byrne into a quick 0–2 count. Wild Bill lived up to his name when he threw the third offering high, hitting Byrne in the shoulder. Tommy Leach came up next and tried to sacrifice the Pirate third baseman to second. He bunted the ball back to Donovan, who looked to second to try and get the lead runner. He found that no one was covering second so he had to go to first base to retire Leach instead.

Trying to put the team in a position where they could get a quick early lead, manager Fred Clarke, who was actually up to bat, called for a hit-and-run. When the Pirate manager missed the pitch, Byrne was left on his own and took off for third, testing Boss Schmidt's questionable arm. The 145-pound Pittsburgh third baseman collided with the Tiger third sacker, who was 40 pounds heavier, sending both to the ground in pain. As both players were rolling around, umpire Jim Johnstone saw that Moriarty held on to the ball, tagging Byrne before the collision for the Bucs second out of the inning. Both players looked seriously injured, with Byrne being the more severe of the two. His ankle was so bad that he had to be carried into the clubhouse by his teammates.

Umpire Bill Klem mistakenly announced that Ed Abbaticchio would enter the contest in place of Byrne. As Klem came towards home plate Clarke leaned over to explain that he would instead use Leach at third and put Ham Hyatt in center. Clarke resumed his at bat forcing a walk, then promptly tested Boss Schmidt's arm too as he stole second. Wagner was also able to coerce a bases on balls from the Tigers veteran hurler. Dots Miller, unfortunately, wasted the opportunity for the visiting team by grounding out to Donie Bush at short, who tossed to Jim Delahanty at second to force Wagner, ending the Pirate threat. The Pirate shortstop thought he was safe and jumped hard on the bag furious at the call.

Banged up, but with a second breath, the Tigers came up hoping to seize the momentum they had, holding the Bucs scoreless in the top of the first despite Donovan's wildness. Davy Jones hit a meaningless popup in foul territory to Leach, who was now at third, to start the frame. Adams then matched Donovan for hit batsmen in the game, plunking Bush in the back. Writhing for a moment in pain at home, the Tigers shortstop got up and took off for first base with his free pass. Cobb failed to move Bush up with an easy fly to Clarke, leaving it to Sam Crawford to keep the inning alive. Adams tossed a strike, which Crawford let go by him. He was angry, kicking the plate hard, irritated at a strike call he didn't agree with. While the Detroit centerfielder was venting his anger, Bush took off for second. He was no match for catcher George Gibson's arm, who threw a deadly strike to Miller, finishing the first for the Tigers.

After skating through the first inning on the edge of blowing up, yet keeping the Pirates off the board, a question about Bill Donovan would be answered in the top of the second. Would it be the veteran hurler who was one of the greatest clutch pitchers of his day, or the one who was given the moniker Wild Bill for his occasional lack of control? As in the first, it appeared as if the clutch pitcher was the version that would face the Bucs, as Donovan pinpointed his first two pitches of the inning once again over the plate for strikes. Then, as in the opening frame, Wild Bill then reared his ugly head as he ended up walking Bill Abstein to lead off the inning. Abstein then attempted to steal second. Schmidt's throw sailed high as the Pirate first baseman slid in safely.

Chief Wilson then laid a good bunt in front of the plate. Schmidt decided to try and get the lead runner at third, throwing it to Moriarty. The ball came in just a tad after Abstein slid into third, putting men at the corners with still no one out. Gibson could not send Abstein home with a lazy pop up to Bush at short. With the pitcher coming to the plate, it looked like Donovan just might be able to get out of a mess for the second consecutive inning. Unfortunately he was wild once again, walking Adams on five pitches to load the

bases for Hyatt. The rookie launched a long shot to center, that while Crawford ran down for the fly out, scored Abstein from third with the game's first
run. The sore-armed Tiger pitcher helped the Bucs plate another run that
was only appropriate for him this day, walking Leach to load the bases and
then doing the same with Clarke, which sent Wilson home. While Wagner
flew out to Cobb to end the inning, it looked like the pitching woes that Jennings had worried about to begin the game were now coming to fruition.

Detroit had been down in the Series before, only to come back, and it
looked as if they were about to turn that trick one more time. Following a
hard grounder by Crawford that ended in the glove of Bill Abstein for the
first out, unassisted, Adams walked Delahanty, and faced Moriarty with one
out and one on. Many wondered if Moriarty would start this contest following
the brutal collision with Chief Wilson to end Game 6. They further were
amazed that he was able to stay in the game after his run-in with Byrne an
inning earlier. Those who were surprised should not have been. Purchased by
the Tigers earlier in the year from the New York Highlanders, Moriarty had
a knack for being tough as nails. A local sportswriter, Joe S. Jackson, described
him the following way: "As a third baseman he had a wonderful whip and as
a base runner he was daring, and especially dangerous after he had reached
third base.... He knows the game thoroughly and is aggressive."[4] His aggressiveness was most on display with his penchant for stealing home, a feat he
is credited doing at least eleven times in his career. His aggressiveness and
toughness showed up in the second inning as he punched an Adams offering
into the right-field seats for a double, sending Delahanty to third. As Moriarty
was pulling up into second, he was limping noticeably. He finally could take
no more as Jennings was forced to replace him on the basepaths with Charley
O'Leary. Formerly the starting shortstop for the Tigers before Donie Bush
took over the spot prior to the 1909 campaign, O'Leary was getting his first
opportunity to play in this Series with the injury to Moriarty. It wasn't the
veteran's first foray in the fall classic though; he played in every game during
the previous two World Series against the Cubs with little success, hitting a
paltry .138 in 36 at-bats.

Tom Jones, with an opportunity to put himself in Tiger lore with a
clutch hit, did no better than an infield popup. Wagner took off for the fly,
losing his cap in the process for the second out. Schmidt then stranded
O'Leary and Delahanty in scoring position with an easy dribbler in front of
the plate, taking the steam out of what originally looked like a productive
frame for Detroit.

Even though the Bucs were ahead, 2–0, they had yet to get a hit. Six
walks and a hit batsman did all the damage. Dots Miller broke that streak

Fiesty George Moriarty was the Tigers' big offseason signing in 1909. The veteran third baseman hit .273 both in the regular season and World Series that year. The season ended on a sour note when he had to leave Game 7 with a leg injury he suffered in the ninth inning of Game 6 (courtesy of Library of Congress, Bain Collection, Prints & Photographs Division, 16989u).

when he hit a bounder over second base for a single to start the third. Donovan the got two quick strikes on Abstein and was infuriated when he claimed the Pirate first baseman's check swing actually went around which what would have been a third strike. It was called a ball instead and Abstein took advantage of the fortuitous call, smacking the next pitch into left field for a double, putting two men in scoring position with no outs.

The Tigers championship hopes were hanging by a string now. Luckily for the Bengals, Donie Bush made the defensive play of the game. Wilson hit a grounder to the future Pirate manager. Bush took the ball and threw a strike to Schmidt at home to tag out Miller who had broken for the plate. Abstein in the meantime had gone for third base and turned back to second when he saw the quick play at the plate. Schmidt threw the ball back to Bush, who missed the tag on Abstein, but he tossed the ball quickly to Delahanty at second for the double play. Wilson, who was safe at first on the fielder's choice, broke for second on the play when he saw Abstein going to third. When the Bucs first baseman went back to second, Wilson had to hustle back to first. After tagging out Abstein, Delahanty threw the ball to Tom Jones trying to complete the most unlikely triple play in the history of the game. He just missed history when Wilson slid into first to beat the throw. Because of the phenomenal defensive sequence, Donovan was able to avoid major disaster in the third, just as he had in the first, by getting Gibson to ground out to Bush to keep Detroit within two runs despite all the Pirate activity in the first three innings.

Even though it was only 2–0, Jennings had seen enough of Donovan and sent George Mullin to pinch-hit for the sore-armed pitcher. Mullin could muster up only a long fly ball to Wilson for the out. Davy Jones tried to get the Tiger offense going and laid down a perfect bunt to Adams, just beating the throw to first for a single. Bush, who had the fine defensive inning in the top of the third, continued his success in the bottom half with his own version of the perfect bunt, sending it to Adams, who looked towards second to see if he could get Jones, but thought better of it, instead getting the Detroit shortstop at first. It set up the Tigers star, the man who could come through in the clutch better than any man in the annals of the game, Ty Cobb, with a man in scoring position. The greatest clutch hitter of them all was anything but on this day as Cobb hit a grounder back to the pitcher to end the third.

Hoping that he still had some steam left after tossing a complete game only two days earlier, Jennings chose to send Mullin to the mound to begin the fourth and hopefully keep the Pirate offense at bay. The Detroit manager's second pitching gamble of the day was again doomed to failure. From the beginning Mullin did not have his normal stuff. The first batter he faced was Babe Adams. While Adams eventually became an acceptable hitter for a pitcher with a .212 average for his 19-year career, during his rookie year in 1909 he was a mere 2-for-39, for a .051 average. On this play he hit the pitch over Davy Jones' head, who eventually ran it down for the first out. Hyatt walked and was followed by Leach, who hit one over the outstretched reach of Donie Bush for a single, putting men on first and second. Fearing that Hyatt, a man who was rarely a threat to steal, would try and take third, Mullin and Schmidt both made attempts to try to keep him at second. Clarke came up and took care of moving his center fielder to third with a perfect bunt that went to Mullin, putting both men in scoring position for Wagner.

Choosing to face Dots Miller, the Tigers hurler put the Bucs legendary shortstop on base via the intentional walk, facing the Bucs rookie with the bases loaded and two out. Despite his 2-for-3 performance in Game 6, Miller was having a less than stellar Series to this point, hitting only .217 following his impressive game only 48 hours before. He continued his hot streak with this at-bat, lining a shot to Cobb in right, plating Hyatt and Leach to increase the Bucs advantage to 4–0. With men on first and third, Mullin did something that Detroit pitchers would do only once in this game, strike out a Pirate batter. The Pittsburgh hitter charged with that dubious honor was none other than first baseman Bill Abstein. It was Abstein's ninth strikeout of the Series, many of them with men on base, to go along with his five errors. So poor was his performance in this fall classic that the *Reach Guide* proclaimed that it was "exceedingly mortifying to himself and painful to his friends."[5]

In the fourth, the Tigers continued to threaten the Pirate rookie hurler with nothing to show for it. While many thought the field would be unplayable in Game 7 due to the heavy rains that plagued the Detroit area the day before, many good plays were made on this less-than-perfect infield, including quite a few by Leach at third, who retired Crawford for the first out of the frame. Delahanty then kept the Tigers' hopes alive with a single to Wilson in right. O'Leary popped up to Wagner at short, sending Tom Jones to the plate with two out. Jones then laced a single to right. Wilson made a nice stab at the ball, keeping Delahanty at second. As he had done so many times on his memorable day, Adams stopped the Tiger rally once again, forcing Schmidt to hit an inning-ending grounder to Leach, who ran to third, beating Delahanty to the bag.

The fifth inning offered the lone time in this seventh and deciding game that both pitchers were able to set down the side in order in the same frame. Mullin seemed to calm down after his shaky first inning of relief by getting Wilson to fly out to short center field, Gibson to ground out to short and Adams, whom the *Pittsburgh Gazette* said "did not seem to care to run,"[6] when he grounded to Delahanty for the third out.

Despite the fact he had allowed no runs to this point, Adams had yet to enjoy a one-two-three inning until the fifth. He induced Mullin into an easy out to Leach then struck out Davy Jones for the second out. Not wanting to give up a bunt single to Bush, Leach broke in for the plate. Bush instead swung away, hitting an easy bounding ball to Wagner at short, leaving the Tigers with only twelve more outs to revive their fading hopes.

One of Jennings' biggest fears before this contest started occurred in the top of the sixth inning when Mullin's over-used arm finally tired out. Following a leadoff ground out to second by Hyatt, Leach came up and launched a ball into the crowd in left-center field for a ground-rule double. Clarke worked Mullin for his third walk of the day, putting men on first and second with Honus Wagner up.

It was a moment made for the movies. Legendary player who has a hugely disappointing World Series in his first go around comes to the plate with a chance to ice away his team's championship in his next venture into the fall classic. Just to make matters more surreal, the Detroit home crowd peppered the great shortstop with taunts, reminding him of his failure in 1903. "It's alright, the Dutchman has ... a yellow streak," the fans chided.[7] Then came the moment that legends are made for. With two on, a chance to put the proverbial nail in the coffin of the Tigers and the crowd mocking the Pirate star, Wagner swung and ripped the ball down the left-field line. Clarke and Leach came home on the hit as Wagner came into third trying to beat Davy Jones throw. The throw was wild, sending the Steel City hero home with the Bucs' seventh run as the small Pittsburgh contingent at Bennett Park erupted.

Detroit protested the play, claiming that the ball went into the crowd, therefore it should be a ground-rule double and Wagner should go back to second. Klem, who was umpiring down the foul line, ignored the Tigers' argument, saying no one touched the ball and the play stood. It would be the one hit in Wagner's magnificent career that would give him the most satisfaction.[8] In Pittsburgh, the thousands of fans who were waiting outside newspaper offices looking for updated World Series news were now uncontrollable with joy when the news came of Wagner's clutch hit.

It wouldn't matter that Mullin was able to retire Miller on a fly ball to Crawford and Abstein on a harmless popup to Bush to end the inning, the Pirates now owned a firm seven-run lead with only three-and-a-half innings left. To make matters worse, there was the now dominant Babe Adams on the mound. For all intents and purposes, the game was over and the championship was Pittsburgh's. All that was left to do was put the finishing touches on this masterpiece that Adams was constructing.

The now-hopeless cause for the Tigers looked more forlorn in the sixth when Cobb tapped a roller to Adams for the first out, Crawford hit an easy fly ball to Clarke in left and Delahanty was retired on a spectacular catch by Leach leaning into the grandstand just beyond third base in short left field. The Tigers could do no better in the seventh except for a lone two-out ground-rule double into the left-field crowd by Schmidt. O'Leary sent a foul pop to Gibson, Tom Jones grounded to Wagner and Mullin stranded Schmidt at second with a fly to Clarke to end the seventh inning.

For the Pirates, their seventh inning was a quiet one too. Wilson flew out to Davy Jones to start the inning, giving way to Gibson. The Bucs catcher fouled several pitches into the grandstand before smacking a ball to the edge of the crowd in center field for a double. Adams came close to getting on base, hitting a difficult grounder that Mullin deflected to Bush, who threw to Tom Jones, just beating the Pirate pitcher to first base as Gibson pulled into third. Hyatt could advance him no further, grounding to Delahanty for the final out of the frame.

While the seventh was quiet for Pittsburgh, the eighth inning would provide the team and their now-euphoric fans an opportunity to make this game much more of a one-sided affair. Leach starting things off easy enough with a roller back to the pitcher for the first out. The Bucs manager continued his unique day, receiving his fourth base on balls of the afternoon. His Game 7 line score read no at-bats, two runs, no hits and an RBI. He then added a second stolen base to his resume for this game, putting himself in scoring position with Wagner coming up. The Bucs Hall of Famer could not repeat his sixth-inning heroics, hitting a meaningless fly ball to Crawford for the second out. Miller then launched a deep fly to center, which should have been the final out for the Pirates in the frame. However, Crawford dropped the ball, scoring Clarke with the Series' final run. Davy Jones saved whatever dignity the Tigers had left with a great running catch of a Abstein fly ball near the left-field line to end the inning.

Down 8–0, the Tigers now looked spent, managing only two harmless infield pop flys to Miller and Wagner by Davy Jones and Bush. The final out came off the bat of Cobb, who, in his final at-bat of what turned out to be a miserable 1909 World Series for the Tiger great, lofted a flyball to Clarke.

The ninth inning proved anti-climatic except for the fact it gave Pittsburgh fans another opportunity to celebrate their soon-to-be world championship club, as they counted down to the now inevitable outcome. Wilson started the top of the frame with a short popup to O'Leary at third. Gibson then hit a hot smash to Bush, who bobbled the ball, allowing the Pirate catcher to reach first base on the error. Adams sacrificed Gibson over to second, before Hyatt fouled out to Schmidt.

Three outs were left for the Tigers, and at this point, they didn't have the spark to try and make this even a competitive game, much less win it. Babe Adams had been superb this afternoon, giving up but five hits to this point, pitching a masterful shutout in what would be the most important start of what turned out to be an impressive career. There was little chance he would fall apart now with victory so close.

It was ironic that fans and experts alike were thrilled at the beginning of this fall classic for the much anticipated matchup between baseball's elite players, Honus Wagner and Ty Cobb. In the end, it was a little-known rookie pitcher in Adams that stole the show with his three magnificent wins.

Crawford led off the Tigers' last-chance inning with a hard grounder to Wagner, who made a great stop tossing him out at first base for the initial out. Not wanting to end this contest without a fight, Delahanty smacked a ball over Clarke's head into the left-field crowd for a double. The hit would prove to be Detroit's last gasp. O'Leary fouled out to Leach as the Pirate faithful were now down to one more out before they could let loose with a joyous celebration that they had waited for since the debacle of the first World Series in 1903. That moment came next when Tom Jones lifted a ball to left field. Fred Clarke got underneath it, cradled it into his glove, and became the first member of an elite fraternity in Pirate history. Clarke along with Johnny Gooch, Bob Robertson and Omar Moreno had the rare opportunity to capture the final out of a World Series for the Pirates (the Bucs of course have won five world championships, but the 1960 title was won off the bat of Bill Mazeroski and did not end on defense).

Pittsburgh now looked forward to a glorious ride home, the parade and adulation that would follow from their loyal following.

Honus Wagner and his merry band of Pirates were elated, having shed the label of chokers from themselves once and for all. For one Pirate, Babe Adams, it was a victory that vaulted him from the status of little-known rookie to World Series legend for his three wins.

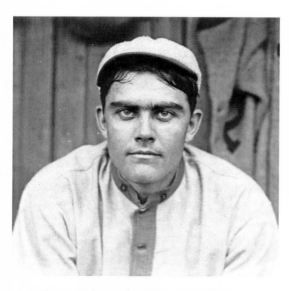

Pirate pitcher Babe Adams saved his best performance for last in the 1909 World Series. Adams shut out Detroit in the seventh and deciding game, 8–0, for his third win of the fall classic, giving the Bucs their first world championship (courtesy of the Pittsburgh Pirates).

For Detroit fans it was a miserable day. Not only did they have to endure the defeat of their hometown Tigers, but their favorite boxer, Stanley Ketchel, was knocked silly by Jack Johnson, losing in the twelfth round via a devastating knockout. The team itself would have an offseason with plenty to think about. It was time to reflect on another fall classic gone badly. While the other two losses in 1907 and 1908 were very one-sided affairs to the Cubs, this one was close, one victory away from a championship. One victory that was at their own facility, following a dramatic Game 6 win when seemingly all the momentum was in their favor, a victory that never came. They would reflect on that as well as the first final and deciding game in World Series history. It not only wasn't as thrilling as most anticipated, but it was a devastating rout, one that would surely stay with them; taste of defeat that was purely bitter and long lasting.

Game 7 Box Score

```
PIT N    0 2 0    2 0 3    0 1 0—8 7 0
DET A    0 0 0    0 0 0    0 0 0—0 6 3
```

BATTING

Pittsburgh Pirates	AB	R	H	RBI	BB	SO	PO	A
Byrne 3b	0	0	0	0	0	0	0	0
Hyatt cf	3	1	0	1	1	0	0	0
Leach cf,3b	3	2	2	0	1	0	4	2
Clarke lf	0	2	0	1	4	0	4	0
Wagner ss	3	1	1	2	2	0	3	4
Miller 2b	5	0	2	2	0	0	2	0
Abstein 1b	4	1	1	0	1	1	10	0
Wilson rf	4	1	0	0	0	0	2	0
Gibson c	5	0	1	0	0	0	2	3
Adams p	3	0	0	0	1	0	0	2
Totals	30	8	7	6	10	1	27	11

BATTING—

2B: Abstein (2,0ff Donovan); Leach (4,0ff Mullin); Gibson (2,0ff Mullin).

3B: Wagner (1,0ff Mullin).

SH: Leach (1,0ff Donovan); Wilson (2,0ff Donovan); Clarke (4,0ff Mullin); Adams (2,0ff Mullin).

SF: Hyatt (1,0ff Donovan).

HBP: Byrne (2,by Donovan).

Team LOB: 11.

BASERUNNING—

SB: Clarke 2 (3,2nd base off Donovan/Schmidt,2nd base off Mullin/Schmidt); Abstein (1,2nd base off Donovan/Schmidt); Miller (3,2nd base off Mullin/Schmidt).

CS: Byrne (1,3rd base by Donovan/Schmidt).

Detroit Tigers	AB	R	H	RBI	BB	SO	PO	A
D. Jones lf	4	0	1	0	0	1	3	0
Bush ss	2	0	0	0	0	0	2	5
Cobb rf	4	0	0	0	0	0	1	0
Crawford cf	4	0	0	0	0	0	4	0
Delahanty 2b	3	0	2	0	1	0	3	3
Moriarty 3b	1	0	1	0	0	0	1	0
O'Leary pr,3b	3	0	0	0	0	0	1	1
T. Jones 1b	4	0	1	0	0	0	9	0
Schmidt c	3	0	1	0	0	0	3	2

Detroit Tigers	AB	R	H	RBI	BB	SO	PO	A
Donovan p	0	0	0	0	0	0	0	1
Mullin ph,p	3	0	0	0	0	0	0	2
Totals	31	0	6	0	1	1	27	14

FIELDING—
DP: 1. Bush-Schmidt-Delahanty.
E: D. Jones (1), Bush (5), Crawford (2).

BATTING—
2B: Moriarty (1,0ff Adams); Schmidt (3,0ff Adams); Delahanty (5,0ff Adams).
SH: Bush (3,0ff Adams).
HBP: Bush (2,by Adams).
Team LOB: 7.

BASERUNNING—
CS: Bush (2,2nd base by Adams/Gibson).

PITCHING

Pittsburgh Pirates	IP	H	R	ER	BB	SO	HR	BFP
Adams W(3–0)	9	6	0	0	1	1	0	34

HBP: Adams (1,Bush).

Detroit Tigers	IP	H	R	ER	BB	SO	HR	BFP
Donovan L(1–1)	3	2	2	2	6	0	0	17
Mullin	6	5	6	4	4	1	0	29
Totals	9	7	8	6	10	1	0	46

HBP: Donovan (1,Byrne).
Umpires: HP—Silk O'Loughlin, 1B—Jim Johnstone, LF—Billy Evans, RF—Bill Klem
Time of Game: 2:10 **Attendance:** 17562

♦ 10 ♦

POST–1909 WORLD SERIES

The first thing the mayor of Pittsburgh, W.A. Magee, did after hearing of the fabulous victory for his hometown Pirates, was to declare October 18 a holiday all over the city of Pittsburgh to honor their champions with a memorable celebration.

It was to be a spectacular day, filled with a celebratory dinner at the Fort Pitt Hotel, to be followed by a parade through the streets of Oakland, on the way to a final stop at their sparkling new facility, Forbes Field, to complete the festivities. There, they would have speeches and what the Pirate players looked forward to, the presenting of their World Series checks. All the Pirates agreed to stay for the celebration after hearing of the plans, before spreading out across the country to their various homes. Even the injured Bobby Byrne was expected to stay.

Dignitaries from around the country who could not attend the celebration, sent their congratulations to Mayor Magee, including one from the mayor of Detroit, Phillip Breitmeyer, who said: "Detroit congratulates Pittsburgh upon the winning of the world's baseball pennant by your crew of Pirates. If Detroit had to lose, nothing could please us more than to lose to Pittsburgh."[1]

The ultra competitive president of the American League, Ban Johnson, was conciliatory in his remarks to Mayor Magee with his telegram:

Dear Sir — Business arrangements prevent me from accepting your cordial invitation to attend the celebration of Pittsburgh's victory in the World Series. Permit me to extend through you to the Pittsburgh players and the patrons of the club my congratulations over the splendid triumph of the ball club. The world's championship was won in a clean-cut and sportsmanlike manner.[2]

The night began at the Fort Pitt Hotel for the club and the local baseball scribes, where president Barney Dreyfuss used part of his World Series profits to fund the elegant affair. There he presented his more honored veterans a

133

After the World Series 23,000 fans filled Forbes Field to cheer on their newly crowned world champions. The players and many local dignitaries addressed the crowd to celebrate the city's first World Series victory (courtesy of the Pittsburgh Pirates).

gold watch. The first was given to manager Fred Clarke in honor of his efforts both as the manager and left fielder. The second was to his ironman catcher George Gibson, who had caught a National League record 134 consecutive games behind the plate during the season. He was considered the unsung hero on the team. Writer Alfred H Spink once wrote, "Wagner, Clarke, and Leach have been set above all others in allotting credit for Pittsburgh's success, but there is a deep impression in many people's minds that 'Gibby' was the one best bet."[3] On his watch, Dreyfuss inscribed, "To George Gibson; In appreciation of faithful efforts. From Barney Dreyfuss, October 16th, 1909."[4]

Following the banquet, the parade took place at 7:30 in the evening. It started downtown and culminated at Forbes Field. Two regiments of the National Guard were present for the parade, as well as a collection of amateur and semi-pro baseball and football teams. Approximately 150,000 rabid fans lined the dusk-lit streets on a cold October evening. The sides of the roads were roped off as the players traveled in automobiles and waved to the crowd. The parade route started at Liberty Avenue in the downtown section of the city, before proceeding to Sixth then Seventh Avenue. The caravan then went approximately three miles down Forbes Avenue to the Oakland section of the city. Noise makers were prevalent everywhere, bands were playing gleefully as the Pirate faithful hollered as their heroes passed by, eventually breaking out in song, chanting "Hail, Hail the Gangs All Here" into the fall Pittsburgh evening. The great Honus Wagner, wanting to make a quick escape after the celebration, drove in his own car.

There was a slew of children that followed the great shortstop's vehicle as he made his way down Forbes. The outpouring of emotion that was being shown by the Pirate faithful made their marks on the players they were honoring. Manager Fred Clarke exclaimed that they "could not have shown their appreciation of us in a better way. It shows that they are loyal to us and that's what makes us feel so good. It touches my heart."[5] Once the team reached their destination, they found 23,000 people jammed in to Forbes Field. The *Pittsburgh Gazette* described the scene there as "several bands were playing, red fire was illuminating the park, and skyrockets were flying."[6]

Dignitaries and players alike approached the podium to address the crown and collect their World Series bounty. Checks were presented for $1,825.22 to each of the world champions. Dreyfuss's take of the receipts amounted to $51,273, although his joy was tempered. His heart was heavy as he thought of the suicide death of his good friend Harry Pulliam. Pulliam was the president of the National League between 1903 and 1909 as well as its secretary and treasurer from 1902 through 1907. Earlier in the year, July 29 to be precise, Pulliam pulled a gun in his third-floor room in the New York Athletic Club, and shot himself in the head. A sensitive man, he reportedly was distraught with the criticism of his performance in his positions with the National League as well as the fact he had been reported in ill health, which was a strain on him.[7] He and Dreyfuss were close friends and associates; Pulliam was named president for both the Louisville Colonels and then the Pirates by Dreyfuss, who owned Louisville before taking over the Bucs in 1900. During the celebration, Dreyfuss said, "I only wish Harry could have lived to see us celebrate our new park with a World Championship."[8]

Many esteemed guests came up to spoke from the podium first that included the Mayor and then Congressman James Francis Burke to name a few. There were bands playing, including Nirella's fourteenth regiment band that played several songs including one that celebrated the Pirates victory named "My Wife Has Gone to the Country" composed by J. Ed Boyle.

What the rabid crowd had been waiting for came next, their world champion Pittsburgh Pirates. They all went up and received incredible ovations, with some giving speeches, as did the dignitaries, through megaphones. As the *Pittsburgh Gazette* described, "The ovations for the stars, however, were almost indescribable. They were demonstrations of fans gone mad with delirious joy — at any rate they acted that way."[9]

Perhaps the most tremendous responses were for Bill Abstein, the first baseman who had one of the single worst World Series performances in the annals of the game, and Bobby Byrne, who hobbled in the event on crutches following his Game 7 injury, and the great Honus Wagner. Wagner was not one for such events and had to be dragged in front of the crowd on the small stage to accept their adulation. The crowd insisted that Wagner speak to them. Instead of giving a speech as many of his teammates had, the bashful Hall of Famer instead ran across the stage sliding into his chair with the fans screaming "safe."[10]

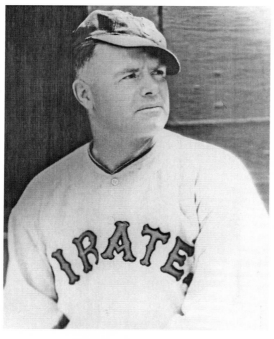

Catcher George Gibson received a gold watch to commemorate his National League record of 134 consecutive games catching at the dinner president Barney Dreyfuss gave for his newly crowned world champions. Eleven years later, Dreyfuss hired Gibson to manage the Bucs (courtesy of the Pittsburgh Pirates).

Out of the group, the team's newest superstar, Babe Adams, reportedly was given the most fervent reception of them all. On top of his winnings from the victory in the fall classic, he was also given an additional $1,264 that teammates and some of the Pirate faithful collected for him to reward him for his heroics, on the trip home from Detroit. For fifteen minutes the crowd was in a frenzy for the rookie pitcher. When they finally calmed down enough for Adams to speak, he said simply "At my farm home in Tipton, my father always taught me to finish any job I started." To which the crowd responded that he certainly finished this job.[11]

For the Tigers, their "World Series celebration" and distribution of checks took place in a much quieter venue, a meeting at the Hotel Tuller.

Honus Wagner, without a doubt the greatest player ever to don a Pirate uniform, is commemorated in a statue that has stood outside of Forbes Field, Three Rivers Stadium and now PNC Park.

The club voted on how to spilt up their Series bounty. They elected to give $500 to the team trainer, a gentleman by the name of Harry Tuthill. There was also a debate on how much to give their former teammate Germany Schaefer, the veteran infielder who was dealt in an August trade to Washington, for Jim Delahanty. After much discussion, they elected to give Schaefer only $500 instead of a full cut. That left the rest of the Tigers a check for $1,180, which took some of the bite from their close defeat by the Pirates.

Team president Frank Navin did the best of course, with his personal take of $51,273.67. It allowed him to pay off Bill Yawkey, the former owner of half of the club, who lent Navin $40,000 at the end of the 1907 campaign to purchase his portion. It was now Navin's free and clear.

While the money did temper some of the team's disappointments, it couldn't take it all away as there was still the fact that the Tigers had been the superior team in the American League for three straight seasons, and had no world championships to show for their efforts.

Cobb perhaps was the most disheartened, being thoroughly outplayed in the Series by Honus Wagner. It was no secret that Cobb was not always a popular player among his teammates, and many felt that his long ventures between Pittsburgh and Detroit to avoid the police in Ohio put Cobb at less than his best for the Series and was a factor in denying them the elusive championship, a fact he would not dispute. "It bothered my play, to think of police coming onto the field to handcuff me," Cobb stated.[12]

He was ready for his winter rest, but Navin would not let Cobb take off until he settled his long dispute with the city of Cleveland over his assault charge. He employed the former mayor of Cleveland, R.E. McKisson, as one of his lawyers. The hope was that the well-connected McKisson would help Cobb get a much reduced sentence. Cobb pleaded not guilty on October 20, claiming he pulled a knife only after the African-American house detective George Stansfield used his billy club on Cobb. The Georgia native then posted $500 bond, as the trial would take place within thirty days. The Tiger great returned to Georgia for the time being to relax and enjoy the banquets given in his honor to celebrate another great campaign.

Cobb returned to Cleveland on November 22 for the trial. In the time between the plea and the trial, McKisson had worked hard, plea bargaining the case to the point that when the trial came up, Cobb was only charged with simple battery and assault. The former mayor of Cleveland argued the point that Cobb had many African-Americans under his employ and that he treated them very well. Because of McKisson's hard work, Cobb got off relatively easy with a $100 fine and court costs. Cobb knew that he was given a very advantageous decision. "It would have meant jail if I hadn't had so much help — a friendly judge, and with the Detroit ball club's bankroll behind me. We bought this one."[13]

Free of the pressure of an imminent arrest, Cobb put it behind him. Things financially for Cobb were also on the uptake too as he was rewarded with a $9,000 per year contract, making him the second highest paid player in the game next to Wagner, the man who had something Cobb did not, a world championship. Certainly Cobb would have other chances to win a

To thank Babe Adams for his spectacular pitching performance in the World Series, his teammates and some Pirate fans collected $1,264 on the train ride home to Pittsburgh from Detroit to give him (courtesy of the Pittsburgh Pirates).

championship, but unfortunately after three futile attempts at winning a World Series, this would be it. The Royston, Georgia, native would never get a chance to play in another fall classic. The failed memory of an 8–0 shellacking in the seventh and final contest of the 1909 Series, a game were he went a feeble 0-for-4, would serve as his last post-season memory despite the fact he still had nineteen years left to go in his legendary career. It was a memory that saw him lose his unforgettable battle with Wagner, the polar opposite of Cobb, who, while also never getting a chance to play in another World Series himself, had the satisfaction of being able to celebrate a title with his team and his hometown, an experience Cobb would never know.

Pittsburgh Pirates World Series Statistics

HITTING

Name	AB	R	H	2B	3B	HR	RBI	W	K	AVG	SB
Tommy Leach	25	8	9	4	0	0	2	2	1	.360	1
Honus Wagner	24	4	8	2	1	0	6	4	2	.333	6
Bobby Byrne	24	5	6	1	0	0	0	1	4	.250	1
Dots Miller	28	2	7	1	0	0	4	2	5	.250	3
George Gibson	25	2	6	2	0	0	2	1	1	.240	2
Bill Abstein	26	3	6	2	0	0	2	3	9	.231	1
Fred Clarke	19	7	4	0	0	2	7	5	3	.211	3
Chief Wilson	26	2	4	1	0	0	1	0	2	.154	1
Ed Abbaticchio	1	0	0	0	0	0	0	0	1	.000	0
Babe Adams	9	0	0	0	0	0	0	1	1	.000	0
Howie Camnitz	1	0	0	0	0	0	0	0	0	.000	0
Ham Hyatt	4	1	0	0	0	0	1	1	0	.000	0
Lefty Leifield	1	0	0	0	0	0	0	0	1	.000	0
Nick Maddox	4	0	0	0	0	0	0	0	1	.000	0
Paddy O'Connor	1	0	0	0	0	0	0	0	1	.000	0
Deacon Phillippe	1	0	0	0	0	0	0	0	1	.000	0
Vic Willis	4	0	0	0	0	0	0	0	1	.000	0
TOTALS	223	34	50	13	1	2	25	20	34	.224	18

PITCHING

Name	G	GS	ERA	W	L	SV	CG	IP	H	ER	W	K
Deacon Phillippe	2	0	0.00	0	0	0	0	6.0	2	0	1	2
Nick Maddox	1	1	1.00	1	0	0	1	9.0	11	1	2	4
Babe Adams	3	3	1.33	3	0	0	3	27.0	18	4	6	11
Vic Willis	2	1	4.76	0	1	0	0	11.1	10	6	8	3
Lerfty Leifield	1	1	11.25	0	1	0	0	4.0	7	5	1	0
Howie Camnitz	2	1	12.27	0	1	0	0	3.2	8	5	2	2
TOTALS	11	7	3.10	4	3	0	4	61.0	56	21	20	22

Detroit Tigers World Series Statistics

HITTING

Name	AB	R	H	2B	3B	HR	RBI	W	K	AVG	SB
Jim Delahanty	26	2	9	5	0	0	4	2	5	.346	0
Donie Bush	22	5	7	1	0	0	3	5	3	.318	1
George Moriarty	22	4	6	1	0	0	1	3	1	.273	0
Sam Crawford	28	4	7	3	0	1	4	1	1	.250	1

Name	AB	R	H	2B	3B	HR	RBI	W	K	AVG	SB
Tom Jones	24	3	6	1	0	0	2	2	0	.250	1
Davy Jones	30	6	7	0	0	1	1	2	1	.233	1
Ty Cobb	26	3	6	3	0	0	5	2	2	.231	2
Boss Schmidt	18	0	4	3	0	0	4	2	0	.222	0
Oscar Stanage	5	0	1	0	0	0	2	0	2	.200	0
George Mullin	16	1	3	1	0	0	0	1	3	.188	0
Bill Donovan	4	0	0	0	0	0	0	0	0	.000	0
Matty McIntyre	3	0	0	0	0	0	0	0	1	.000	0
Charley O'Leary	3	0	0	0	0	0	0	0	0	.000	0
Ed Summers	3	0	0	0	0	0	0	0	2	.000	0
Ed Willett	2	0	0	0	0	0	0	0	0	.000	0
Ralph Works	0	0	0	0	0	0	0	0	0	.000	0
TOTALS	232	28	56	18	0	2	26	20	22	.241	6

PITCHING

Name	G	GS	ERA	W	L	SV	CG	IP	H	ER	W	K
Ed Willett	2	0	0.00	0	0	0	0	7.2	3	0	0	1
George Mullin	4	3	2.25	2	1	0	3	32.0	23	8	8	20
Bill Donovan	2	2	3.00	1	1	0	1	12.0	7	4	8	7
Ed Summers	2	2	8.59	0	2	0	0	7.1	13	7	4	4
Ralph Works	1	0	9.00	0	0	0	0	2.0	4	2	0	2
TOTALS	11	7	3.10	3	4	0	4	61.0	50	21	20	34

◆ 11 ◆

THE BALLPARKS

Exposition Park
Home of the Pittsburgh Pirates
1891–1909

For the first three months of the Pirates championship campaign in 1909, the club played in antiquated Exposition Park before moving into its palatial palace in the Oakland section of the city, Forbes Field. Located on the same site as Three Rivers Stadium, which is now a parking lot between PNC Park and Heinz Field, home of the Steelers, Exposition Park was the third unsuccessful attempt to build a ballpark by the river in Pittsburgh's northside.

The issue with building a stadium at that location during the turn of the twentieth century was the fact that it was next to the river, so flooding was a constant occurrence. On one occasion, Independence Day in 1902 to be exact, over a foot of water stood in the outfield, but the club decided to go on with its doubleheader against Brooklyn that day. The team had to institute a special ground rule that all balls hit into centerfield would be singles. Brooklyn could not take advantage of the new rules, though, being shut out by the Bucs on both occasions, 3–0 and 4–0.

Other than the wet outfield, the other distinguishing aspects of Exposition Park included the twin spires on the roof behind home plate and the massive outfield, which measured 400 feet down the left-field line, 380 feet in right field and 515 feet to straight away center. Because of this, only one home run ever cleared the fence during the tenure of the park, when Tim Jordan of Brooklyn parked one over the right-field wall on July 22, 1908. Perhaps the biggest event ever to take place in the facility was when it hosted Game 4 of the first World Series ever on October 6, 1903, the first game a National League team hosted in the Series. Pittsburgh broke out to a 5–1 lead that day, holding off the Boston Americans, who scored three in the ninth inning to win, 5–4.

Tiring of the constant floods, Pirate president Barney Dreyfuss announced plans to build a new stadium in the Oakland section of the city after the 1908 campaign. On June 29, 1909, the Pirates said good bye to Exposition Park, defeating the Cubs, 8–1, in front of 5,545 fans, 25,000 less than would see their first game at Forbes Field.

Five years later the Pittsburgh Rebels of the Federal League refurbished Exposition Park, expanding its capacity from 6,500 to 16,000. Unfortunately the team and the league only lasted two years, folding in 1915. It was the last major league season ever played at the park.

Recently several members of the Society for American Baseball Research in Pittsburgh found the exact parameters of the facility and painted a marker in the exact location of where home plate stood in Exposition Park, to commemorate the stadium that not only housed the first Pirate teams of the twentieth century, but also where the American institution, the World Series, was first played.

Forbes Field
Home of the Pittsburgh Pirates
1909–1960

Sick of his wooden stadium by the river that had severe flooding issues, Pirate president Barney Dreyfuss set out to not only build an adequate replacement in the Oakland section of the city, but also construct the most magnificent facility the sport had ever seen. His effort, Forbes Field, turned out to be all that and more.

Wanting to build "the finest base ball grounds in the country" Dreyfuss hired architect and engineer Charles W. Leavitt Jr. from New York to build his field of dreams at the entrance of Schenley Park.[1] The new ballpark was named after a British general war hero in the French and Indian War, John Forbes, who led the British to overtake Fort Duquesne in Pittsburgh, renaming it Fort Pitt after the French burned it down and the British rebuilt it. Forbes Field was to be the first steel and concrete facility in the National League (Shibe Park, home of the Athletics of the American League opened a couple months earlier on April 12, 1909).

Louis Brandt of the Nicole Building Company, who was commissioned to build the new stadium, said, "Pittsburgh's new ball park is going to be one of the show pieces of the greater city, and we are glad to be able to cooperate

In 1909, Pirate owner Barney Dreyfuss gave Pirate fans his greatest gift by build-ing the magnificent Forbes Field. Dreyfuss felt it necessary to replace the team's old stadium, Exposition Park, as it was built by the river and often flooded the outfield (courtesy of the Pittsburgh Pirates).

with President Dreyfuss in an enterprise of which the people are bound to be proud." He further went on to describe the park. "The stands and offices will form one of the most ornamental structures in the Oakland district. The base of the grandstand will be concrete and tile, and the balcony and box tiers will be made of structural steel."[2]

Within a year Forbes Field was ready. A capacity of 30,000 gathered for opening day in July 1909. It included 18,000 in the magnificent new grand-stands, 6,000 in the concrete left-field stands with the remaining capacity housed in a temporary stands that was to be replaced by a concrete one in the future. The then world record crowd for a baseball game of 30,338 jammed every corner of Forbes Field to see their league-leading club take on the defending National League champion Chicago Cubs to christen this new modern marvel.

Over 40 older retired players were on hand for the opening ceremonies, helping to raise a huge American and city of Pittsburgh flag in the park. Also attending was Mayor W. A. Magee, who threw out the first ball to Director of Public Safety John M. Martin, who in turn tossed a strike across home plate to begin the opening contest. Despite the fact that they were defeated, 3–2, the day was a huge success. Forbes Field was lauded as an architectural marvel by almost all who came to see it. As *The Sporting News* claimed, "It was impossible to properly describe Forbes Field. It requires a personal visit to permit one to understand just how big and magnificent it is."[3]

Dubbed "The House That Wagner Built" by Dreyfuss's son-in-law William Benswanger, who took over as president of the club following the Hall of Fame owner's death in 1932, Forbes Field was as magnificent as was reported.[4] It drew 98,000 fans in its first five games and hosted a World Series

Wanting to preserve parts of historical Forbes Field when it was torn down in 1972, the University of Pittsburgh saved home plate, encasing it in the bottom floor of Posvar Hall about 10 feet from where it actually stood when Forbes Field was open.

in its first year of existence. In the opening contest of that memorable fall classic, Dreyfuss's new field made the record books once again as 29,264 patrons filled the facility, a World Series record.

As the years went on, Forbes Field went through many changes and saw many memorable events. Stands were built in right field in 1925, lessening the distance for a home run by 76.5 feet. Seven years later a net was constructed over the right-field wall to make it more of a challenge. During the 1935 season, Babe Ruth hit his last three homers in his illustrious career at Forbes Field, becoming the first player to clear those same right-field stands, sending one of his three long balls over the roof.

In 1946, a brick wall replaced the wooden one and ivy was grown on it. The farthest point from the wall to home plate was a mammoth 457 feet. Only one time in the regular season did a ball clear the wall in center field, by Dick Stuart in 1959. Because it was so difficult to hit a homer to deep center, the team felt comfortable enough to store the batting practice cage there in front of the fence.

There were Greenberg Gardens constructed in 1947 after the Bucs secured the services of Hall of Famer Hank Greenberg. The fence that was built there in front of the left-field wall cut the distance of a homer by 30 feet, making it easier for their new addition to hit long balls. It was taken down in 1954, returning the left-field line to a mammoth 365 feet, just about the exact distance Bill Mazeroski hit a ball in Game 7 of the 1960 World Series, allowing the fans at the classic stadium to see their beloved Pirates actually win the World Series for the only time in Forbes Field with his classic home run.

While Maz's homer is the greatest moment in the history of Forbes Field, there were many other events outside of baseball where fans of many other sports could enjoy its ambiance.

During the losing era of Pittsburgh Steelers football, the club called Forbes Field its home from 1933 to 1963. The city's three ranked major college clubs also played there. The University of Pittsburgh was there before the construction of Pitt Stadium, as was Carnegie Tech (now Carnegie Mellon University), who hosted the final regular season appearance of Notre Dame's Four Horseman, and Duquesne University that was a national power in the late 1930s and early 1940s.

For boxing fans, hometown hero Fritzie Zivic beat Jake Lamotta there in 1943 while Jersey Joe Walcott captured the world heavyweight championship in 1951 against Ezzard Charles. That same year a movie was filmed in Forbes Field, *Angels in the Outfield*.

Baseball fans not only got a chance to see their Bucs, but also some of the greatest players and teams ever to take the diamond. Forbes Field hosted

This section of the outfield wall at Forbes Field still remains in place today. It was the farthest point in center field where it was deemed so difficult to hit a homer that the team had a flag pole, batting cage and a monument to Barney Dreyfuss in front of it.

the 1944 and 1959 All-Star Games as well as three other World Series following the 1909 classic: 1925 against Walter Johnson and the Washington Senators, 1927 versus arguably the greatest major league team ever to take the field, the 1927 New York Yankees, and 1960, when Mazeroski's homer upset those same Yankees. Perhaps the best teams ever to play at Forbes Field were not major league clubs, but those of the Negro Leagues who wore the uniform of the Homestead Grays.

By the late 1960s the luster of the greatest baseball grounds ever built had worn off. You could not see home plate from the upper left-field stand and the fans were no longer enamoured with its magnificence. Ninety-four year old Pirate fan Domenic Finoli explained his joy at the construction of Three Rivers Stadium, saying that the time for Forbes Field had come to pass. Having seen many games at Forbes Field, he explained, "The seats were tight and uncomfortable, you had a poor sight from the left field stands and the place smelled like urine." The players were also looking forward to a new sta-

Beautiful Schenley Fountain is still a favorite place for people who visit the Oakland section of Pittsburgh. The fountain provided Pirate patrons quite a sight as it could be seen over the left-field fence when Forbes Field was open between 1909 and 1970.

dium. Pitcher Steve Blass said, "Well, we were very excited. Even though Forbes was a plus for the pitchers, it was like a 1,000 years old. Everything about Three Rivers was new and exciting, including air-conditioning in the clubhouses."[5]

The end came on June 28, 1970 when the Bucs defeated the Chicago Cubs who opened Forbes Field 61 years earlier in a doubleheader, 3–2 and 4–1. A year later, the facility was destroyed to make room for what is now Posvar Hall on the campus of the University of Pittsburgh.

Even though it has been four decades since Forbes Field has been gone, baseball fans can still take some comfort that some of its intricacies still remain. A portion of the wall still stands, including the 457-foot sign that Stuart cleared in 1959, with the green ivy hanging over it. Home plate remains encased in glass on the bottom floor of Posvar Hall as well as a marker where Mazeroski's homer cleared the wall.

On October 13 every year, hundreds of Pirate faithful comeback to these

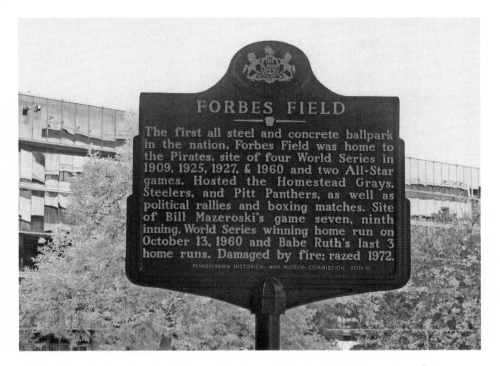

This historical marker is right outside the park in the Oakland section of Pittsburgh that honors Forbes Field. Every year on October 13, hundreds of Pirate fans come to this place where Forbes Field used to stand to hear the original broadcast of game 7 of the 1960 World Series, when Bill Mazeroski homered in the bottom of the ninth inning to defeat the Yankees.

grounds to celebrate Mazeroski's series winning homer its anniversary. They come to remember a great moment in what was at one time so many years earlier, the most spectacular baseball grounds ever.

Bennett Park

Home of the Detroit Tigers

1896–1911

While only in existence for 15 years, a pittance for most stadiums, it's where they put Bennett Park that made it memorable. Tiger management built the ballpark at the corner of Michigan Avenue and Trumble Avenue, the precise spot where Tiger Stadium was erected.

Constructed in 1896 to house the original Detroit Tigers who played in the Western League, the park was named after a former catcher for the Detroit Wolverines, Charlie Bennett, who lost both his legs in an 1894 train accident. Bennett was beloved by the baseball fans of Detroit. Not only did he have the honor of having the park named after him, but for 31 years, he became a tradition, throwing out the first pitch on Opening Day for the Tigers.

Housing only 5,000 fans when it was first built, the park was constructed on the property of William Woodbridge, the Michigan governor and U.S. senator from Michigan, who owned a farm on the site, as well as a place called Haymaker, where farmers would go to weigh their hay.

The land was rocky and the infield was laid over cobblestones. It made for a troublesome infield and allowed the Tigers to make more than their share of errors over the years. Perhaps the most interesting feature of this small facility was the fact the fans built what were called "wildcat bleachers" on top of the houses and barns that surrounded the short wall in left field, allowing fans to get a view of the game without paying.

By 1901, the Tigers moved to the new American League, becoming a major league franchise and expanded the park to 8,500 fans. The first "official" major league game was played in Bennett Park on April 25, 1901, when Detroit gave the overflow crowd a thrill, scoring ten times in the bottom of the ninth inning to defeat the Milwaukee Brewers, 14–13. The first two years the Tigers played in the AL, they couldn't use Bennett Park on Sundays, instead playing its Sunday games in a facility by the name of Burns Park.

Other interesting features of the stadium included a clubhouse in deep center field with a small scoreboard (left) and a groundskeeper's shed (right) surrounding it. All three items were considered in play. Bennett Park also featured a covered grandstand, running right past third base and almost to first base on the right-field side. The home plate area also had a lake around it, Cobb's Lake. It was the area where the groundskeepers kept well watered so Cobb's bunts would stay fair.

Over the course of the years the stadium was in existence there were several changes to Bennett Park. In 1907, there were temporary stands built in right field. The next season Detroit bought the lumberyard located beyond right field and then moved home plate 40 feet towards the outfield. The intention of the move was to build grandstands behind home plate. The team removed the clubhouse the same year and installed a larger scoreboard in right field.

When the Pirates played the Tigers in the 1909 World Series, Frank Navin had temporary bleachers constructed in left field, making them permanent the next season. By having the permanent bleachers built there, Navin finally was able to block the free view of the wildcat bleachers.

After all the changes had been made, the capacity had increased in the old wooden ball park to 14,000, allowing a record attendance of 490,490 to attend Tiger games during their last championship season in 1909.

By 1911, Bennett Park had become antiquated and was considered too small. The new capacity installed over the years had made the field one of the smallest in the game. The wooden park needed replaced. Taking a cue from the Pirates' Barney Dreyfuss, Navin tore down Bennett Park after the 1911 season came to its conclusion, building a much larger facility, seating 23,000. When it opened, it went by the name of Navin Field. Later on the facility was renamed to its more familiar name, Tiger Stadium.

◆ 12 ◆

THE TEAM PRESIDENTS

Barney Dreyfuss
1865–1932

Owner — Louisville Colonels 1888–1899
Pittsburgh Pirates 1900–1932
President — Louisville Colonels 1888–1899
Pittsburgh Pirates 1900–1929, 1931–1932

Championships as President

National League: 1901, 1902, 1903, 1909, 1925, 1927
World Series: 1909, 1925

"America is and always has been the land of opportunity," Pirate legendary owner and president Barney Dreyfuss used to say.[1] To the German immigrant from Freiburg, Germany, who came to this country in 1885, he lived that statement to the fullest.

Dreyfuss was one of the great innovators in the game of baseball. He contributed so much to the city he adopted, Pittsburgh, but today few realize who this smallish man was. Rob Ruck, a well known professor of Sports history at the University of Pittsburgh, once said, "For a city that adores sports and has a two-story sports museum as part of its history center, he is one of the figures we ought to know more about. He was a mensch. He meant as much to the identity of the city as Art Rooney and Cumberland Posey (the Hall of Fame owner of the Homestead Grays)."[2]

An energetic worker who would often work long hours, six days a week as a book maker in his cousin's distillery business, Dreyfuss' doctor suggested he come up with something more relaxing to do with his free time for fear his intense schedule would do irreparable harm to his health. Dreyfuss chose the game of baseball to unwind. His new "hobby" turned into a passion, as

Pirate owner Barney Dreyfuss (top row, fourth from the left) stands among his fellow owners in the National League. Dreyfuss came to Pittsburgh in 1900 after his former club, the Louisville Colonels, was forced out of the National League (courtesy of Library of Congress, Bain Collection, Prints & Photographs Division, 13107u).

he invested in the American Association's Louisville entry, the Colonels, which was consolidated into the National League following a merger in 1892 with the American Association. He eventually became the sole owner in 1899.

When the National League contracted teams after the 1899 season, Louisville was one of the four clubs that folded. Dreyfuss worked out a deal. By taking less money from the National League for giving up the Colonels, he would get the opportunity to purchase half of the Pittsburgh Pirates, a team that had spent most of their eighteen-year existence in the bottom half of the pennant chase. Bringing with him from his former team was a nucleus of young players, the likes of Honus Wagner, Fred Clarke, Rube Waddell, Tommy Leach and Deacon Phillippe, which would form the first dynasty of the twentieth century. Borrowing money from his cousins, Dreyfuss bought the remaining ownership of the club a year later, becoming its sole owner and set out to make the Pirates the envy of all of baseball.

In his first season as owner, the club finished in second place, which got them a spot in the 1900 Pittsburgh Chronicle Telegraph Cup Series. They would lose the series to the first-place Brooklyn Superbas, but it was a prelude to the greatness that would come as the Bucs captured its first of three consecutive National League crowns in 1901.

This came at a time though when Ban Johnson and the new upstart American League were raiding National League clubs for their biggest stars.

Johnson had a list of 46 players on his list that he wanted from the NL and got all but one by the beginning of the 1902 campaign. There were also reports that he had a hands-off approach to Pittsburgh players in an attempt to make sure they ran away with the pennant by such a large margin, that it would end whatever fan fervor there was for the race to result in less attendance, thus hurting the senior circuit financially.[3] The margin of victory the Pirates had over Philadelphia was only seven and a half games, so if there was in fact a conspiracy by Johnson to force a runaway pennant, it failed to materialize.

In 1902, Johnson went hard after Pirate players and there were rumors that the rival league was going after several Pirates. The main goal was to ink the Pirates shortstop. Johnson offered Honus Wagner an unheard of amount at the time, $10,000, to leave the Bucs. Whether it was loyalty to Dreyfuss, or the fact he loved playing in his hometown, Wagner signed for a much less, $3,600 to be exact, to stay, saying, "I loved my team and Associations. They meant much more to me than money."[4]

Dreyfuss demanded loyalty, and by the time the dust settled in 1902, he only lost three players, Jack O'Connor, whom he dropped after detectives Dreyfuss hired to follow him caught him meeting with American League officials, and two pitchers, Jesse Tannehill and Jack Chesbro. Both ended up jumping to the New York Highlanders (Yankees) following a wonderful 1902 campaign in Pittsburgh, when they went 20–6 and 28–6, respectively, for the Bucs. Angry at the situation Dreyfuss issued the following decree: "if ... any of our players at the expiration of their contracts choose to leave the Pittsburgh club, well and good. But I will not stand for any treachery or disloyalty from anybody while in my employ. No player can be a stool pigeon for the American League and draw a salary from the Pittsburg club at the same time."[5]

By some accounts, one of the reasons the team was able to stay intact despite the fact the new league was offering so many riches to lure players, was that Dreyfuss seemed to be a decent, generous owner, unlike some of his contemporaries. In 1901, he treated his players to a top-of-the-line hotel while in Chicago, kept an injured Sam Leever on the payroll with his career in doubt due to an injury suffered while being hit by a Christy Mathewson pitch, and paid for an all-expense-paid trip for the club to Atlantic City to rest up during an extended break in the schedule. Some say he did this to try and keep his players in Pittsburgh, but two years later when the two leagues were at peace, he did something else that proved his generosity. After losing the 1903 fall classic, he gave his share of the receipts to the players, allowing the losing Pirates to have a bigger share per player than the victorious Boston Americans did. He made the checks out to their wives so he made sure the players saved some of their well-deserved bounty. Dreyfuss also did another thing for his players in an attempt to make sure they didn't squander their earnings. He would set up bank accounts for those who wanted one and even offered to invest their money for them, guaranteeing the principle.

Because of some of the above reasons, the team stayed in tact, even though it was rumored that at one point most of the Pirates were offered a contract in the AL. They ended up being more than worth the money Dreyfuss was paying them as they crushed the rest of the National League in 1902, with a 103–36 mark, running away with the senior circuit crown by 27.5 games.

They won the pennant again in 1903, a year that saw Dreyfuss become the architect of what would become an American institution — the World Series. After helping to broker a peace between the leagues that season, Dreyfuss challenged the Boston Americans, champions of the upstart league, to a best-of-nine series at the end of the season to determine who was the best team in all of major league baseball. It was the first official World Series, one that saw his injury-riddled club lose to Boston in eight games, and a contribution to the game that will be the one he is most remembered for.

The other major contribution the Pirate owner gave to baseball and the city of Pittsburgh was its magnificent monument that housed many a Pirate and Pirate fan throughout its 61-year history, Forbes Field. When Dreyfuss took over the club, they played in a dilapidated stadium by the name of Exposition Park. Located what is now a parking lot in between PNC Park and Heinz Field, the outfield of the stadium stood right at the shore of the three rivers and often times would flood. Looking to house his club in a more stable environment, Dreyfuss built a park in the Oakland section of the city in 1909, far away from the water, and named it Forbes Field. The first modern steel and concrete baseball stadium in the league, Forbes Field was a sight to behold. It housed three world championship clubs over its existence, the first in its inaugural season of 1909, when the Bucs president put together a powerful unit that not only won the National League pennant with 110 wins but defeated the Tigers in the first seven-game series in the history of the fall classic.

The victory ended a decade of excellence that Dreyfuss had a big hand in. The great Branch Rickey once said that the Pirate president was the greatest judge of talent.[6] He used that ability to build his dynasty. That ability to spot talent came into question, though, in his second decade of ownership as his team fell apart. Names like Cozy Dolan, Bob Harmon, Ed Konetchy, Mike Mowrey, King Cole, Solly Hofman and Marty O'Toole replaced the names of some of the greatest players ever to wear a Pirate uniform only a few short seasons before.

The team stumbled out of championship contention for a few years, until he rebounded, using his skill to secure players like Max Carey, Pie

Traynor and the Waner brothers, all four of whom would eventually earn membership to baseball's ultimate fraternity, the Hall of Fame. This collection of players led Dreyfuss to a second world championship, one of the greatest comebacks in World Series history in 1925. It also secured him a National League crown two years later when Murderers Row, the 1927 Yankees, overwhelmed the Bucs. It was a fall classic, according to his great-grandson Andrew, that "our great-grandfather was mortified that the Pirates were beaten so badly."[7] He, of course, had nothing be mortified of, as he was by far the most successful Pirate owner in the history of the franchise.

In 1930, Dreyfuss turned over the reigns of the franchise over to his son Sam, as he turned his attention to his other duties, vice president of the National League. Sadly, a year later Sam died of pneumonia. A heartbroken Dreyfuss took control of the club for one more season, passing away himself in 1932 of pneumonia and prostatitis.

Seven decades after his death, his immense contributions to the city and the game had been forgotten, save a well-hidden plaque in PNC Park and a historical marker near where a portion of the Forbes Field wall still stands on the University of Pittsburgh campus. It wasn't until the twenty-first century when a new 12-person Veterans Committee, which was constructed of Hall of Fame members, veteran media members, and current and former executives, took a look at exactly what Barney Dreyfuss meant to the game. In 2008 they gave him the ultimate honor by selecting him to be enshrined in Baseball's Hall of Fame.

An historical marker near where Forbes Field once stood commemorates Pirates owner Barney Dreyfuss. For 32 years, Dreyfuss ran the club, winning two world championships and six National League pennants. He was elected to the Hall of Fame in 2008.

In the acceptance speech given by his great-grandson Andrew, he concluded by telling of yet another honor that would be bestowed upon his great grandfather that day.

"I'll close with a story that illustrates our great-grandfather's generosity and dedication to baseball. In the 1920s, Pittsburgh had a minor league team, the Comers, in Columbia, South Carolina. In 1926, Columbia's wooden stadium burned to the ground and the city did not have the resources to build a new one. Barney Dreyfuss was so passionate about baseball that he donated the necessary funds to build a new stadium. Columbia's Dreyfuss Field opened for play in 1927 and has housed minor league and college baseball teams for the past 81 years. Tonight at 7:00, the Columbia Blowfish of the Coastal Plain League will play on the original Dreyfuss Field wearing 1927 replica jerseys to honor Barney Dreyfuss' induction into the Hall of Fame. What a wonderful tribute to our great-grandfather and to one of baseball's pioneers."[8]

Frank Navin
1871–1935

Business Manager — Detroit Tigers 1902–1907
President — Detroit Tigers 1908–1935
Owner — Detroit Tigers 1907–1935

Championships as President

American League: 1907, 1908, 1909, 1934, 1935
World Series: 1935

A humorless man who was dubbed "Old Stone Face," Frank Navin was the leader of the Tigers for four decades, building one of the twentieth century's first dynasties at the beginning of his tenure and then constructing a second at the end, winning his elusive world championship only a month before his death.

Born in Adrian, Michigan, to Irish immigrant parents, Navin began his trek to the Tigers by working in the insurance industry for Samuel Angus after graduating from what is known today as Michigan State University. Angus eventually invested in the Tigers, becoming the owner in 1902. He brought Navin over to run the day-to-day operations as the business manager, which began a 33-year tenure that saw the club through some of their most successful eras.

A year later, Angus sold the club to William Yawkey Sr. who decided to retain the 32-year-old Navin. In 1908 Yawkey passed away and left the team to his son, who had little interest in the game, so he sold almost half his interest in the team to the Adrian native for $40,000, loaning Navin the money to make the first payment. Yawkey also named Navin as president of the team with full control of the Tigers. With his generous receipts from the 1909 World Series, Navin was able to pay off Yawkey to own his portion of the club free and clear.

By all accounts the Tiger president was a frugal man, to say the least. He was notorious for keeping his payroll among the lowest in the circuit. Despite this tendency, he was able to assemble a powerful squad, grabbing Sam Crawford from the Cincinnati Reds in 1903 and Bill Donovan from Brooklyn the same season.

He also seemed to be a fine judge of young talent. He bought a young hurler from Toledo, Ohio, who was playing for Fort Wayne in the Western

Tigers owner Frank Navin (top row, first on left) poses with his fellow American League owners. Navin came to the Tigers in 1902 as a business manager and by 1908 became the club president (courtesy of Library of Congress, Bain Collection, Prints & Photographs Division, 17210u).

Association in 1901 by the name of George Mullin. Navin then invested a small amount, only $700, for a feisty southern outfielder in the South Atlantic League who went on to become one of the greatest hitters the game has ever known, and one of its most controversial figures, Ty Cobb.

As he was building a title contender, Navin was in need of someone to run the ship. His manager, Bill Armour, was not getting the team to play to its potential, finishing the 1906 campaign at 71–78. Navin had eyed 38-year-old Hughie Jennings, who was managing Baltimore of the Eastern League. When he approached former major league great Ned Hanlon, who owned the minor league club, to inquire about purchasing Jennings, he was given the outrageous price of $5,000 for the services of the manager. True to his frugal nature, Navin found out that Baltimore had signed Jennings to a player's contract, as he was also their shortstop. Because of this, Detroit was able to secure his services for a much more reasonable $1,000, the going price for drafting a player from the minor league circuit, and immediately named him to replace Armour.

With the 1907 campaign quickly approaching, Navin now had the pieces in place to begin the incredible run of three consecutive American League championships.

The club responded to Jennings, winning 21 more games than the year before with a 92–58 mark to capture the pennant. It was here that Navin showed his legendary frugalness by paying his two Hall of Famers, Crawford and Cobb, a combined $8,000, far under the market value for players of their kind. The great Cobb was not complementary of the way Navin doled out money. "Paying a ball player his worth pained old Stone Face deeply," the Georgia legend remembered.[9] Navin and Cobb had various run-ins during their 22 seasons together. In 1911, Cobb protested, and held out, until Navin made good on a promise he backed off on, to raise the right fielder's salary to $10,000. Cobb would blame Navin for the failure of the club to maintain its championship form following their 1909 championship claiming, "It wasn't hard for me to guess. Navin and his scouts couldn't make a good trade if it bit them."[10]

Unlike his manager Hughie Jennings, who often irritated his players by giving Cobb preferential treatment, Navin was unafraid to confront the Georgia native when the situation dictated it. One such moment occurred when Cobb refused to play in the field next to center fielder Davy Jones after the Tiger great reportedly fumed because he thought Jones had missed a hit-and-run sign. Jones recalled what Navin said to Cobb. "Suppose he did miss that sign, which the other players tell me he didn't. So what? That's no reason for you not to play. You're just making an excuse because you're not hitting...."

Now you're going to play today, and that's all there is to it. Otherwise you'll be suspended without pay. And it's out of the question to take Jones out of the game, so forget it."[11]

While Navin had his many altercations with Cobb, he had the utmost respect for the way his other Hall of Fame outfielder Sam Crawford played. "Sam Crawford was without a doubt one of the greatest natural hitters who ever lived," Navin stated. And he combined with great hitting strength a timeliness in delivery which made his batting doubly effective."[12]

Described by writer Fred Lieb as a man who "rarely smiled, seldom laughed, and couldn't have cried if he had wished to, Navin showed little emotion at a ballgame, whether the Tigers were winning with a late-inning rally or were being routed 11–0."[13] Then there was another side to the Tiger president, though. While he lived up to his Old Stone Face image most times and was excessively cheap with his payroll, Lieb pointed out that underneath he was very caring of his players. Lieb also painted a picture of the man, one that he claimed would easily forgive a player that left the team under strained circumstances. He told the story of pitcher Ed Willett who left the Tigers to sign with the rival Federal League in 1914. Lieb went on to say that despite that fact that Willett jumped ship, Navin took care of him when he had a bad financial situation later on and gave his wife financial help after his death.[14]

Whether a stone-faced tyrant or warm compassionate man, Navin was a wonderful businessman. By 1912 the club had made profits of $365,000 and had raised the value of the franchise to $650,000, an incredible amount for the time.[15] Yawkey and Navin took some of their profits and built a new facility to replace rickety old Bennett Park, which would eventually become one of the most legendary fields in baseball, Navin Field. Navin put a significant amount of money into the stadium, making several improvements over the next decade.

As much as he put into the club's incredible new ballpark, he continued to hold salaries down which caused yet another controversy with Cobb in 1921. The Hall of Famer was named that season as the club's manager and claimed in his autobiography that he asked Navin how much help he was going to give him, to which the club president responded, "Everything you need to win. My partners will go along with that."[16] In a bitter moment remembering the situation, Cobb shot back in his memoirs, "His weak spine showing all the way, Navin did nothing of the sort. He sabotaged his own ball club. In my six years as manager I had the worst ownership manager ever suffered. At the same moment, Navin wasn't giving the government an honest tax account on his gate receipts."[17] The latter statement was a claim that Navin lowered his actual turnstile count at the Tiger home games so he didn't have to report the financial take to the government. By 1926, the heated feud came to a boil when Cobb was forced to resign due to a gambling scandal and was replaced by former third baseman George Moriarty.

Within the next few years, Navin's fortune began to falter at the hands of the Great Depression. The stock market crashed and his accumulated gambling debts had made Navin more dependent on Walter Briggs, the man who had purchased a portion of the club from Yawkey, to run his team.

Eventually he was able to rebuild his club, adding such greats as Goose Goslin, Mickey Cochrane and a young slugger by the name of Hank Greenberg, who recanted similar stories about what a tough negotiator Navin was. Greenberg remembered his first encounter with Navin over a contract dispute. "My salary was $3,300 in 1933, and I asked for $5,500 in 1934, figuring I had a pretty good year. They only wanted to give me $5,000, though, and that $500 led to my first holdout. Mr. Navin wrote me a letter in which he said something like 'I've had many better ballplayers than you on my team.' Ty Cobb once thought he was bigger than the game and I told him if he didn't want to play he could stay home. The same thing goes for you. If you don't want to play with us, you can stay home."[18] Eventually the two settled their dispute when Navin offered to give him a $500 bonus if the team finished in the top three in the American League.

In 1934 the team improved incredibly, capturing the American League crown, so Greenberg did collect the bonus. The Tigers repeated in 1935, a year when Navin finally lived his long-awaited dream as the team finally won its first World Series crown. The Tiger president was elated, but unfortunately a month later, on November 13, Navin suffered a fatal heart attack while horseback riding.

Navin was at times a tyrant, a confidant to baseball dignitaries, frugal and difficult to deal with, but what he was most of all was a man that directed the Tigers through one of the most successful eras in the franchise's history.

♦ 13 ♦

THE MANAGERS

Fred Clarke
1872–1960

Years	Wins	Losses	Pct
19	1602	1181	.576

Manager — Louisville Colonels 1897–1899
Pittsburgh Pirates 1900–1915

Championships as Manager

National League: 1901, 1902, 1903, 1909
World Series: 1909

As a manager, Fred Clarke was a paradox, a man who expected his players to be feisty and aggressive on the diamond, but gentlemen off it. He was also a paradox himself.

A brilliant manager, Clarke was also a talented inventor who developed and patented things such as a pulley system for tarpaulins so four men could easily pull it over the flood-ravaged fields of Exposition Park and smoked glasses that clipped to a players hat, which he developed after Honus Wagner lost a ball in the sun.[1] On top of that, he was a talented businessman, which allowed him to amass a fortune of $1 million by 1917. While those two patents were his most important contribution to the game from an invention stand-point, he also developed and patented a rubber slip placed in front of the pitching rubber to prevent a pitcher from slipping, as well as a small equipment bag.[2]

He was a paradox to his boss, Barney Dreyfuss, often butting heads with him. He was extremely intense and fiery on the field, doing whatever he had to in order to win a game, especially in the early days managing in Louisville,

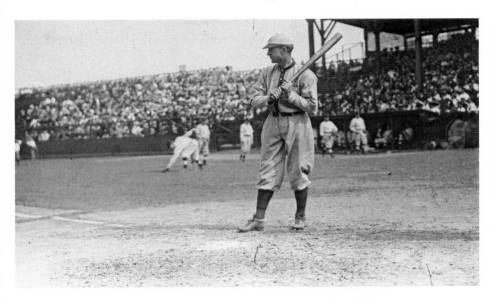

Fred Clarke was the most prolific manager in the history of the Pittsburgh Pirates. Clarke won 1422 games in his 16-year career at the helm of the Pirates, with four National League crowns and a championship in the 1909 World Series (courtesy of Library of Congress, Bain Collection, Prints & Photographs Division, 9310u).

in contrast to Dreyfuss who was more intent on winning with dignity. In one instance, Clarke sent catcher Chief Zimmer to hide in the outfield to steal the catcher's signs and send them to the bench. Another time he kicked Dreyfuss out of the locker room, insisting if he had something critical to say that he say it in private and not in front of the players.

While at odds at time, he also credited Dreyfuss with making him a success, not only as a manager and player, but in life. He said that the Pirate president taught him moderation, from Clarke's early days as a carouser. Clarke said that Dreyfuss once asked him as a young player with Louisville, when it was becoming apparent his lifestyle was affecting his play on the field: "Are you fair with yourself? ... You will live in the major league a few years only if you continue to dim your batting eye and weaken your physical self by carousing around. Then you will go back to the minors and be swallowed up, and you never will have been any one. It's up to you. Think it over."[3]

Even though such conflicts would put a strain between some managers and owners, the Pirate owner stated to Clarke after he apologized for one particular situation, "Fred, I wouldn't give a darn for a fellow who always agrees with me."[4]

He was very loyal to Dreyfuss as they formed a very successful partnership that lasted 19 years. He turned down many lucrative offers to join the American League, and in turn, Dreyfuss gave him a percentage of the team's profits and a generous salary. It was so successful that he was one of the few people elected to the Hall of Fame that had the credentials to be selected both as a manager and a player.

His 1602 victories are the 16th best mark all time, while his .576 winning percentage ranks 15th, as does his four pennants won. Bill James named him not only the most successful manager of the first decade of the twentieth century, but also the 13th best all time, in his book *The Bill James Guide to Baseball Managers*. On the other hand, James also stated, "Clarke's ability as a manager decreased significantly as soon as Honus Wagner began to grow old, however, and he was forced out after the 1915 season."[5] Despite the fact James may not completely appreciate his greatness behind the bench, Clarke still had a style that helped form the first true dynasty of the twentieth century.

He once stated that his philosophy in managing was "the successful manager must, of course, know baseball." Then, he must have "the shrewdness, cheek, information and money" to get good players. And finally, he had to be able to shape the players "into a big, happy whole, both on and off the field." He went on further to tell of his lack of patience with disruptive players, especially Hall of Fame hurler Rube Waddell, who pitched for him in the beginning of the 1900s that a player who was disruptive could not be part of his roster, "no matter how good a ball player he [was]."[6]

He had a tendency to change his batting order often, a mark of the modern-day manager. He also had a proven philosophy in bringing up a young pitcher. While many managers of the day would often throw talented young pitchers on the mound early in their career, Clarke preferred to keep them in the bullpen until they were ready to be slotted into the rotation. An example of this was rookie pitcher Babe Adams, whom he brought along slowly in 1909, yet felt he was ready to start Game 1 of the World Series that year over his much more experienced hurlers, a move that allowed Adams to win three games and hand Clarke his only world championship. His philosophy with pitchers allowed him to never lead the league in two important categories, hits or walks allowed. Clarke especially had little patience with pitchers who couldn't get the ball over the plate," which was another reason perhaps no teams never led the circuit in bases on balls.

He was described on the website *The Baseball Page* as one of the men "who were born without the ability to kiss anyone's ass. He would tell you exactly what he thought, even if you didn't ask."[7] As a result of that character trait, Clarke had more than his share of run-ins with teammates and opposing players.

Clarke, who owned a lucrative ranch called "The Little Pirate Ranch" near Winfield, Kansas, was also a huge believer in fundamentals and defense, which was evident in the fact the Pirates never led the league in errors during his tenure.

Offensively Clarke helped usher one of the most potent offenses in the senior circuit during his tenure. The great Honus Wagner credited his manager for helping his batting stance. "Fred Clarke, who was one of the wisest baseball players I ever saw and a great hitter, taught me the foot shift (the stance is explained further in Wagner's biography in chapter 14) as an aid to batting. I have always depended on the foot shift ever since."[8]

While Clarke was well aware of everyone's weaknesses on the team, he needed to have another eye on himself as a player as he had a difficult time picking up his own deficiencies. "When I was manager of the Pirates, I knew every weakness and every strong point of every batter on the team. When they were not hitting right, I knew why and could tell them so. But, and here is the rub, I could never tell what was wrong with my own batting when I was off stride. And there was only one man on the team who could. That was (Ginger) Beaumont. So I used to get him to look me over and diagnose my ailment."[9]

After a series of unsuccessful seasons following the Bucs victory in the 1909 World Series, Clarke retired from the bench in 1915 to spend more time on his ranch and with his family. The Hall of Famer eventually returned to the team as vice president of the club and a bench coach on Bill McKechnie's staff. He got some credit for helping the club to mature and win the 1925 World Series. According to Jack Gallagher of the *Los Angeles Times*, "McGraw's old baseball enemy, Fred Clarke, stepped into the picture again as adviser to the Pirate team ... and, after that, the baseball world witnessed the boys from Pittsburgh literally smash their way to the top of the parent [league].... After the Pirates missed three or four pennants that seemed to be within their grasp, Dreyfuss decided that something was lacking and that Clarke could supply that particular something. He did."[10]

When the team voted on sharing part of their winnings for the '25 series, they voted on a $1,000 share to Clarke, far under the full share of $5,332.72. Whether it was because they knew Clarke had money and didn't need it or was a show of disrespect, in 1926 Clarke's career on the bench ended in an ugly way.

As the story goes, Clarke and the manager McKechnie got into a discussion on how to deal with the slump of aging star Max Carey. The former Pirate manager wanted Carey replaced, while the then current Bucs skipper didn't want to put Cuyler there. After Clarke shot back that the batboy could do a better job than Carey, there was a thought that Clarke was trying to over run McKechnie and return as the manager. Carson Bigbee heard what had been said and Babe Adams and Carey called for a team vote to have Clarke removed from the bench. True to his nature, Dreyfuss did not like controversy and through his son Samuel (the elder Dreyfuss was on vacation in France at the time) dropped all three players from the team (in what is known as the ABC Affair, i.e., Adams, Bigbee and Carey). At the end of the year, McKechnie was fired and Clarke was removed from the bench. While McKechnie went on to a Hall of Fame managing career with the Cardinals, Braves and Reds, Clarke never returned to the bench again, ending a long career in a less than stellar way as the greatest manager ever to don a Pirate uniform.

Hughie Jennings
1869–1928

Years	Wins	Losses	Pct
16	1184	995	.543

Manager — Detroit Tigers 1907–1920
New York Giants 1924–1925

Championships as Manager

American League: 1907, 1908, 1909
National League: 1924

He was a vibrant red-haired Irishman, born in the mining town of Pittston, Pennsylvania, who took over the Detroit Tigers from Bill Armour in 1907, turning around a second-division club into one of the most powerful teams in the early twentieth century.

Hughie Jennings was not only a great manager, but had enough quirks to fill a book. He had a memorable smile, and constantly chattered from the third-base coaching box, while chewing grass blades to the point that grass that surrounded the coach's box was nothing but dirt by the time he finished the game. Perhaps the one thing that Jennings was more noted for than anything else was a spine-curdling yell he would let lose, "Ee-yah." So noted was he for the scream that it became his nickname. As he screamed "Ee-yah" he would position himself in sort of position like an Indian doing a rain dance. His hands were in a fist in the air and his right leg would be in the air as well.

It was believed that the yell emanated from saying, "that's the way" and kept getting shorter until it came out in its more familiar form.[11] He also claimed to have invented the saying "attaboy" which he yelled often too.

After winning three American League pennants in his first three seasons at the helm of the Tigers, manager Hughie Jennings never won another title in the next eleven campaigns. Owner Frank Navin finally relieved Jennings of his duties in 1920 following a 61–93 season (courtesy of Library of Congress, Bain Collection, Prints & Photographs Division, 16448u).

A lawyer also, who attended the Cornell Law School before passing first the Maryland bar exam in 1905 then doing the same in Pennsylvania two years later, he came to the Tigers from the Baltimore Orioles of the Eastern League. Detroit owner Frank Navin was rebuffed from getting Jennings, whom he felt could be the manager to lead his club to a pennant, when Orioles boss Ned Hanlon demanded $5,000 for his services. When Navin found out Baltimore had signed Jennings to a player's contract, he was able to draft him as a player for the much more reasonable cost of $1,000. It was the best money he ever spent as Navin was correct in his assumption; Jennings was in fact the man to manage the Tigers to a pennant.

The Mansfield University alumnus was a manager who wasn't above anything to help his team win. He would try and get under the skin of players and umpires alike, even resorting to such things as buying shiny balls, rubber snakes or jack-in-the-boxes to try and confuse the great Rube Waddell, who was prone to be distracted by such things.

Jennings inherited a 20-year-old outfielder who may have been a troublemaker, but was one of the greatest hitter the game has known by the name of Ty Cobb. At first the new manager wanted to trade his budding superstar. Cobb had a rough spring training that season, full of many fights and conflicts. He had gotten into a fight with catcher Boss Schmidt and almost one with outfielder Matty McIntyre. With the situation becoming more intolerable, Jennings and Navin tried to deal their young superstar to the Indians for Elmer Flick. Cobb walked out of camp and returned to his home in Royston, Georgia, until a solution was reached. The trade never materialized, as it was the Indians who actually turned down the trade, thinking the Georgia native was too troublesome and that Flick was actually a better player. Flick suffered from stomach ailments that kept him out of most of the 1908 campaign, and probably led to his retirement two years later, while Cobb went on to lead the Tigers to three straight pennants and become one of the top ten players in the history of the game.

Jennings and Navin once again tried to deal their disgruntled star, this time to New York for pitcher Bill Hogg. This trade would have been even more one-sided than the Flick deal, as the curveballer was only 23–26 in the previous two campaigns. Bill Yawkey, the owner of the Tigers at the time, nixed the deal and Cobb remained a Tiger.

Once the trades fell through, Jennings sang his praises. "Hear me! This boy has it. He has the makings to become the greatest player who ever lived."[12] He gave Cobb carte blanche, seemingly with no rules. It was a policy disdained by many of his players over the years who did not like Cobb.

Jennings knew that Cobb was the key to his offense, which was the staple of his championship clubs. Over the course of his 16-year managerial career, teams headed by Hughie Jennings led the league in hits seven times, runs scored and batting average on six occasions and slugging percentage during five seasons.

When it came to hitting, the Detroit manager had very strong philosophies. He said that he had "little faith in paper averages. A ball player must have talents and talents, if they are good enough, will win him a place."[13] He further went on to say: "A batter must not only have ability, but he must make the most of this ability, otherwise he is merely a mechanical workman. The successful player has energy, perseverance, aggressiveness and ambition. All are important and all enter very largely into his success."[14]

The Pennsylvania native didn't like to waste too many positions on the field with weak hitters. He even had a modern philosophy of managing on the subject, wanting to make sure he was strong offensively at first base and in the outfield. "Their positions are not so difficult in a fielding sense and gives them an opportunity to develop their batting eye. Other infielders should hit, but you can stand for one weak hitter on your infield if he is good enough as a fielder. Generally you will get that weak hitter at shortstop. You can forgive a catcher for not hitting, for he has so much else on his mind and you hardly expect a pitcher to hit."[15]

Hitting took him to three league titles, and his thoughts of a strong outfield and first baseman when it came to offense proved to be correct. He led the league three straight times between 1907 and 1909 in batting average with a devastating outfield that included Cobb, Hall of Famer Sam Crawford, Davy Jones and Matty McIntyre and first basemen Claude Rossman and Tom Jones.

While leading his club to three consecutive American League championships, Jennings never could get his club over the hump, losing twice decisively to the Cubs and once to the Bucs in 1909. Their run ended in 1910, partially because of the dissention on the club. The main reason was due to the players' combative relationship towards Cobb as well as the fact their pitching staff fell apart compared to their 1909 performance.

Through all the problems, the *Spalding Guide* in 1911 gave Jennings credit for keeping the team together as well as he had. "Occasional rumors were heard that there was dissention on the part of the Detroit players. If this were the case the manager must be given credit for handling the differences with some diplomacy, for it was not until the season was in its extremity that Detroit could no longer depend upon beating the Philadelphia's (the Athletics)."[16]

Four years into his job, Jennings was wildly successful sporting a 366–243 record with a .602 winning percentage. As tantalizingly close as he was to a world championship in that time period, he would never lead the Tigers to the World Series again.

Often times late in the 1910s, the red-haired Irishman's job was on the line with rumors of Cobb taking over the helm. Cobb discounted the rumors. In his book about Cobb, writer Al Stump stated that "Cobb discouraged it (the rumors)."[17] He went on further to say that one of the main reasons was that he liked Jennings.

As the Tigers continued to fail in their quest for a championship, the rumors persisted. Finally after a seventh-place finish in 1920, with his popularity among his players waning, Hughie Jennings resigned by mutual consent as Navin finally made the change, replacing him with Cobb.

Soon after Jennings left Detroit, New York Giant manager John McGraw hired him as a coach on his club. With McGraw suffering from sinusitis among other maladies, Jennings took over several times over the course of the 1924 campaign, leading the Giants to a 32–12 mark in the games he managed, helping them to the National League crown. Once again he lost in the World Series, this time to the Washington Senators in seven games.

In 1925, the red-headed manager once again took control of the Giants for a time as McGraw continued to suffer with his sinus issues. A 21–11 record wasn't quite good enough to get New York back to the Series as the Giants finished 8.5 games behind Jennings' 1909 nemesis, the Pittsburgh Pirates.

After the 1925 season, Hughie Jennings was diagnosed with tuberculosis and did not return to coach, ending his long career in baseball. Two years later he suffered from meningitis and died in Scranton on February 1, 1928, at age 58.

Seventeen years later, when the first Veterans Committee was formed, Hughie Jennings was selected to join baseball's elite in the Hall of Fame, ironically the same year Fred Clarke went in. While many believe his selection mainly was due to his outstanding 17-year career as a feisty shortstop primarily with Louisville and Brooklyn (he is still the all-time leader in hit by pitches with 287), he certainly had the credentials to enter baseball's hallowed halls as a manager too.

◆ 14 ◆

THE 1909
PITTSBURGH PIRATES

Infielders

Bill Abstein

First Base
Born 2/2/1883
Pittsburgh Pirates 1906, 1909

Died 4/8/1940
Major League Career 1906, 1909–1910

If the Pittsburgh Pirates had lost the 1909 World Series, the name Bill Abstein would rank with Fred Merkle and Bill Buckner among baseball's biggest goats of all time. Fortunately for the memory of Bill, the Pirates were victorious over the Tigers and, hence, his poor play in the Series makes for only a laughable footnote.

The Pirates had struggled with finding an adequate first baseman since letting go of Kitty Bransfield following a .223 season in 1904. In 1908, Fred Clarke tried four men at the position, with Harry Swacina seeing more time there (51 games) than anyone else. He batted a weak .213 with only seven extra-base hits. The team recalled Abstein following the season. He had played briefly with Pirates as a second baseman/outfielder with the Pirates in 1906, but was thought to need more experience and moved to first base in the minor leagues. Although there were rumors the Pirates were trying to land the Cardinals' Ed Konetchy in an off-season deal, when nothing came of the rumors, and Dreyfuss waived on the Reds' Jake Ganzel, Abstein became the heir-apparent to the first base job.[1] Bill had hit .272 with 41 extra-base hits, including 19 triples, playing for Providence of the Eastern League.[2]

Although he battled tonsillitis in May, the early reviews on Bill were good. Tommy Leach claimed Abstein was the best receiver of throws at first since Bransfield.[3] In September, Ralph Davis wrote, "Bill Abstein has done grand work at first base."[4] Bill hit a respectable .260 for the season, adding 20 doubles and 10 triples, to help drive in 70 runs, the sixth highest total in the National League.

Abstein's World Series play was, however, another matter. Whereas Merkle, Buckner and others etched their place in ignobility with one horrendous play, Abstein's performance was akin to a recurring nightmare. He struck out nine times, some sources say 10 times, in 26 at-bats.[5] He committed five errors and appeared lost at times on the bases. With no one out and representing the tying run on third in the ninth inning of Game 6, he tried to score on a groundball to first base and was thrown out. George Cantor wrote that he spiked Tiger catcher Boss Schmidt out of anger rather than as an attempt to score the winning run, as the Detroit team had been riding him.[6] Fred Clarke considered replacing him for Game 7, but because the only other player who was on the roster who had seen action at first that season was Ham Hyatt, who had played in only two games there, he stuck with Bill. He scored the first run of the game after opening the second inning with a walk, but he had already paid for his ticket out of Pittsburgh. Contrary to legend, he was not released immediately following the Series, but was placed on waivers during the offseason and sold to the St. Louis Browns.

Things didn't get any better for Bill in St. Louis. He hit only .149 with 3 RBIs in 87 at-bats for the Browns in 1910. Abstein returned to the minor leagues later that year. He had one strong year for Los Angeles in 1914, batting .308, but his averages tended to be in the .240–.260 range most of the time.

Dots Miller

Second Base
Born 9/9/1886   Died 9/5/1923
Pittsburgh Pirates 1909–1913   Major League Career 1909–1921

One of the biggest on-field improvements for the Pirates in 1909 came at second base, where rookie John "Dots" Miller supplanted veteran Ed Abbaticchio early in the season. Miller had just one year's professional experience, split between Easton of the Atlantic League and McKeesport of the Ohio-Penn League, when he joined the team in spring training. Given his limited experience, it was not surprising that Miller was not considered a strong candidate to make the squad, but when Honus Wagner announced he would arrive late, Clarke gave the rookie some playing time at short. Miller opened some eyes with his fine play, most importantly those of Clarke. The youngster even impressed Wagner, who inadvertently gave Miller his nickname. When a reporter asked the Pirate star who the new kid was, the scribe misheard Wagner's reply, "That's Miller," and thought Honus had said, "Dot's Miller."[7]

When Abbaticchio struggled at the start of the season, Clarke placed Miller at second. With the Pirates "Big Three" of Tommy Leach, Clarke and Wagner batting in front of him, Miller ended the season third in the National League with 87 RBIs. His .279 average ranked behind only Larry Doyle among National League second basemen. Physically a large man, Miller was compared to Wagner by Jack Ryder in *The Sporting News*. "This would not be a compliment from the standpoint of physical beauty, but when applied for ballplaying ability, it is the sincerest of flattery."[8]

Dots knocked in a run with a double in the second game of the World Series that year, but Bill Donovan shut out the Bucs the rest of the way for a 7–2 win. In Game 3, Miller stood at the plate as the Pirates scored two runs. The first came on a throwing error by Boss Schmidt and the second on a wild pitch. Dots eventually walked in that at-bat and scored. In the sixth, Miller again stood at home as another run crossed the plate when Leach came in on another error. Dots collected two hits each in Games 6 and 7. His two-run single in the fourth inning of the final game gave the Pirates a 4–0 lead and Babe Adams some room to breathe.

As pleasantly surprising as Miller's play was in 1909, it was just as disappointing in 1910. There was some thought he and Wagner were enjoying socializing too much.[9] Miller returned with solid seasons from 1911 through 1913. He drove in between 78 and 90 runs during this span. Having moved to first base in 1913, Miller put together one of the Pirates' best seasons at that position to date. In addition to his 90 RBIs, which ranked fourth in the NL, Miller finished second with 20 triples and fourth in total bases. The Pirates, however, were an aging team. Following the season Dreyfuss pulled a blockbuster trade by sending Miller with Chief Wilson, Art Butler, Cozy Dolan and Hank Robinson to the Cardinals for pitcher Bob Harmon, first baseman Ed Konetchy and third baseman Mike Mowrey.[10] The trade might have worked out fine for the Bucs if Konetchy and Mowrey didn't jump to the Federal League after their first season in Pittsburgh. Miller, for his part, had another fine year in 1914, finishing fourth in the Most Valuable Player voting following a .290, 88-RBI performance, then steadily declined as a hitter until his swan song season of 1921 when he hit .297 in 343 at-bats for the Phillies.

Miller then managed the San Francisco Seals of the Pacific Coast League before contracting tuberculosis in 1923. He passed away on September 5 that year. Miller's nephew, Jack Tighe, managed the Tigers in 1957–58.

Ed Abbaticchio

Shortstop–Second Base
Born 4/15/1877   Died 1/6/1957
Pittsburgh Pirates 1907–1910   Major League Career 1897–1898, 1903–1905,
                                        1907–1910

Expected to be the Pirates everyday second baseman in 1909, veteran Ed Abbaticchio was replaced by Dots Miller following a slow start after appearing in a handful of games that season. Abbaticchio was a terrific athlete, thought to be the first man to play both professional football and baseball and is considered the first man of Italian heritage to play in the major leagues.

In 1895, Abbaticchio was a member of the first all-professional football team, which was located in his hometown of Latrobe, Pennsylvania. He is credited with developing the first spiral punt. In 1898, Ed reached, what at the time, was the pinnacle of professional sports in the United States, becoming a player in the National League with the Philadelphia Phillies. He appeared in three games that season, and 25 the next, but hit only .228 and was let go. He resurfaced with the Boston Beaneaters in 1903 after back-to-back seasons with averages above .350 for Nashville of the Southern Association.[11]

Abbaticchio started for the Beaneaters for three consecutive seasons, the first at second and the final two at short. His hitting improved each year, and Ed had raised it to .279 in 1905, after which he walked away from baseball to assist in his family's hotel business in Latrobe. Some thought Abbaticchio's father offered him a handsome sum of money to manage the business as a way of coaxing his son away from baseball, which was viewed by some as a profession for lazy and unsavory characters. However, when the opportunity arose for Abbaticchio to be traded to the nearby Pittsburgh Pirates, "Abby" returned to the diamond. Abbaticchio's skills were so prized by the Pirates that Barney Dreyfuss parted with the .300-hitting Ginger Beaumont, defensive whiz Claude Ritchey and pitcher Patsy Flaherty to obtain the local boy.

Moved back to second base, Ed drove in a career high 82 RBIs, the second best total in the senior circuit in 1907, despite collecting only 23 extra-base hits all season. His RBIs dropped to 61 the following year before Miller's play kept him mostly on the bench. Abbaticchio saw some action in midseason, filling in when Honus Wagner was injured. He batted only once in the World Series, striking out as a pinch-hitter on the ill-fated play that ended Game 6.

Abbaticchio got into only three games, batting the same number of times as the 1910 calendar turned to July. On the first day of the month, the Pirates sold him back to the Boston franchise, which was now calling itself the Doves. After hitting .245 in 52 games, Eddie returned back to Latrobe.

Honus Wagner

Shortstop
Born 2/24/1874   Died 12/6/1955
Pittsburgh Pirates 1900–1917   Major League Career 1897–1917

During the thirty years following Honus Wagner's retirement in 1917, there were some outstanding shortstops. Luke Appling won a pair of batting titles and almost always was topping .300. Joe Cronin was a Most Valuable Player, solid defensively and noteworthy at the plate. Arky Vaughn broke Wagner's Pirate record for highest batting average in a season by hitting .385. No one considered them a rival for the title of greatest shortstop of all time.

Ernie Banks was an outstanding slugger and sure-handed fielder as the Cubs shortstop in the 1950s. A two-time Most Valuable Player while playing on weak teams, Banks topped 40 home runs five times in his career, twice leading the National League. Although he was easily the best shortstop since Wagner, he was never considered as good of an all-around player.

Cal Ripken, Jr., played every day, breaking a hallowed record for endurance. Also a two-time MVP, Ripken hit 431 home runs and was the best all-around shortstop of the 1980s and 1990s, an era that also produced strong hitting shortstops Robin Yount, Barry Larkin and Alan Trammell. But neither Ripken nor any of his contemporaries have been called the second Wagner.

Recently, Derek Jeter became the all-time leader for hits as a New York Yankee and won his second Gold Glove Award. So strong a defensive player and extremely alert on the ball field that when superstar Alex Rodriguez joined New York, he agreed to move to third base. There is talk that if Jeter continues to stay healthy and hit at his current pace, he could pass Pete Rose to become baseball's all-time hits leader. But no one is writing that he should be considered the game's greatest shortstop.

By 1909, Wagner was acknowledged as not just the young professional sport's best shortstop, but its greatest player of all time. He had amassed six batting titles and at one point or another had led his league in just about every category as a hitter. Honus had also topped the National League in doubles six times, slugging, on-base percentage and stolen bases five times, RBIs three times, runs twice and total hits once. Although he had hit as high as .381 in 1900, Wagner was coming off his best season in 1908 as he dominated the league-leader categories as no one ever had done before. He paced the NL in hits (201), doubles (39), triples (19), RBIs (109), average (.354), on-base percentage (.415), slugging (.542) and stolen bases (53) while tying his personal high by playing in 151 games. Wagner had almost single-handedly carried an offense in which no other player topped .265 to the pennant before the Pirates lost to the champion Cubs in their final game of the season.

Honus Wagner (center) stands in the middle between two fellow Hall of Famers, George Sisler (left) and Pie Traynor (right). Wagner is considered one of the greatest players ever to take the diamond, finishing his incredible career with 3,415 hits, the eighth best total of all time (courtesy of the Pittsburgh Pirates).

Wagner had just turned 35 before his teammates reported to spring training in 1909. Having proven during a salary holdout in 1908 that he kept himself in playing condition during the offseason, Wagner informed Dreyfuss he would be starting his play just before the opening of the season. The Pirate owner reportedly did not object.[12] Honus hit well in the early going with his average rising to .420 at one point.

Ralph Davis quoted an unnamed reporter as saying, "I note that they are not comparing Wagner and (Nap) Lajoie any more. There is no comparison between them. Lajoie is a second baseman. Wagner is a ball player — and the greatest ever, at that. Patrons are wise enough that they recognize the superiority of the Dutchman, and he is always given a great reception in every city he visits."[13] Bill Dahlen, another fine shortstop of that time, kept his comments brief, but to the point, saying, "The Flying Dutchman is playing better than ever this season."[14]

Honus cooled off in midseason, then missed time when he was injured in an on-field collision in Cincinnati.[15] As great a player as he was, Wagner was able to show a sense of humor on the field as well. On the Fourth of July, Wagner came to bat with a "torpedo," fireworks shaped as a bat, which exploded when he swung at the first pitch he faced.[16] Getting back to work, Wagner ended up 1909 having another dominant season. He outhit the National League average by 95 points and, defensively, Wagner was considered as good, if not better, than any shortstop in the National League.

The World Series promised to be a showdown between the beloved, long-standing giant of the game and Ty Cobb, the belligerent, angry young man who put up even greater numbers than Wagner in ruling the American League. Legend had it that on one play, Cobb tried to intimidate Wagner. Standing on first base, the brash Cobb yelled at the shortstop, "I'm coming down, Krauthead!" Wagner supposedly told him to come on down. Cobb did, spikes glistening as he came in at Wagner. Honus received the catcher's throw, deftly stepped aside and planted a tag so squarely on the Georgia Peach's mouth that it drew blood. It is a wonderful story, a great legend, but one that never happened.

Cobb flatly denied the play. Wagner, later in life, embellished it as a good story, claiming it to be true.[17] In reality, Cobb and Wagner exchanged pleasantries before the start of the Series and compared notes on hitting. The two actually used similar, hands-apart grips at the start of their swings, but Wagner tended to punch at the ball less often than Ty. Both had similar hitting philosophies, however.

"You hear about batters who swing from the handle and there are others who choke up on the bat. I do both," said Wagner. Often I swing from the handle, but a good deal of the time I choke up ... Fred Clarke ... taught me the foot shift as an aid to batting. I have always depended on my foot shift ever since. I always stand on my right foot when I am batting. The weight of my body comes on that foot. But I stand in such a manner that I can shift my left foot around. You can cover a great deal of ground by shifting that foot. You can step away from the plate to hit a ball close up or you can lunge right into the plate to hit a ball that is on the outside."[18]

F.C. Lane noted that Cobb's thoughts on successful hitting mirrored Wagner's, quoting the Georgia Peach as saying, "My idea of a real batter is a man who can choke up on the bat when he feels like it or slug from the handle when it is necessary. And he can accommodate himself to almost any kind of ball a pitcher gives him by stepping away if it's too close, and wading into it if it's on the other side of the plate. A combination of proper handling the bat and good footwork will go a long way to offset any system of pitching that has ever been devised."[19]

Salutations and myths aside, Wagner was not exaggerating when he talked about the Series being hard fought.[20] Nor was it an exaggeration to say that the old king had bested the young dark knight during the seven-game classic.

After Fred Clarke tied the opening game, 1–1, with a fourth-inning home run, Tiger ace George Mullin served notice that Honus's status as baseball's best player would not immune him from retribution and hit Wagner with a pitch. Honus did not advance from first, but in the sixth, Wagner opened with a double. He appeared to be picked off second, but catcher Boss Schmidt made a poor throw and Wagner took third. He scored on a Bill Abstein groundout, the final run in the Pirates 4–1 win.

After collecting a hit in the Pirates Game 2 loss, Wagner enjoyed an outstanding Game 3. He reached on an error, which produced an RBI for Wagner, and later scored on a wild pitch in the first, then added three hits and another run batted in later in the game as the Pittsburgh held on to an 8–6 nail-biter. Hitless in the Pirates' second loss of the Series in Game 4, Honus singled and scored a run in Game 5, which not coincidentally was another Pirate win. Wagner also was hit by a pitch following another Clarke home run, which had broken a 3–3 tie, also not thought to be a coincidence. Honus was not about to take this assault lying down. He stole second and third and continued on to score when Schmidt's throw sailed into the outfield.

Wagner doubled in two runs in the first inning of Game 6 to make the score Pittsburgh 3, Detroit 0, but Vic Willis could not hold the lead and the stage was set for Game 7. Honus had only one hit, but it was a big one as he tripled in two runs to put the game on ice and scored himself on the play when Davy Jones made a bad throw. For a man who had many great days on the ball field, it is truly a testament to his team sentiment that Wagner called that day, October 16, 1909, his greatest day in baseball.[21]

The Flying Dutchman could still be called the greatest player in baseball as he outhit Cobb .333 to .231, collecting eight hits, a pair of doubles, the Series' only triple and six stolen bases. He scored four runs and drove in six and while Tommy Leach (.360) and Clarke drove in seven and hit his two home runs, it was Honus who enjoyed the best all-around Series.

Wagner continued to play at a high level for another four seasons. He started 1910 slowly, and there was talk Wagner was drinking too much.[22] Such talk decreased as Wagner's hitting increased. He missed out on his eighth title, finishing fifth in the NL, but only 11 points behind the new champion Sherry Magee with a .320 average. However, Wagner finished tied for the top spot in hits (178) with teammate Bobby Byrne. Wagner captured that eighth batting title the following season when he hit .334 and he continued to be a .300 hitter for two more seasons. Beginning in 1914, Wagner's average never returned to the charmed circle. A disappointing .252 in an injury-plagued 1914 had critics saying the 40-year-old should retire, but Honus played three more seasons. His 45 extra-base hits in 1915 reflected his better health as Honus led the National League in games played with 156. His power numbers fell off again in 1916, but he hit .287, still 40 points better than the average National Leaguer. Honus had not intended to play in 1917, but with the Pirates struggling as they had not done since the Dutchman had flown into Pittsburgh, Dreyfuss encouraged him to return. Primarily playing first base, Wagner's .265 was second on the team behind the club's new star Max Carey's .296. Wagner was also coaxed into managing that season, but Honus had never wanted the job and after sampling it for three games, he decided the responsibility definitely was not for him.[23]

Wagner had maintained a home in his native Carnegie, Pennsylvania, just a few miles outside of Pittsburgh during his playing days. In his youth, the town was called Mansfield. The Wagners were German coal miners and Honus had built his legendary strength mining coal before becoming a ballplayer. (In fact, Honus's given name was John, but people sometimes Germanized it to Johannes, which was shortened to his nickname that he became nationally known by.) He began raising a family in Carnegie in his retirement. He later coached baseball at Carnegie Tech and invested in a sporting goods store, but when his business failed during the Great Depression, Wagner found himself in financial straits. Following an article in which Fred Lieb wrote of Wagner's plight, the Pirates invited him to join their coaching staff in 1933. Honus accepted and remained on the coaching sidelines until 1952. With his health failing, Wagner attended the dedication of a statue in his honor a few months before his death in 1955. That statue followed the Pirates from outside of Honus's kingdom of Forbes Field to Three Rivers Stadium to its new home, appropriately, in front of the main gate at PNC Park.[24]

Alan Storke

Third Base–First Base
Born 9/27/1884   Died 3/18/1910
Pittsburgh Pirates 1906–1909   Major League Career 1906–1910

Alan Storke was so talented a ballplayer that Barney Dreyfuss allowed him to report late to the Pirates in order to pursue his Harvard education. Storke's father was an attorney and Alan was following in his footsteps as well as pursuing a career as a major league infielder. He saw his most action with the Bucs in 1907, a season when he played every infield position while appearing in a total of 112 games. Storke hit in the .250's each of his first three seasons in Pittsburgh. In 1909, the scholar-athlete hurriedly reported to the

Pirates to fill in when Bill Abstein was taken ill in May, leading to a mini-controversy. After Alan assisted in a Pirate win against Cincinnati, the Reds filed a protest with the National Commission, arguing that he was ineligible to play as he had not formally petitioned for reinstatement to the league. Dreyfuss scoffed at the protest, pointing out that Storke had not retired and had not been a holdout. Indeed, Alan had signed a contract the previous December and as such was not required to report to his team by May 1.[25] Storke filled in at third and first for Dreyfuss' team until he was traded in August to the Cardinals, along with Jap Barbeau, for Bobby Byrne. St. Louis played him extensively at shortstop and, after again hitting in the .250's for the Pirates, Storke improved his average to .282 for his new employer while appearing in 48 games. Despite his success, Storke was included in a multi-player deal with the Reds following the season. Tragically, the young man with a bright future died of empyema, a streptococcus infection due to discharge into the body's natural cavities, such as the lungs. The condition is rare today as it can be treated with antibiotics.[26]

Bobby Byrne

Third Base
Born 12/31/1884   Died 12/31/1964
Pittsburgh Pirates 1909–1913   Major League Career 1907–1917

The acquisition of third baseman Bobby Byrne from the Cardinals, for infielders Jap Barbeau and Alan Storke in August 1909, solved the Pirates' third-base problems and gave the Pirates one of the better hot-corner men in baseball for the next four seasons.

A small man weighing only 148 pounds, who the Pirates had coveted for almost a year before the trade was consummated, Byrne was considered a strong defensive player.[27] So strong was his glove that the Pirates had expressed interest in him following the 1908 season in which he hit but .191 in what was his second major league season. The team's interest continued into 1909 even though Bobby was only hitting .214 at the time of the trade. However, Byrne had greatly improved his batting eye and had drawn 46 walks, whereas he had walked only a total of 58 times in his two previous seasons. His all-around play shot up with the Pirates as the newest Buccaneer posted an excellent .387 on-base percentage in 46 games, thanks to a respectable .256 average and 32 walks as Byrne took over the leadoff spot on Fred Clarke's lineup card. He committed just two errors in the field, a huge improvement over Barbeau, whose fielding average with Pittsburgh had been .891. Byrne also added to his value with 29 stolen bases for the year. His combined total of 92 runs scored ranked third in the senior circuit and his 78 walks ranked second.

Hitless in Games 1 and 2 in the World Series, Byrne collected pair of singles in Game 3, scoring a run in the team's 8–6 win. He collected two more hits and scored twice in the Pirate's next victory, an 8–4 triumph in Game 5. But the play Byrne is most remembered for occurred in Game 7. After the Pirates lost Game 6, a contest in which two Tiger players had been injured on consecutive plays in the ninth inning, Detroit starter Wild Bill Donovan opened the game by hitting Byrne with a pitch. Tommy Leach sacrificed him to second. Then Bobby broke for third. When Clarke swung and missed at Donovan's pitch, Bobby came into the Tiger's third baseman and chief agitator, George Moriarty, with spikes high. Both players were injured on the play. Byrne suffered a broken ankle and had to be helped from the field. Moriarty initially stayed in the game with a gashed knee, but had to leave the game shortly afterwards, replaced by a pinch-runner after doubling in the second. Although criticized by some for the play, Byrne received a standing ovation from a partisan Pittsburgh crowd during the team's victory celebration at Forbes Field.[28]

The speedy leadoff man enjoyed his finest season in 1910, tying Wagner for the NL lead in hits with 178 and surpassing everyone with 43 doubles. He batted a career high .296. Byrne's on-base percentage was .366 and he scored 101 runs to place second. He continued to play well through August 1913, when he was traded to the Phillies with former ace pitcher Howie Camnitz for Cozy Dolan and cash. Byrne was moved to second base in 1914, but a .209 season for the National League champions in 1915 began to signal the end of regular duty for Bobby, who appeared as a pinch-hitter in that year's World Series. Waived to another Series-bound team, the White Sox in 1917, Bobby got into one game in September, but was not eligible for the World Series. His major league career came to an end with his solo appearance in pale hose.

The trade for Byrne in 1909 would be replayed in Pittsburgh with a similar move some 70 years later, when the Pirates dealt for another third baseman who greatly contributed to their championship team. While Byrne was never as good a player as Bill Madlock, his play greatly tightened the Pirate infield and completed their powerful batting order.

Jap Barbeau

Third Base
Born 6/10/1882   Died 9/10/1969
Pittsburgh Pirates 1909   Major League Career 1905–1906, 1909–1910

A 5'5" infielder, William Joseph "Jap" Barbeau was obtained following the 1908 season, drafted from Toledo of the American Association. Barbeau had gained major league experience with Cleveland in 1905 and 1906, but after a poor showing in the latter season (.194, .830 fielding percentage) was sent back to the bushes. Averages of .295 and .282 impressed the Bucs enough to give him another chance. Winning a utility role in spring training, Barbeau was given regular duty once it was decided Ward Miller was not the answer to the team's center field problems. Fred Clarke moved Tommy Leach to center and Barbeau became an everyday third baseman.

Despite some strong early season reviews, Barbeau again posted a sub-.900 fielding percentage and could manage only .220 batting and .302 on-base averages in 91 games before he was traded with Alan Storke to Cardinals for Bobby Byrne. Like Byrne, Barbeau hit better in his new uniform, batting .251 and showing a strong .370 on-base percentage in 48 games. The Cardinals, however, were not overly impressed and Jap appeared in only seven games in 1910 before Mike Mowrey took over as the guardian of the hot corner in St. Louis.

Outfield

Fred Clarke

Left Field
Born 10/3/1872
Pittsburgh Pirates 1900–1911, 1913–1915

Died 8/14/1960
Major League Career 1894–1911, 1913–1915

While most of the acclaim Fred Clarke has received for the success of the 1909 Pirates has centered on his managing, the 36-year-old left fielder remained a solid offensive performer with enough speed to steal 31 bases. Clarke, who would end his career with a .312 batting average, hit .287 and set a career high with 80 walks, tops in the National League. In spite of his age, Clarke played in 152 games that season, also the highest figure of his career. On the surface, it might appear Clarke's statistics were not overwhelming, but he finished in the top ten in average, on-base percentage, OBPS, games, runs scored (trailing only Honus Wagner with 97), hits, triples, singles, runs batted in and runs scored, in addition to his number one status in the receipt of receiving free passes.

In the World Series, Clarke's average was only .211, but he was one of the stars of the seven-game classic. His fourth inning home run in Game 1 posted the Pirates first run of the Series. In his team's Game 3 victory, Clarke singled and drove in a run. With the Series tied, 2–2, and the score knotted, 3–3, in Game 5, Clarke smashed a three-run homer, a shot to center field, which gave the Bucs a lead they would not relinquish. Fred's RBI and run scored wasn't enough to stop Detroit from retying the Series in Game 6. In Game 7, the player-manager posted one of the strangest lines ever in a World Series box score. Clarke went to the plate five times without being charged with an at-bat. He walked four times and sacrificed. Fred also stole a pair of bases. He scored a pair of runs and was credited with an RBI. Even his sacrifice was a key play as it set up Pittsburgh's third and fourth runs.

A .312 hitter in his 21-year career, Fred Clarke stole 503 bases and hit 220 triples, the seventh best figure in major league history. The Veterans Committee elected him to the baseball Hall of Fame in 1945 (courtesy of the Pittsburgh Pirates).

The world championship was the crowning feather in Clarke's cap, but the beginning of the player-manager's career was equally impressive. Clarke debuted by going 5-for-5 after arriving on the major league scene with Louisville on June 30, 1894. He showed some power with seven home runs and then posted his first .300 season a year later when he batted .347. His most impressive average came a couple of years later, in 1897, when Clarke hit .390 to finish second to Wee Willie Keeler who connected at a .424 pace. For years, Clarke was credited with a .406 mark that year, but researchers found that his totals had been mistakenly calculated.

The left-handed-hitting Clarke had become a favorite of Barney Dreyfuss after he heeded the owner's advice to quit carousing when Clarke was a young player. Dreyfuss rewarded Clarke's brains and maturity by naming him his manager and brought him to Pittsburgh in 1900 with a bushel full of his best Louisville players when Dreyfuss took over the team. After injuries dropped him from the .300 circle in 1900 for the first time since his rookie campaign, Clarke stormed back with a vengeance, hitting .324, .316, .351 and .306 before missing .300 for a fifth straight season by one point in 1905. In 1903 Clarke had his most productive hitting for the Pirates. In addition to finishing second to Wagner in hitting by just four points, Clarke led the NL in doubles with 32 and slugging at .532. His 70 RBIs was the best of his Smokey City career and his 15 triples tied his best figure in a Pirate uniform.

Prior Fred's heroics in 1909, his average had dipped to .265 in 1908, although during his three-year stretch under .300 (1907–1909), Clarke was drawing more walks than ever before. There were rumors Clarke, who was certainly well off financially by this time, might retire to his Little Pirate Ranch after achieving his championship, but he returned as both player and manager in 1910.[29] Still an effective player, Clarke began needing more time off as his legs were beginning to go. His last season as a regular player was 1911 when Fred hit .324 and still was able to swipe 24 bases. After that year, Clarke put in only cameo appearances through 1915, collecting the final two hits of his career in 17 at-bats. Fred led the team off the field as well through 1915, but the Pirates were a fading club as its stars were all aging together. At the close of the season, Clarke decided it was time he quit the game.

But Fred's involvement with the Bucs didn't end there. He invested money in the franchise and in 1925 began assisting with coaching duties, sitting on the bench next to one of his former players, Bill McKechnie, who had taken over the club in 1922. Clarke's second tour of duty began with as much promise as his first as the Pirates won the World Series, but in 1926 Clarke touched off what became known as the A-B-C Affair (which is explained in Clarke's managerial biography in Chapter 13). Following the season, McKechnie was not retained and Clarke decided to return to Kansas full time.

Sadly, Fred would never see his Pirates win another title as he died on August 14, 1960, less than two months before Bill Mazeroski's World Series winning homer.

Tommy Leach

Center Field
Born 11/4/1877   Died 9/29/1969
Pittsburgh Pirates 1900–1912, 1918   Major League Career 1898–1915, 1918

It is somewhat strange that the third member of what was sometimes referred to as "Pittsburgh's Big Three" behind Honus Wagner and Fred Clarke was a man who was called "Wee Tommy," but in many ways Thomas William Leach may have been the biggest of all Pirates in 1909.

Leach's offseason the year before began tragically when his wife, who had been ill for years, passed away, leaving Tommy and a son named Nelson to fend for themselves.[30] (Sadly, the Pirates' trainer, Ed LaForge, also lost his wife around the same time.)[31] Tommy made it through a grieving winter and reported to spring training uncertain of where the Pirates would ask him to play. A fine third baseman, Leach opened the season at that position, but Tommy had played significant time in center field in 1905 and 1907 and had the speed to cover that position, even if he did not have a cannon for an arm.

When rookie center fielder Ward Miller got off to a terrible start, Clarke asked Leach to again switch positions. Tommy obliged, and although his .261 average was not outstanding, he led the league with 126 runs scored, about 30 more than the runner-up, who happened to be Leach's boss. The 5'6" Leach, who had led the National League in triples (22) and home runs (with the lowest total ever for a champion, six) previously, hit a career-high 29 doubles and walked 66 times in '09, and his 27 stolen bases also aided his ability to score runs.

Leach enjoyed a stellar World Series, leading the victors with a .360 average, nine hits and four doubles. Following Bobby Byrne's first-inning injury in Game 7, Clarke moved Leach again, this time back to third base. He played the field flawlessly that afternoon and coming to plate five times, Tommy collected a pair of hits, a walk, scored twice and added a sacrifice to spark the Pirates' Series–winning offense.

But as noted above, Leach's excellent play in 1909 was not unexpected. He had starred for the Pirates since coming to Pittsburgh from Louisville with 13 other players in 1900. Tommy had grown up as a neighbor to the Delahanty family and when Ed Delahanty became a star player for the Phillies, Tommy's father supported his diminutive son's decision to become a professional ballplayer. "If Ed can do it, so can you," the elder Leach encouraged.[32]

After struggling in the low minors, Tommy attracted big league attention while playing for Auburn in the New York State League. Two teams showed equal interest in Leach and his team offered to sell him to whichever club he preferred. Seeking his manager's advice, Leach chose Louisville as the manager informed him Washington had a good third baseman by the name of Wagner. It turned out the Wagner playing in D.C. was Butts Wagner, and to Leach's astonishment another Wagner, this one nicknamed Honus, was playing third for Louisville. Leach was both awed and worried when he saw Honus in action for the first time, immediately recognizing this Wagner was the greatest player he had ever seen. Butts, on the other hand, was just an ordinary player. Leach, as good as he was, was not about to replace the budding superstar, and became a utility player. He hit well enough in limited play to impress Barney Dreyfuss, and got his chance at real playing time in 1901, after the Pirates' third baseman, Jimmy Williams, had jumped to Baltimore and hit .305.

In 1902, Leach played a role in Wagner becoming the greatest shortstop of all time. Clarke had asked Wagner, capable of staring at any position, to try his hand at shortstop after Bones Ely had left for the American League, but Honus was reluctant. Leach, who had been playing short, agreed to encourage Wagner, who had a much stronger arm as well as incredible range, to switch positions with him. Honus eventually agreed. For his part, Wee Tommy enjoyed his home run championship that year.

Leach continued to play well throughout the decade and helped lead the Pirates to three early-century pennants and into the first World Series in 1903 after scoring 97 runs and driving in 87. Leach hit four triples in that first World Series, a record which still stands, and collected nine total hits as well as tying for the Series lead with seven RBIs, but the Bucs were outdone by Boston behind the pitching of Bill Dineen.

During the team's close but no cigar seasons of 1904–1908, Tommy continued to be one of the top players in the game. As noted above, he split most of his playing time between third base and center field. With Leach around, Clarke knew that at least one of those positions would be well covered. Leach's best offensive campaign during these years was 1907 when scored 102 runs, collected a career-high 166 hits and 43 stolen bases and hit .303.

From 1910 until the end of his career, Leach played mostly center field. Ralph Davis, as early as 1909, wrote that Leach, now past 30 years old, might be better suited "away from the rigors of third base." He noted that Leach's successor at third, Jap Barbeau, had a stronger arm.[33] Indeed, Davis had reported prior to 1909 that the Pirates were trying to obtain Bobby Byrne to play third rather than trading for an outfielder or bringing back Roy Thomas, once a walking machine for the Phillies, who had covered center for the Bucs in 1908. Leach's best post–1909 season was 1913, when he led the National League in runs scored with 99 in 131 games, but by then Leach was "Wee Tommy of the Chicago Cubs." Leach also led National League outfielders with a .990 fielding percentage that year and batted a solid .287. After one more year with the Cubs and a disappointing 1915 with the Reds, the aging ballplayer went to the minor leagues for a few seasons. After back-to-back seasons hitting just .244, Leach was off to a .291 start in 67 games for Chattanooga, when his old employer in the Steel City, facing a wartime shortage of players, beckoned. He hit only .194, but was cagey enough to draw 19 walks to boost his on-base percentage to .363.

Tommy then moved to Florida, played baseball there in the minors for a few years, and was active in the game of life for another 51. He passed away at the age of 92 in 1969.

Ward Miller

Center Field
Born 7/5/1884   Died 9/4/1958
Pittsburgh Pirates 1909   Major League Career 1909–1910, 1912–1917

Although Ward Miller had led the Wisconsin-Illinois League in hitting with an eye-popping .383 mark, the Cubs, who held an option on him, allowed him to slip through waivers to the Pirates in the fall of 1908. A left-handed hitter with impressive speed, Miller had an outstanding spring training and won the Pirates' center field job. He was referred to as Ty Cobb II and expressed confidence in his abilities.[34] The Pirates' leadoff hitter in the season opener, Miller yelled at the first major league pitcher he faced, Cincinnati's Art Fromme, to "put the ball over." Adding, "I want to kill your third baseman." The cocky youngster then tripled down the left field line and scored the Bucs' first run of the year.[35] This was the highlight of Ward's Pirate career. He hit only .143 in 56 at-bats before being sent to the Reds for Kid Durbin on May 28.

Chief Wilson

Right Field
Born 8/21/1883   Died 11/23/1948
Pittsburgh Pirates 1908–1913   Major League Career 1908–1916

Babe Adams did more for the 1909 Pirates than winning a dozen games during the season and three more in the World Series. In a way, Adams' ability as a scout helped win several more games that year, for when Babe came to Pirates in 1907, he recommended that owner Barney Dreyfuss purchase a hard-hitting outfielder Adams had pitched against in the Western League. That player was Owen Wilson, a left-handed batter with a powerful throwing arm.

The Pirates must have trusted the Babe's judgment as Fred Clarke put the raw rookie in right field for the 1908 season. The manager must have seen something beyond Wilson's statistics to stay with him in 1909 as Wilson had a poor rookie year, hitting only .227 with 18 extra-base hits in 529 at-bats. Or, perhaps, it was that Clarke didn't have any adequate replacements for Wilson as his backup outfielders, Danny Moeller, Spike Shannon and Beals Becker, all hit less than .200 and combined for only seven long hits in 88 games. It was Clarke who gave Wilson his nickname Chief. Unlike several players of his generation who carried the nickname, Wilson was not Native American. A native Texan, Wilson was very familiar with how to use a lariat and impressed his manager so much that Clarke called him "Chief of the Texas Rangers."[36] In the off season, there was some thought that new recruit Hamilton Hyatt, a strong hitter, would push for playing time in right, but Wilson's defense and improving hitting kept him in the lineup. Ralph Davis noted that Wilson already boasted the strongest arm in the league.[37]

Wilson proved the Pirates' patience was no mistake as he batted almost 30 points higher than the league by hitting .272 and increased his extra-base hits to 40. Still not a patient man at the plate, Wilson walked only 19 times while appearing in 154 games. Playing in his only World Series that fall, Wilson struggled, going just 4-for-26 with a single double and RBI. He was

In his second major league season, Owen "Chief" Wilson had a breakout campaign, hitting .272 in 1909. Three years later Wilson etched his name in the history of the game when he hit 36 triples, a record that still stands today (courtesy of Library of Congress, Bain Collection, Prints & Photographs Division, 09308u).

called out trying to steal third with the Pirates trailing by a single run to end Game 6.

But unlike most of his teammates, Wilson's best seasons lay ahead of him, including one in which he set a record which has continued to afford him a modicum of fame and which likely will never be broken. In 1912, Chief hit an astounding 36 triples, breaking the record of 31 set by Dave Orr in 1886 and tied by Heinie Reitz in 1894.[38] This followed another excellent season in which Wilson topped the National League with 107 RBIs. In both seasons, he hit .300 on the nose.

Chief's 1913 season was not nearly as impressive and following the season he was traded in a headline-making trade along with Dots Miller and three other players in return for two regular infielders, first baseman Ed Konetchy and third baseman Mike Mowrey, plus pitcher Bob Harmon, a one-time 20-game winner. Wilson won two fielding titles in St. Louis, but his hitting was not as impressive as it had been in Pittsburgh and after hitting .239 in 1916, Wilson's major league career ended at the age of 33.

Hamilton Hyatt

Outfield
Born 11/1/1884
Pittsburgh Pirates 1909–1910, 1912–1914

Died 9/11/1963
Major League Career 1909–1910, 1912–
1915, 1918

Hamilton Hyatt, who Fred Lieb would describe 40 years later as "one of the game's greatest pinch hitters," contributed clutch hits off the bench as a 24-year-old rookie for the 1909 Pirates.[39] Obtained following a 15-home-run, .323 season for Vancouver of the Western League, Hyatt was called the "The Washington Giant" for his size, strength and success in that state.[40] He hit .437 in the early games, including going 6-for-7 as a pinch-hitter. His defense was said to be a different story and likely kept Clarke from playing him in the field more than eight times (six in the outfield and twice at first base) all season. Ham ended the year hitting .299 in 67 at-bats. His nine pinch-hits topped the National League, although he ended up hitting less than .250 in that role.

Hyatt got into two World Series games. His first appearance was in his familiar pinch-hitting role, but in Game 7, Ham went into center field, a position he had not played all season, when Tommy Leach moved to third to replace the injured Bobby Byrne. Hyatt drove in the game's first run with a sacrifice fly in the second inning. As well as Babe Adams pitched, it was the only run Hyatt's fellow freshman needed. Perhaps luckily, no balls were hit to him in the outfield.

Hyatt was given a chance to further establish himself in 1910 when Clarke played him at 38 games at first, but Ham hit .263 and was sent back to the minors. Playing for Kansas City, Hyatt had another big year in bushes, batting .327. Among his 210 hits were 31 doubles, 13 triples and 14 home runs.[41] This earned him another try with the Pirates, but Clarke continued to use him primarily as a pinch-hitter. He enjoyed fine years in 1912 and 1913, hitting .289 and .333, respectively and he led the NL in pinch-hits for a second time in 1914, but hit only .214 overall. Hyatt went to the Cardinals in a waiver transaction following that year. He saw the most action of his career in 1915, appearing in 106 games and batting 295 times, but his final average of .268 with 19 extra-base hits could not outweigh his inability in the field. Again he returned to the minors and again he hit well enough for another trial, this time during 1918 when he resurfaced with the New York Yankees, but a .229 average in 53 games ended his playing career.

Kid Durbin

Pinch-Runner
Born 9/10/1886   Died 9/11/1943
Pittsburgh Pirates 1909   Major League Career 1907–1909

Blaine Alphonsus "Kid" Durbin, an outfielder obtained from the Reds for Ward Miller on May 28, was used only once as a pinch-runner by manager Fred Clarke, appearing in his final big league game on June 30.[42] Durbin had been a seldom-used outfielder and pitcher with the Cubs in 1907 and 1908, prior to going to Cincinnati for the start of 1909 in a trade with Tom Downey for John Kane. With the Reds, Durbin had gone 1-for-5.

Catchers

George Gibson

Catcher
Born 7/22/1880   Died 1/25/1967
Pittsburgh Pirates 1905–1916   Major League Career 1905–1918

An excellent defensive catcher and game-caller who would establish records for durability, George Gibson held the Pirates' team record for games caught for almost 90 years. But more astonishing was his ironman performance in 1909 when he caught 150 out of 152 games the Bucs played that season. Along the way to his record for total games caught in one year, Gibson shattered Chief Zimmer's record of 111 consecutive days behind the plate without a rest when on September 9, he donned the tools of ignorance for the 112th straight game.[43]

Gibson never carried a big enough bat to be considered a superstar, but after struggling for a few seasons (he batted .178 in both his freshman and sophomore years), Gibson hit a more than respectable .265 in 1909, a year in which the league as a whole hit .244, and drove in a career-high 52 runs. He caught every inning of the World Series that fall when speed-demon Ty Cobb was safe only once against Gibson's arm as Cobb's other theft was a steal of home. While the Tigers were credited with making six steals in the Series, their success rate was only 50 percent. Gibson also contributed some at the plate, doubling and scoring the go-ahead run in Game 1 and singled and scored on Ed Summers' wild pitch in the second inning of Game 5 and improved the Pirates' 6–4 lead by driving home another in the eighth. Both games were won by the Pirates. However, in Game 6, George came to bat with the tying run at third in the ninth and hit a sharp grounder to Sam

Catcher George Gibson set a National League record in 1909 when he caught 134 consecutive games for the Pirates. Between 1908 and 1910, Gibson caught an amazing average of 144 games a year (courtesy of Library of Congress, Bain Collection, Prints & Photographs Division, 3273u).

Crawford at first. On the play, the baserunner, Bill Abstein, tried to score, but was thrown out as the Pirates went down without squeaking out the tying run.[44]

Gibson was born in London, Ontario. He decided he would rather be a ballplayer than lay brick for his father. After establishing himself as a fine defensive player, George arrived in Pittsburgh via Montreal in 1905. Despite Gibson's weak bat, he took over regular duty from the aging Heinie Pietz in 1906. His batting slowly improved into the .220's before Gibson's finest all-around season in 1909. Although George carried a workload perhaps comparable to heavy labor, he led all National League catchers in fielding with a .983 mark. In addition to his 52 RBIs, Gibson set career highs with hits (135), doubles (25) and triples (9). George even had a career year on the bases, stealing nine times.

Nicknamed "Moon" because of his round face, Gibson had another fine season in 1910, batting .259 with 44 runs batted in and again led the league in games caught with 143, a total 26 more than his nearest competitor, Chief Meyers, and fielding percentage. But the toll of untold foul tips, collisions and other assorted dangers that catchers endured in those days began leave lasting craters on Moon. He caught under 100 games in 1911 and 1912, although he did take his third fielding title with a .990 percentage, the highest of his career, in the latter year. He appeared in only 48 games in 1913 before enjoying better health in 1914 and 1915. He hit a career high .285 in 102 games in 1914, but by 1916, three other backstops saw more action for Pittsburgh than did Gibson. He was waived to the Giants that season, but refused to report, citing a handshake agreement he had made with Barney Dreyfuss years before. Dreyfuss had agreed never to sell Gibson on waivers when the player was in his declining years.[45] The Giants' John McGraw got him to reconsider for the next season and George served as a backup catcher and pitching coach (he actually only caught four times in 1918) for the next two seasons, before returning to Canada to manage Toronto in the International League. When Dreyfuss sought him out to manage the Pirates in 1920, Gibson asserted his feelings about the Pirates owner having waived him to New York a few years before. Dreyfuss agreed to pay Gibson the $1,800 waiver price he had received for him as well as pay him the remainder of his salary for the time George had sat out in 1916. Gibson took the job and the Pirates improved under him, but Dreyfuss thought him to be too soft on some of his heavy partying players and replaced him with Bill McKechnie in 1922. After coaching and managing the Cubs and in the minor leagues, Gibson came back to Pittsburgh once again when Dreyfuss offered him a second chance to manage the club. The Pirates finished a surprising second in 1932 and repeated as runner-up in 1933, but with the club off to a lackluster start in 1934, Gibson resigned and Pie Traynor took over the team.

Gibson's career total of 1,155 games caught as a Pirate remained the team's record until Jason Kendall surpassed it in 2004. Fred Lieb, writing in 1948, considered Gibson the team's all-time greatest catcher.[46]

Mike Simon

Catcher
Born 4/13/1883
Pittsburgh Pirates 1909–1913

Died 6/10/1963
Major League Career 1909–1915

Mike Simon was a 26-year-old rookie backstop for the Pirates in 1909. He appeared in only 12 games that season, going just 3-for-18 with a couple of RBIs. Simon did not appear in the World Series and caught only 14 more games in 1910 as George Gibson continued his sturdy work. But when Gibson was injured in 1911, Simon began to catch more. He never appeared in 100 games during his seven-year career. He hit .225 with only one home run in 1,069 at-bats. After 1913, Simon jumped to the Federal League. Playing for St. Louis, he played in a career-high 93 games, but hit just .207. Simon's batting was even worse (.176) in 47 games in 1915 with the Brooklyn Tip Tops and he was not invited back to the major leagues once the Federal League folded.

Paddy O'Connor

Catcher
Born 8/4/1879
Pittsburgh Pirates 1908–1910

Died 8/17/1950
Major League Career 1908–1910, 1914–1915, 1918

A seldom-used third-string catcher during his time with the Pirates, Paddy O'Connor caught three games in 1909 and made his only appearance at another defensive position in his career when he played a game at third that season. O'Connor, who was born in Kerry, Ireland, went 5-for-16 (.313) with three runs batted in. Other than 70 games with the Pittsburgh Rebels of the Federal League in 1915, O'Connor's most action came as a rookie in 1908 when he played in a dozen games. O'Connor did not play in the 1909 World Series.

Pitchers

Howie Camnitz

Right-handed Pitcher
Born 8/22/1881
Pittsburgh Pirates 1904, 1906–1913

Died 3/2/1960
Major League Career 1904, 1906–1915

After his highly successful 1909 campaign, Howie Camnitz went on to win 20 games on two other occasions, finishing his 11-year major league career with a 133–106 record (courtesy of Library of Congress, BainCollection, Prints & Photographs Division, 15423u).

A three-time 20-game winner, Howie Camnitz had his grandest year in 1909, going 25–6 to post a National League best .806 winning percentage. The 5'9" right-hander's victory total tied the immortal Christy Mathewson for second in the league behind another future Hall of Famer, Three Finger Brown's 27 wins. Camnitz's 1.62 ERA placed fourth and his 133 strikeouts seventh. There were rumors, however, that Howie was drinking heavily by the end of the season. Similar talk occurred the year before.[47] Officially, it was stated he suffered from ptomaine poisoning in mid–August[48] and/or a throat infection later in the year.[49] Whatever the reason, Camnitz was ineffective in the World Series, getting hit hard in his Game 2 start as well as his lone relief inning in Game 6.

Samuel Howard Camnitz, called "Red" or "The Kentucky Rosebud" because of his hair color, had first arrived in the majors with Pittsburgh in 1904. He was an unimpressive 1–4 that season before being sent to the minors for the rest of that season and all of 1905 and most of 1907. When he returned to the Pirates, Camnitz had made a major adjustment. He no longer telegraphed his curveball, considered by most his best pitch.[50] Howie gradually became an important figure on the Pirate staff, working his way into 31 games, including 19 starts in 1907 and 38 games and 26 starts in 1908. His records those years were 13–9 and 16–9. He gave a preview in 1908 of his stellar season by posting an even better ERA, 1.56, which placed him fourth that season as well.

Following a very disappointing 1910 season, in which Barney Dreyfuss singled out Camnitz in the owner's criticism of players imbibing, noting Camnitz had broken the temperance clause in his contract,[51] Camnitz bounced back to win 20 games in 1911 and 1912, but his pitching went into a deep slump from which it would never recover in 1913. He started the season 6–17 before a late-season trade to the Phillies. Splitting six decisions in the City of Brotherly Love, Camnitz finished the season with 20 losses. The next year, Howie returned to Pittsburgh, but this time he was doing his pitching in the upstart Federal League. Although facing watered-down competition, Camnitz would lose only one less game than he had the year before, finishing 14–19. When Camnitz also attempted to lure former Pirate teammates to the new Pittsburgh club, Barney Dreyfuss got an injunction to stop him from doing so.[52]

Camnitz became trouble for his new employers in 1915. Again struggling on the mound and out of shape, Camnitz was released following an altercation in New York.[53] The 34-year-old pitcher said he would continue to report to the Rebels and demanded he be paid accordingly, but eventually he returned to his native Kentucky and retired from the game.

Vic Willis

Right-Handed Pitcher
Born 4/12/1876   Died 8/3/1947
Pittsburgh Pirates 1906–1909   Major League Career 1898–1910

Vic Willis figured he had plenty of bargaining power following three consecutive 20-win seasons for the Pirates since coming to Pittsburgh in 1906. The Pirates had finished a game behind the Cubs for the 1908 pennant and although Willis had lost the final game of the season to Chicago, which dashed the Pirates' World Series dreams, his 23 wins were tied with Nick Maddox for tops on the club. If the Pirates were going to have a chance in 1909, Willis thought they would have to meet his salary demands.

Willis first wrote to a friend that he was quitting baseball when he did not receive what he thought was a suitable salary offer. However, Ralph Davis, the Pittsburgh correspondent for *The Sporting News*, and most assuredly Pittsburgh owner Barney Dreyfuss remembered Vic's talk of retiring the year before when negotiating his contract and did not take Willis's thoughts that he "would never play another game of professional baseball, except as such as he might participate in about his own home" seriously.[54]

Willis was said to be asking for a salary of $5,100. Dreyfuss had offered $4,100, but then pulled the offer. Willis, who had claimed he was pursuing business interests in his hometown of Newark, New Jersey, eventually settled for the same reported base salary of $3,500 that he had received the year before.

Once in tow, Vic returned to being one of the best pitchers in the game. It was a good thing for the Bucs he had returned, given Maddox's early-season arm problems. He won 22 games, the fourth highest total in the NL, including 11 in a row at one point. Willis also pitched two one-hitters in 1909, but one game he did not win was the first game ever played at Forbes Field, which he dropped to the Cubs, 3–2. That season would prove to be Willis's last great season in what many years later would be honored as a Hall of Fame career.

Vic had started out with the Boston Beaneaters in 1898. He had an overpowering curveball and an impressive slowball, and won 25 and 27 games, respectively, in his first two seasons.[55] His biggest year was 1902, when Willis again won 27 and led the National League in games and starts. He also led in complete games, finishing 45 of the 46 games he began, and strikeouts with 225. He and teammate Togie Pittinger led a weak Boston team to respectability, but the quality of his teammates' play continued to decline and dragged Vic down to three consecutive losing seasons, including 18–25 and 12–29 marks in his last two years in Boston. In fact, Willis's 29 losses in 1905 is the modern low point for decisions. The Pirates, though, did not think he was washed up and traded four young players to obtain him. Willis thanked the Pittsburgh franchise by going 89–46 in his four years playing for Clarke & Co.

Bypassed by Clarke as a starter in Games 1 and 2 of the World Series, Willis relieved Howie Camnitz with the Pirates trailing 4–2 in the third inning of Game 2. Ty Cobb, standing on third, saw that the hurler was bearing down on the first hitter he faced, so Cobb took advantage of this to steal home against him. Willis's pitching then shut the door on the Tigers, but the Pirates would score no more runs against Bill Donovan in their 7–2 loss. Clarke finally called on Willis to start in Game 6, but Vic was shaky, allowing three runs in five innings.

Perhaps Dreyfuss had had enough of Willis's holdouts and threats of retirement, or had worried that Willis's drinking was having a bad influence on the team's younger pitchers.[56] With the emergence of Babe Adams as a likely replacement for the ace right-hander, Dreyfuss sold Willis to the Cardinals. Willis struggled to a 9–12 mark in his final major league season, electing to retire rather than report to the Cubs who had claimed him on waivers following the season.[57] In 1995, the Veterans Committee opened the doors to Cooperstown for the man who had won 249 games in his career and had enjoyed eight 20-win campaigns, 85 years after he had retired and nearly a half century after he had passed away.

Lefty Leifield

Left-Handed Pitcher
Born 9/5/1883   Died 10/10/1970
Pittsburgh Pirates 1905–1912   Major League Career 1905–1913, 1918–1920

The epitome of the crafty southpaw, Albert Leifield was a sturdy pitcher for the Pirates, winning between 15–20 games six years in a row from 1906 to 1911. Better known by his nickname Lefty, Leifield did not possess an overwhelming pitch, although Johnny Evers, in *Touching Second* (quoted by Bill James and Rob Neyer) noted he threw "a high fastball which breaks with an odd little jump" that was difficult to hit.[58] Another thing Leifield did that contributed to his success was that he was able to, in today's lingo, "pitch backwards." In other words, Leifield would throw his breaking ball in what is generally considered fastball counts.[59] He also had a very deceptive motion he could employ with a runner on first, making it impossible for the runner to get a good jump or steal against him.[60]

A fine late-season performance following his recall in 1905 (5–2, 2.89) gave Lefty a shot at regular duty in 1906 and he had one of his best years, going 18–13 with a career low 1.87 ERA. He followed that up with the only 20-victory season in 1907. Leifield, bothered by arm ailments, struggled to break .500 in 1908 and came under criticism by Pittsburgh fans. Fred Clarke staunchly defended his pitcher, who finished 15–14. Off to a so-so start in 1909, Leifield came on strong to finish seventh in the National League with 19 wins, and his ranking in winning percentage was even higher, fifth, thanks to a .704 mark. Like the Pirates' two other big winners, Leifield struggled against the Tigers in the World Series. Making the start in Game 4, Leifield was treated rudely by the Detroit hitters, giving up seven hits and five runs in four innings.

Leifield's pitching continued to be strong the next two years, but as his teammates' abilities declined so did his won/loss record. A sore arm added to his problems and after starting only once in six appearances in 1912, Albert and his aching left arm were traded with Tommy Leach to the Cubs for another has-been pitcher, King Cole, and utilityman Solly Hoffman. Leifield found new life in Chi-Town and went 7–2 for the Cubs, but his arm bothered him even more in 1913 and this time, after six games, he was sent packing again, only this time to the minors. In 1918, with his arm having made significant improvement, Lefty was given a chance to return to the majors at the age of 35.[61] Unlike other players from the 1909 world champions who were given new life in the big leagues due to the player shortage during the First World War, Leifield performed well, much better than his 2–6 record, and came back again in 1919 to go 6–4 before further arm problems ended his career the following year. Lefty stayed in baseball as a coach for the Browns, Tigers and Red Sox and managed in the minor leagues following his playing days. Leifield was the last living man who could claim he was on the World Series winning team when he died in 1970.

Nick Maddox

Right-handed Pitcher
Born 11/9/1886   Died 11/27/1954
Pittsburgh Pirates 1907–1910   Major League Career 1907–1910

A 22-year-old Nick Maddox burst onto the big league scene as no other Pirate pitcher before or since in 1907. He triumphed by pitching a shutout in his debut, then no-hit Brooklyn one week later, winning the contest 2–1.[62] Maddox's effort was the franchise's first no-hitter and remained the only no-hitter pitched in Pittsburgh until the Cardinals' Bob Gibson fired one against the Bucs in another world championship season, 1971. Maddox's line in six late-season games that season was 5–1 with a 0.83 ERA and only 32 hits and 4 walks allowed in 53 innings.

Nick really looked like the real deal the next season when he tied Vic Willis for the team lead with 23 wins (fourth best in the National League) and posted a 2.28 ERA in 260 innings. Not overpowering, Maddox fanned only 70 while walking 90 in his first full season. However, Maddox's arm began giving him discomfort in 1909 and he was nursed along at points during the year. His ERA remained an impressive 2.21 and he fanned more (56) than he walked (39), but won 10 fewer games while losing the same number as he had in 1908.

Fred Clarke gave Maddox the ball for Game 3 of the World Series and Nick held the Tigers to just four harmless hits through the first six innings. By this time, the Pirates had run up a 6–0 lead. A shaky defensive play aided Detroit in scoring four runs, but the Bucs added two more in a rain-soaked ninth inning, allowing Clarke to stick with the right-hander even after an error and Ty Cobb's double keyed two more scores for the Tigers. Nick recovered to retire Sam Crawford and got Jim Delahanty to line out to left to end the game. Five of the Tigers' six runs scored against him that day were unearned, although Nick ended up allowing 11 hits.

Maddox continued to allow few hits, but was pitching in fewer games in 1910, going 2–3 with a 3.40 ERA in 20 games, including seven starts. He was sold to Kansas City and although he showed durability in 1911 and topped 20 wins, his WHIP was 1.389 and increased to 1.528 during a 10–13 campaign the next year. He pitched two more years in the minors, later returning to Pittsburgh to live until he passed away in 1954. His gravestone reads "Pirate Pitcher; First No Hitter 1907."[63]

Babe Adams

Right-Handed Pitcher
Born 5/18/1883
Pittsburgh Pirates 1907, 1909–1916,
  1918–1926

Died 7/27/1968
Major League Career 1906–1907, 1909–
  1916, 1918–1926

An 0–3 pitcher with an ERA of 7.61 in five major league games for the Cardinals and Pirates in 1906 and 1907, Charles "Babe" Adams came into spring training in 1909 looking to establish himself as a big leaguer. He left that year as a national celebrity, the winner of three World Series games against the Detroit Tigers.

Adams, who had acquired his nickname when a female fan remarking on his good looks said he was a "babe," started the 1909 season pitching mostly relief, but showed much more promise than the other inexperienced pitchers Fred Clarke had brought north with him. With Nick Maddox, Deacon Phillippe and Sam Leever not always physically able to go, Adams began to get more mound time. He won seven of his last nine decisions, dropping one by a 1–0 score and another on an error, and overall pitched three shutouts in 12 starts, and set a team record for strikeouts in a game when he fanned 12. His final stats were 12–3 and he would have won the ERA title with a 1.11 mark, except the feat required he pitch 154 innings. As it was, Babe pitched only 130, but he gave up only 88 hits for an opponent batting average of .196. Adams secret to his new success was his fine control of his fastball and variety of curves. "I use about ten different forms of the curveball and when speed is a factor, it gives me a wide scope in melting in a mixture of balls that only the best have a right to negotiate."[64]

Clarke chose Adams to start the opening game of the Series, it is said, following a tip from National League President John Heydler. Heydler had seen a Washington pitcher named Dolly Gray stifle the big Detroit hitters during the season and felt Adams' repertoire was similar to Gray's. Authors Dennis and Jeanne Burke Delaveria have called this story into question, noting Gray was a left-hander who could experience struggles with control at times and who went just 5–19 for the Senators in 1909.[65]

Adams, on the other hand, appeared in complete control of the Tigers. After winning the opening contest, 4–1, Clarke started Adams in Games 5 and 7 and Adams won them as well. He completed each of his starts, throwing a shutout in the finale and finished the Series with a 1.33 ERA against the best-hitting club in the American League. Ty Cobb went just 1-for-10 against him with one walk. Sam Crawford roughed him up a bit in Game 5, but Adams held Wahoo Sam hitless in the deciding game.[66]

For the next half dozen seasons, Adams was Pittsburgh's best pitcher and had three seasons in which he won at least 18 games. In 1914 and 1915, the Pirates as a whole struggled, winning 133 times while losing 174. Given this fact, Adams combined 27–30 mark is better than it looks on the surface and in 1914 he posted the lowest WHIP (1.032) in the National League, the second time in his career he had topped the league in this important category. Arm problems ruined Babe's 1916 season and he returned to the minor leagues for a third time. Following a combined 34–16 record in the minors, Adams returned to the Bucs at the end of 1918. He split a pair of decisions, but pitched very effectively as his 1.19 ERA proves, and earned a chance for regular duty in 1919. Adams reclaimed his spot in the rotation and among the top pitchers in the NL, going 17–10 with a 1.98 ERA, fifth best among senior circuit hurlers. He duplicated his win total in 1920. In 1921, needing more rest between starts, the 39-year-old went 14–5. In his three seasons since returning from the minors, Adams topped the league in WHIP each season. In fact, Babe's career WHIP of 1.092 is the sixteenth best of all time. He finished in the top five in this category 10 times in his career.

Adams stretched his career another five seasons, pitching in the majors beyond his 46th birthday. His best season in his twilight years was 1923 when he went 13–7, but his control was still excellent. No doubt he was losing something off his pitches and the lively ball caused earned run averages, including the Babe's, to skyrocket. Adams went 6–5, but with a 5.42 ERA for the Pirates' World Series team in 1925. Clarke gave him a cameo appearance in the Series and Adams pitched another scoreless inning, becoming the only man to appear in both the 1909 and 1925 fall classics. In 1926, Babe, never one to engage in controversies, made an off-the-cuff remark which embroiled him in the A-B-C affair and led to his release. He pitched for two teams, including Johnstown, Pennsylvania, in the low minors in 1927, combining for a 6–1 record and even managed the Johnnies for part of the season before giving up the professional game.

Deacon Phillippe

Right-Handed Pitcher
Born 5/23/1872   Died 3/30/1952
Pittsburgh Pirates 1900–1911   Major League Career 1899–1911

Deacon Phillippe had been an ace pitcher and World Series hero since joining the Pirates in 1900. Including his rookie year with Louisville in 1899, Phillippe had opened his career with five consecutive 20-win seasons and added a sixth in 1905, but by 1908, he was a sore-armed pitcher, restricted to five poor relief appearances. It was thought Phillippe would retire to his farm in Butler County, Pennsylvania, following the year, but he reported his arm was better and asked Fred Clarke for another try in 1909. The Pirate manager could not refuse the man who received his nickname due to his clean living and affability.[67] In the best-of-nine 1903 World Series, Phillippe had taken the slab five times when Clarke asked and Phillippe won three times, the only victories the Pirates recorded in falling to Boston, five games to three.

Phillippe's performance on the mound in 1909 proved the Deacon to be a man of his word. Although he started only 13 times and added nine relief appearances, Phillippe went 8–3 with a 2.32 ERA. He pitched six scoreless innings of relief in appearances against the Tigers. Some fans hoped Clarke would start Phillippe, by now a sentimental favorite, in Game 7, but Deacon watched from the bench as Babe Adams dominated in his third Series victory.

Phillippe continued to star in his swingman role in 1910, going 7–1 in both starting and relief roles. His arm finally gave out in 1911 and he retired after pitching just three times.

Charles, which was Deacon's given name, later managed a minor league team in Pittsburgh called the Filappinos, a play on his last name, in what was the forerunner to the Pittsburgh Federal League team. He held a series of jobs until he passed away in 1952, including a stint as a clerk in Honus Wagner's sporting goods store.[68] In 1969, Phillippe was honored by Pittsburgh fans by being named the Pirates' all-time greatest right-handed pitcher. A great control artist who relied on a fastball and curve, Phillippe still holds the record for being the stingiest control artist in the history of major league baseball, as he permitted only 1.25 walks per nine innings during his career.[69]

Sam Leever

Right-Handed Pitcher
Born 12/23/1871   Died 5/19/1953
Pittsburgh Pirates 1898–1910   Major League Career 1898–1910

    A schoolteacher in the offseason, Sam Leever served many a lesson to National League hitters during his 13-year career with the Pirates. One of the few pieces Fred Clarke inherited when he arrived in Pittsburgh in 1900, the Goshen Schoolmaster had led the league in starts and innings pitched in 1899. Sam would finish his career in 1911 with 194 victories, all for Pittsburgh, the only major league team he ever pitched for. Those 194 wins are tied with Babe Adams for the second highest total in team history, behind only Wilbur Cooper.

    Three times Leever won 20 games. His best season was 1903 when his .781 winning percentage and 2.06 ERA were the best figures in the NL and his 25 wins ranked him in a third place tie with his teammate Deacon Phillippe. But with the World Series just around the corner, Leever injured his shoulder while skeet shooting. He was ineffective, losing both his starts against Boston.

    Sam's shoulder recovered and he was an effective pitcher through 1908, again leading the league in winning percentage in 1905 when Sam harnessed a 20–5 record. In 1906, he went 22–7, but he began to be used more conservatively in 1907 and won 14 and 15 games in the two ensuing seasons. There was talk his sharp curve had taken too much out of his arm for Leever to continue to contribute to a winning team. Leever scoffed at such assumptions. "I am very anxious to show some of the fans who are of the opinion that I am a dead one, that I can still pitch, even though they have ordered a coffin for my arm," Leever wrote to Barney Dreyfuss.[70]

    Sam's contributions in 1909 were limited, but were important. He went 8–1 in 19 games, including four starts. His 2.83 ERA showed he was still a credible pitcher if used wisely, but Clarke did not use him in the World Series that fall. Sam returned for one more time in 1910. He pitched more often and more consistently than most of the young pitchers who were fighting to take his place, but requested his release the next spring when he was first insulted by Dreyfuss's contract offer, then by the owner's offer to sell him to a minor league team, with Sam getting the proceeds.[71]

Sammy Frock

Right-Handed Pitcher
Born 12/23/1882   Died 11/3/1925
Pittsburgh Pirates 1909–1910   Major League Career 1907, 1909–1911

A new recruit the Pirates had high hopes for in 1909 was Sammy Frock, a hard-throwing right-hander the team had obtained after a big year in the Eastern League. Pitching for Providence, Frock had gone 24–14 with 149 strikeouts in 325 innings pitched. It was Frock's third consecutive 20-win season in the bushes.[72] Sam had had a cup of coffee with Boston two years earlier, going 1–2. This time around, Frock reversed his record, posting a 2–1 record. Although he was on the Pirates' roster all season, Fred Clarke saw fit to use him only eight times, with four of those being starting assignments, all season and did not call on him in the World Series.

After mopping up in one game in 1910, Sammy, along with first baseman Bud Sharpe, was sent back to the Boston Doves for Kirby White, another pitcher. He was one of the Doves' best pitchers in that year, although his won-loss record was just 12–19 as he finished third in the league in strikeouts. Frock started only once in 1911 and allowed 29 hits in 16 innings as he tried to regain his power on the mound before the Boston team, now called the Rustlers, sold him to Atlanta in the Southern Association.[73] One final piece of trivia about Frock: He was born on Sam Leever's eleventh birthday.

Chick Brandom

Right-Handed Pitcher
Born 7/8/1887   Died 10/7/1958
Pittsburgh Pirates 1908–1909   Major League Career 1908–1909, 1915

Chick Brandom finished 1909 with the same excellent ERA as Babe Adams, 1.11. Unfortunately, Brandom would never gain the acclaim of his rookie teammate. As low as Brandom's earned run average was in 1909, it was nearly double what he had posted in 17 innings for the Pirates in 1908. This time around, Chick threw 40 innings in 13 games, including two starts. He won his only decision for the second year in a row, but did not play in the World Series.

Brandom had a birth defect in which his second toe overlapped his first on one of his feet. Ralph Davis wrote that this caused Brandom "considerable discomfort and pain" when pitching and added that the young pitcher was planning to have the second toe amputated.[74] Whether or not he actually did is unclear, but Chick was sold to Kansas City for 1910.[75] Although he won 20 games for KC that year, he went just 1–14 the next season and it wasn't until 1915 that Brandom returned to the majors, going 1–1 for Newark in the Federal League in 16 games.

Bill Powell

Right-Handed Pitcher
Born 5/8/1885   Died 9/28/1967
Pittsburgh Pirates 1909–1910   Major League Career 1909–1910, 1912–1913

"Big Bill" Powell was obtained from Springfield in the Connecticut League following a 20-win season in 1908. Reported to be a hard thrower with a moving fastball, the 6'2" 182-pound pitcher appeared in three games for the Pirates despite being at Clarke's disposal for the entire season in 1909, walking six in seven innings while fanning only two. He lost his only decision. Powell started nine times in 1910. Pitching in a dozen games, Bill went 4–6, but had a respectable 2.40 ERA when he was sold to Kansas City in midseason. He was drafted by the Cubs for 1912, but made only one appearance for them before making his final big league start for the Reds in 1913. He lasted only one-third of an inning, allowing two hits and two walks. Apparently control remained an issue for Powell, who even during a huge 27-win season for KC in 1912, walked 166 men in 340 innings.[76]

Harry Camnitz

Right-Handed Pitcher
Born 10/26/1884   Died 1/6/1951
Pittsburgh Pirates 1909   Major League Career 1909, 1911

Harry Camnitz, the younger brother of Howie, made one appearance early in the season for the Pirates in 1909, allowing six hits in four innings of relief. Sent to McKeesport, a nearby Class C team, Camnitz won 27 games. Promoted to a higher minor league with Jersey City, Camnitz struggled to a 6–16 record. He returned to the majors a year later with St. Louis and picked up his only major league victory as he made two more relief appearances.

Gene Moore

Left-Handed Pitcher
Born 11/9/1885   Died 8/31/1938
Pittsburgh Pirates 1909–1910   Major League Career 1909–1910, 1912

Left-hander Gene Moore was pitching for Dallas in his home state of Texas when he was purchased by the Pirates in July 1909. With the Bucs having only one reliable left-hander, Albert Leifield, it was hoped Moore would provide some late-season balance to the staff.

A letter to Barney Dreyfuss recommending Moore sang his praises, "Moore is by far the best southpaw I've seen this season."[77] The letter went on to say Gene was more impressive than Leifield or Jack Pfiester, the Cubs' star southpaw. Apparently, Fred Clarke wasn't as impressed, as he used Moore only once, in a late-season game when Gene did not fare well. Moore appeared in four games for the Bucs in 1910 and five with the Reds in 1912, finishing his career 2–2 with an unsightly Deadball Era of 4.76. A son, also named Gene, was born in 1909 and eventually would become a better ballplayer, appearing in over 1,000 games as a major league outfielder from 1931–1945 and batting a respectable .270.

Charlie Wacker

Left-Handed Pitcher
Born 12/8/1883 Died 8/7/1948
Pittsburgh Pirates 1909 Major League Career 1909

Charles James Wacker, a 27-game winner with Evansville in the Central League in 1908, did most of his pitching for Milwaukee in the respected American Association in 1909, going 7–7, after making the only major league appearance of his career when he pitched two innings for the Pirates on April 28.

POS	Name	How They Came to Pittsburgh
C	George Gibson	Purchased from Montreal of the Eastern League in 1905
1B	Bill Abstein	Purchased from Shreveport of the Southern Association in 1906
2B	Dots Miller	Purchased from Easton of the Atlantic League in 1908
SS	Honus Wagner	Trade with Louisville along with Tommy Leach, Fred Clarke, Bert Cunningham, Mike Kelley, Tacks Latimer, Tom Messitt, Deacon Phillippe, Claude Ritchey, Rube Waddell, Jack Wadsworth and Chief Zimmer for Jack Chesbro, Paddy Fox, Art Madison, John O'Brien and $25,000
3B	Jap Barbeau	Signed as free agent in 1909
3B	Bobby Byrne	Traded in August 1909 from the Cardinals for Alan Storke and Jap Barbeau
OF	Tommy Leach	Trade with Louisville along with Honus Wagner, Fred Clarke, Bert Cunningham, Mike Kelley, Tacks Latimer, Tom Messitt, Deacon Phillippe, Claude Ritchey, Rube Waddell, Jack Wadsworth and Chief Zimmer for Jack Chesbro, Paddy Fox, Art Madison, John O'Brien and $25,000

POS	Name	How They Came to Pittsburgh
OF	Fred Clarke	Trade with Louisville along with Tommy Leach, Honus Wagner, Bert Cunningham, Mike Kelley, Tacks Latimer, Tom Messitt, Deacon Phillippe, Claude Ritchey, Rube Waddell, Jack Wadsworth and Chief Zimmer for Jack Chesbro, Paddy Fox, Art Madison, John O'Brien and $25,000
OF	Chief Wilson	Signed as free agent in 1908
UT	Alan Storke	Drafted in the Rule 5 draft in 1905 from Providence of the Eastern League
UT	Ed Abbaticchio	Trade with Boston Beaneaters in 1906 for Ginger Beaumont, Claude Ritchey and Patsy Flaherty
UT	Ham Hyatt	Purchased from Vancouver of the Northwestern League in 1908
OF	Ward Miller	Signed as Free Agent in 1909
C	Mike Simon	Purchased from the Boston Doves in 1909
UT	Paddy O'Connor	Drafted in the Rule 5 draft in 1907 from Springfield of the Connecticut League
PR	Kid Durbin	Trade with Cincinnati in May 1909 for Ward Miller and cash
P	Vic Willis	Trade with Boston Beaneaters in 1905 for Dave Brain, Del Howard and Vive Lindaman
P	Lefty Leifield	Signed as free agent in 1905
P	Nick Maddox	Drafted in the Rule 5 draft in 1906 from Cumberland of the Pennsylvania-Ohio-Maryland League
P	Babe Adams	Purchased from Denver of the Western League in 1907
P	Deacon Phillippe	Trade with Louisville along with Tommy Leach, Honus Wagner, Bert Cunningham, Mike Kelley, Tacks Latimer, Tom Messitt, Fred Clarke, Claude Ritchey, Rube Waddell, Jack Wadsworth and Chief Zimmer for Jack Chesbro, Paddy Fox, Art Madison, John O'Brien and $25,000
P	Sam Leever	Signed as free agent in 1898
P	Sam Frock	Purchased from Providence of the Eastern League in 1909
P	Chick Brandom	Purchased from Kansas City of the American Association in 1908 for $5,000
P	Bill Powell	Signed as free agent in 1909
P	Harry Camnitz	Purchased from McKeesport of the Ohio-Pennsylvania League in 1909
P	Gene Moore	Purchased from Dallas of the Texas League in 1909
P	Charlie Wacker	Signed as free agent in 1909
P	Howie Camnitz	Drafted in the Rule 5 draft in 1903 from Vicksburg of the Cotton States League

◆ 15 ◆

THE 1909
DETROIT TIGERS

Infielders

Claude Rossman

First Base
Born 6/17/1881
Detroit Tigers 1907–1909

Died 1/16/1928
Major League Career 1904, 1906–1909

The Tigers thought they had obtained the long-term answer for their first baseman when they purchased Claude Rossman from Cleveland following a .308 season in 1906. Rossman had a couple of solid offensive years, helping Detroit to the World Series in 1907 and 1908 by hitting .277 and .294. But there was concern about Claude's defense. More specifically, Rossman had developed a mental block about making throws.[1] The first baseman would either heave the ball wildly or hold onto it even though observers felt he had a play on a baserunner. Benched in favor of George Moriarty, Rossman briefly reclaimed his position when Moriarty fell ill. His hitting was welcomed by his teammates, but Rossman continued to struggle in the field and was traded to the St. Louis Browns in August for Tom Jones.

The trade, however, did not ease Rossman's anxiety about playing first base. "If I could not do it for Detroit," he said, "I can not possibly help St. Louis. I want to quit the infield and play in the gardens. My arm is strong and my hitting will come back if they put me out there. All I'm asking is that (Manager Jim) McAleer give me a trial in the outfield."[2]

Rossman got his trial in the outfield, but only for two games. He was sent to the minors the next season, playing for Minneapolis in the American Association. Rossman had three big seasons there between 1911 and 1913, hitting between .302 and .356, but did not get another shot in The Show. After a .252 season in 1914, Rossman was gone from professional baseball.

Rossman was later confined to a mental hospital, where he died in 1928 at age 46.[3] His confinement leads one to wonder if Rossman's issue with making throws from first base was an anomaly, a la the later-day Steve Sax, or did it signal the beginning of deeper mental health problems?

Tom Jones

First Base
Born 1/22/1877   Died 6/19/1923
Detroit Tigers 1909–1910   Major League Career 1902, 1904–1910

Ironically, the man Claude Rossman was traded for, Tom Jones, also died at the age of 46. Jones had been the Browns' regular first baseman since 1904. He was generally thought of as a good defender and led the league in putouts and double plays in 1908. A right-handed hitter, Jones was an extremely consistent, although not an outstanding, batter. He hit between .242 and .252 every year for St. Louis and led the league in games played in 1904, 1907 and 1908. He started 1909 playing at his usual level, batting .249, but with just twelve extra-base hits in 97 games prior to his trade to Detroit. Coming to the Tigers, Jones hit better than expected, batting .281 with nine doubles in 44 games. Jones played one more season in the majors, batting .255 while adding his fourth career home run in 1910.

Not surprisingly, Jones hit .250 in the 1909 World Series. He had a pair of RBIs, including a single which tied Game 6, 3–3, in the fourth.[4]

Del Gainer

First Base
Born 11/10/1886   Died 1/29/1947
Detroit Tigers 1909, 1911–1914   Major League Career 1909, 1911–1917, 1919, 1922

Twenty-two-year-old Del Gainer, a right-handed hitter, appeared in two games at first base, collecting his first major league hit in 1909. He went on to appear in big league games for the Tigers, Red Sox and Browns over 10 different, nonconsecutive seasons, but never was more than a semi-regular. Gainer did help the Red Sox to a World Series championship in both 1915 and 1916, including delivering a winning pinch-hit in Game 2 of the 1916 Series. His best seasons were 1911 when he hit .302 in 70 games for the Tigers and 1915 when he batted .295 in 82 appearances for Boston.

Hughie Jennings

First Base
Born 4/2/1869　　　　　　Died 2/1/1928
Detroit Tigers 1907–1918　　Major League Career 1891–1918

Manager Hughie Jennings, a Hall of Fame shortstop during the 1890s for the Baltimore Orioles, appeared in two games at first, going 2-for-4 with a pair of RBIs, but did not participate as a player in the World Series.

Germany Schaefer

Second Base
Born 2/4/1877　　　　　　Died 5/16/1919
Detroit Tigers 1905–1909　　Major League Career 1901–1902, 1905–1916, 1918

Herman "Germany" Schaefer was a veteran infielder in 1909 who began the season as the Tigers' regular second baseman after spending 1908 as a supersub who appeared in 153 games, but no more than 68 at any one position. A showman and something of a flake, Schaefer was a decent hitter and fielder and had stolen a career-high 40 bases in '08 while hitting .259 with 33 extra-base hits, but it was his zany antics on the field for which he is best remembered. According to *The Sporting News*, Schaefer's play slumped in midseason during 1909 and he was replaced at second by Red Killefer, then by Charlie O'Leary before being traded for the man who would guard the keystone base during that year's World Series, Jim Delahanty.

Depending on the source, Schaefer may or may not have "stolen" first base while with the Tigers.[5] It is a fact, however, that Schaefer later accomplished the feat while playing for the Washington Senators in 1911. With quick-footed teammate Clyde Milan on third base and Schaefer on first in the bottom of the ninth against the Chicago White Sox, a double steal was called for. Schaefer easily took second as the White Sox catcher held onto the ball. Still attempting to draw a throw, Schaefer headed back to first on the next pitch. White Sox manager Hugh Duffy came out to protest, but apparently did not call time. Seeing another opportunity, Schaefer broke again for second and got caught in a rundown, but all of the comedic drama went for naught as Milan was thrown out trying to score.

Another Schaefer story definitely took place during Germany's days with the Tigers.[6] Schaefer had been coaching third one day, but in the ninth inning he came into the game as a pinch-hitter against White Sox star Doc White with Detroit trailing, 2–1. Schaefer announced to the crowd, "Ladies and Gentleman, you are now looking at Herman Schaefer, known as Herman the Great, acknowledged by one and all as the greatest pinch hitter in the world. I am now going to hit the ball into the left field bleachers. Thank you."

What happened next belongs in a "Ripley's Believe It or Not" column. Schaefer not only made good on his boast, but announced his trip around the bases as though he was running in a horse race. As he touched first, he yelled, "Schaefer leads at the quarter" and as he slid into second, "Schaefer leads at the half." He dramatically slid into home with victorious glee, "Schaefer wins by a nose," then jumped up, adding "Ladies and Gentlemen, I thank you for your kind attention."[7] Herman the Great's blast that day accounted for one half of his season's home run total. In fact, the most home runs tallied by Schaefer in a season was three and he cracked only nine during his career, but at least one more brought about another grand performance.

Against future Hall of Famer Rube Waddell, Schaefer once carried his bat around the bases after a fence-clearing shot, pointing it at the great fireballer, pretending to shoot him as Germany rounded the bases.[8]

Obviously, not everyone was always amused by Schaefer's antics. He was reportedly ejected by a disapproving umpire for wearing a raincoat and boots to the plate during a rainy game and another time for appearing in "disguise" by doffing a black mustache.[9] Still, Germany had a long career, but the Tiger portion of it ended when he was traded to Washington for Delahanty as the Tigers felt Delahanty would provide more punch in the middle of the lineup.

Schaefer played and coached for the Senators for the next 5½ years, continuing to entertain fans. Considering the poor quality of the Washington teams of that era, it is not surprising that owner Clark Griffith was said to approve of Schaefer's antics. Schaefer had a career year in 1911, batting .334, but his defensive skills were probably eroding as he played first base that season. His playing time greatly decreased after that, but after clowning his way through his career as a player and coach, Schaefer got serious during World War I, asking his nickname be changed to "Dutch" as, of course, the U.S. was at war with Germany.

Jim Delahanty

Second Base
Born 6/20/1879   Died 10/17/1953
Detroit Tigers 1909–1912   Major League Career 1901–1902, 1904–1912, 1914–1915

If one were to take a quick glance at Jim Delahanty's career in *The Baseball Encyclopedia*, one could easily mistake him for a modern ballplayer. His eight teams in a 13-year career is akin to many current players and the fact that one of his relocations sent him to a pennant-contender in the heat of an August race is a story featured on ESPN several times during the modern baseball seasons. Additionally, Delahanty's .283 career batting average would be more common today than it was during baseball's Deadball Era. Perhaps it wouldn't be until the reader saw that Delahanty had played for the Browns and not the Cardinals during his time in St. Louis that he would realize Jim's career began at the start of the twentieth century.

A younger brother of the tragic future Hall of Famer Ed Delahanty, as well as three other brothers who played in the major leagues, Jim had grown up in the same neighborhood as Tommy Leach. By 1909, Big Ed had been dead for five and a half years and Jim was entering his seventh full season as a big leaguer, playing for his sixth team in a career which included token appearances for the Chicago Cubs as far back as 1901. Subsequently, Delahanty had played for the Giants, Braves, Reds and Browns before coming to the Senators in 1907. After splitting time between third and second earlier in his career, Delahanty played exclusively at second for Washington, hitting .317 in 83 games. His playing time was cut by a combination of penalties and unusual sportsmanship by Delahanty's manager, Joe Cantillon.[10] During an August game in Cleveland, Delahanty was ejected for arguing with umpire Silk O'Laughlin. He made matters worse by screaming profanities loud enough to be heard by fans. American League president Ban Johnson further penalized him by fining him and banning him from playing in Cleveland for the remainder of the season. The Senators, as usual, were out of the pennant race, but to be fair to the other contenders, Detroit, Chicago and St. Louis, Cantillon decided he would not play Jim in those cities as well.

Returning against all competition by 1909, Delahanty struggled. He was hitting only .222 when he was traded to Detroit in August. His bat improved somewhat for the stretch run, as he hit .253 and drove 10 doubles in 150 at-bats. For the season, Delahanty's 23 doubles and 30 extra-base hits represented a respectable total for an AL second baseman as he ranked third in both categories behind the elite keystoners of the day, Eddie Collins and Nap Lajoie.[11]

Delahanty was the Tigers' top hitter against the Pirates that fall with a .346 mark; his four doubles tied his old neighbor Tommy Leach for the Series lead. He enjoyed a big performance in Game 3, collecting three hits in his first four at-bats, including a pair of doubles, but on the final at-bat of the game, representing the tying run, flew out to left.[12]

Jim enjoyed some good seasons after 1909. He hit .294 in 1910 and had a career year with a .339 season in 1911, adding 94 RBIs and 43 extra-base hits. He played less, although he hit .286 in 1912 and was released. It was thought his salary and declining defensive skills (he saw considerable time as a left fielder that season) were the reasons and his encouragement of the Tigers striking in support of Ty Cobb, who had been suspended by Johnson for pummeling a fan that season, didn't help.[13] He played minor league ball in 1913, but returned for a final try with his last big league team, the Brooklyn

Tip Tops. Delahanty's career in the Federal League lasted less than the two full years the league was in existence, as he was released after playing in less than 20 games in 1915.

Although Jim's final batting average was over 60 points less than his Hall of Fame brother, his .283 ranked thirty-third among Deadball Era hitters with 3,500 or more at-bats and fifth among second baseman behind Lajoie, Collins, Larry Doyle and Danny Murphy. Bill James ranked him eighty-first among second basemen all-time and he would have undoubtedly finished higher had he done more with the leather, as James listed only Rogers Hornsby and Rod Carew as having a greater percentage of their career value being as a hitter rather than a fielder at that position.[14]

Red Killefer

Second Base
Born 4/13/1885   Died 9/4/1958
Detroit Tigers 1907–1909   Major League Career 1907–1910, 1914–1916

Another player whose major league career would not equal that of his sibling was a player dealt to Washington in the trade for Jim Delahanty, Wade "Red" Killefer. Killefer was a utility player for Detroit for a third successive season in 1909. In 79 at-bats, Killefer hit .279, appearing in 23 games, including 17 as a second baseman. The Senators gave him more playing time, but his hitting slumped by 105 points and he hit an unimpressive .229 as a semi-regular in 1910. It was four years before Killefer would get another shot in the majors, this time with Cincinnati. He hit well during the two years the talent level in the league was diluted by the existence of the Federal League, batting in the .270's both seasons, but dropped down to .247 in his final year, playing for the Reds and Giants.

Although he played only one season as a regular, Killefer twice led his league in being hit by pitches, 1910 and 1915. Red's younger brother Bill was a standout defensive catcher, mostly for the Phillies and Cubs, and managed and coached in the majors for 15 years.

Donie Bush

Shortstop
Born 10/8/1887   Died 3/28/1972
Detroit Tigers 1908–1921   Major League Career 1908–1923

With the Tigers locked in a September battle for the 1908 pennant and facing a discombobulated infield, due mainly to shortstop Charlie O'Leary's illness, Frank Navin exercised a right previously negotiated with the Indianapolis

Shortstop Donie Bush had a stellar rookie year in 1909, leading the American League in plate appearances with 676, 82 walks and 52 sacrifices. He went on to play 16 seasons finishing fifth on the all-time list for sacrifices with 337 (courtesy of Library of Congress, Bain Collection, Prints & Photographs Division, 14678u).

Indians to recall a 20-year-old speedster who had gained a reputation as an outstanding defender. His name was Owen Bush, but he became better known by his nickname, Donie, which was the result of a telegraphic error announcing the transaction.[15]

Thrust into Detroit's everyday lineup, the young switch-hitter batted .294 and scored 13 runs in 20 games. Donie's arrival settled the team's problem at shortstop and would do so for the next dozen years, but Bush was called up too late in the season to be placed on the Tigers' 1908 World Series roster.

Bush opened the 1909 season as the Tigers' regular shortstop and appeared in 157 games. He gave Hughie Jennings an excellent all-around player in his rookie season. At 5'6", 140 pounds, Donie may have played "the little man's game," but he did so in a gigantic way, leading the league in walks (88) and sacrifices (52). He scored 114 runs, a figure topped only by his spectacular teammate, Ty Cobb, and Bush's .273 average was the highest among American

League shortstops. Defensively, Bush established a new league mark with 567 assists, but on the negative side, he committed a league-high 71 errors, and his .925 fielding percentage was one of the lower figures among shortstops. Still, the picture one gets of Bush in 1909 is of a wide-ranging fielder who could get to a great many ground balls, if not always successfully. His World Series play seemed to magnify the qualities he showed during the season, as he hit .318 with a .483 on-base percentage, but also committed five errors in the seven games. An error in the sixth inning of Game 1 kept the inning alive for the Pirates, who tacked on their third run later in the frame en route to the 4–1 win. Donie's flub in the first inning of Game 3 allowed the Pirates' first run to score in another Detroit loss, but he helped key the Tigers' do-or-die victory in Game 6 with a hit, a pair of walks and two runs scored. Donie was hit by a pitch in the Series' finale, but did not score. His final error was inconsequential.[16]

Although Bush would not top his rookie batting average until 1917, when he hit .281, he led the league in walks four times in the five years following his freshman season and in 1915 set a personal high of 118 while batting only .228. Bush also set a career-high with 44 RBIs that season and his patience at the plate paid off with 99 runs scored. His 1915 season marked the seventh consecutive year of 90 or more runs scored, including a career-high of 126 set in 1911. When Bush's average established his new full season high in 1917, he led his circuit in runs with 117. Bush continued to play regularly for the next four years, including 1921 when he was sent to Washington in a waiver transaction.[17]

Defensively, Bush established some impressive records, but also posted high error totals during his career. His 425 putouts in 1914 tied the major league record, which had been set by his manager Jennings in 1895. Additionally, Bush led the AL in putouts in 1911 and 1919, assists four times in five years between 1911 and 1915 and total chances per game in 1911, 1912 and 1914. He also topped the league in errors for a second time in 1911.

Owen was seen as a fiery player and a student of the game, so it made sense that he would move into managing once his playing days ended. He posted a 75–78 record for the Senators in his first year as field boss in 1923, but was replaced for 1924 by the team's 27-year-old second baseman, Bucky Harris. Bush then managed Indianapolis for three seasons before getting another shot at a major league managing post. That came when Barney Dreyfuss hired him to run the Pirates in 1927 after the club had endured a disappointing season, which featured the lowlight of a player revolt, which cost the easy-going Bill McKechnie his job. Dreyfuss wanted a rigid hand at the helm and turned to the no-nonsense former shortstop.[18]

Bush put his mark on Pirate history by leading the Bucs to the 1927 pennant. Perhaps his most significant move was installing another small player, Lloyd Waner, into the daily lineup. Bush also decided to add more thump by placing the offensively minded George Grantham at second and getting Joe Harris's .300 hitting bat into the lineup at first. Bush's time with the Pirates might have been longer than three years had he not run into clashes with some of his players, most notably star outfielder Kiki Cuyler in 1927. The two initially clashed when Bush wanted Cuyler to hit second, a spot Cuyler did not feel he was suited for. Later, when Cuyler did not slide into second on a double play ball and was subsequently tagged out on the play, Bush did not care to hear that Kiki had thought by going in standing up he would have made it harder for the opposing team's shortstop to complete the play. Bush benched Cuyler, a man who had been runner-up for the National League's Most Valuable Player award in 1925, and refused to play him during the remainder of the season or in the World Series. In 1928, star shortstop Glenn Wright found himself in the manager's doghouse and was dealt away. The Pirates had previously given up on another shortstop, future Hall of Famer Joe Cronin, during this time and Bush was slow to recognize Dick Bartell's potential. In 1929, the Pirate field boss came under criticism for overusing his ace pitcher Burleigh Grimes, but in defense of Bush, the Pirates had a very shallow staff that year. By August, Dreyfuss decided the man he had only two years earlier called "the best manager I ever had" might not be as effective as coach Jewel Ens, so Bush was let go.[19]

Bush had less success the rest of his time as a major league manager, as he took jobs with the struggling franchises in the south side of Chicago and in Cincinnati. Bush, however, was a man of his word. After agreeing to manage the White Sox, an offer came to manage the powerful New York Yankees, but Bush would not renege on his commitment to the pale hose. He later managed in the minor leagues and bought an interest in the Indianapolis club, where the stadium was eventually renamed in his honor. Bush remained involved in the business of baseball until his death in 1972. In fact, he was still active as a scout for the White Sox when he passed away.[20]

George Moriarty

Third Base
Born 6/7/1884   Died 4/8/1964
Detroit Tigers 1909–1915   Major League Career 1903–1916

The 1909 Tigers certainly had their share of men who had great success in life outside of their baseball careers. Ty Cobb became a millionaire due to sharp investments, most notably General Motors and Coca Cola. Sam Craw-

ford raised walnuts and coached baseball at University of Southern California.[21] Davy Jones earned his degree in pharmacy and owned successful drug
stores.[22] Donie Bush became "the man" in Indianapolis sports, eventually
having a stadium named in his honor.[23] But perhaps the true Renaissance
Man on the ballclub turned out to be its battling third baseman, George
Moriarty.

Moriarty joined the Tigers after three years with the New York Highlanders. An all-purpose utility player with good speed, Moriarty had hit well
in 1907 when he batted .277, but this came sandwiched between two years
of hitting in the .230's. The Highlanders were a last-place club in 1908, so
once Hal Chase was reinstated with the team, Moriarty became expendable.
The Tigers placed Moriarty in the lineup full-time, although George initially
played first base, due in part to a muscle strain and in part to Jennings' dis-
satisfaction with Claude Rossman's defense.

Moriarty's .273 average with the Tigers justified his status. Moriarty
came to be considered a fine defensive third baseman, but there were two
other things he became better known for as a player. The first was his propensity for stealing home, the second his pugnacious nature. Moriarty claimed
to have stolen home 17 times between his last season in New York and his
first in Detroit.[24]

Moriarty's fighting spirit and artful stealing of home may be best illus-
trated in an incident during May of his initial year in a Tigers uniform. George
attempted to steal home with two outs in the ninth and the Tigers trailing
the Red Sox, 3–2. The Boston catcher, Bill Carrigan, added insult to injury
by not only tagging out Moriarty to end the game, but spit tobacco juice on
him. George reportedly clobbered Carrigan with a punch, knocking the backstop to the ground.[25]

Following the publishing of an editorial by William J. Cannon in the
Detroit News titled "Don't Die on Third," supporting Moriarty's decision to
tie the game on his own devices, the Detroit newcomer became known as The
Man Who Won't Die on Third. In the 1909 World Series, Moriarty's tactics
caused ire among the Pirates. Tommy Leach remembered in *The Glory of
Their Times* that Moriarty was an agitator who would try to intimidate the
opposition. "I got a single and went to third on a hit by Honus. I'm standing
on third base, not thinking about anything in particular, when this Moriarty
comes over and kicks me in the shin. Just like that."[26] Leach, who was pre-
maturely balding in 1909, went on to explain how he had shaved his head and
had been applying a liniment in an effort to thicken his hair, and Moriarty
grabbed the cap off Leach's head and slapped him with it.[27]

Undoubtedly, some of the Pirates thought Moriarty got his just due when Bobby Byrne cut open the Tiger's knee on a stolen base attempt in the first inning of the final game. Moriarty remained in the game long enough to double in his first at-bat, but had to be replaced by a pinch-runner.

Moriarty remained a Tiger through 1915, usually as their regular third baseman, although he played 71 games at first in 1912 and only 33 at the hot corner. His averages during this time were always within 15 points of each other, with a low of .239 in 1913 and a high of .254 the following year. Moriarty moved to a utility role in 1915 and batted just 38 times. He started 1916 with the Chicago White Sox, but was released to become player-manager at Memphis.[28]

Prior to making the major leagues, Moriarty had worked in a typewriter factory, but following his playing days, he held a variety of positions, most notably as manager of the Tigers in 1926 and 1927. Charlie Gehringer recalled that even during the Lively Ball Era, Moriarty was intrigued with stealing home: "He had everybody stealing home, whether you could run or not. He'd even get you in the hotel lobby and show you how it should be done. He would show you how to get a lead. He'd start jockeying around between the potted palms and the furniture and people would look at him like he'd gone balmy. I'll bet we set a record that year for having guys thrown out trying to steal home."[29]

Later, Moriarty became an umpire in the American League and continued to build on his reputation as a fighter. He challenged the entire Chicago White Sox team to a fight in 1932, knocking out Milt Gaston, who had unwisely decided to accept Moriarty's challenge. Moriarty ended up on the losing end of the brawl, however. Not only did George break his hand hitting Gaston, but was physically overwhelmed by Gaston's teammates.[30]

During the 1935 World Series, Moriarty told the Cubs to stop their ethnically charged verbal abuse of Hank Greenberg.[31] Later in the Series he ejected manager Charlie Grimm and two others, but Commissioner Landis apparently did not like how George handled the situation, as a rule had been put in place for that World Series that Landis would have to be consulted before a player could be ejected. Moriarty was fined along with those he banished.[32]

Moriarty later scouted for the Tigers, signing 1950s staples Harvey Kuenn, Bill Tuttle and Billy Hoeft.[33] He died in 1964, a decade before his grandson, Michael Moriarty, rose to prominence as an actor.

Charlie O'Leary

Infielder
Born 10/15/82   Died 1/6/41
Detroit Tigers 1904–1912   Major League Career 1904–1913,   1934

A light hitter even by Deadball Era standards, Charlie O'Leary was the Tigers' regular shortstop from his rookie season in 1904 until illness shortened his season in 1908. Defensively, O'Leary led the American League in putouts, total chances per games and errors in 1906 and putouts again in 1907, but with Donie Bush impressing the Tigers brass during the '08 pennant race, O'Leary was moved to a backup role for 1909, despite having recovered enough to start all five World Series games in 1908. O'Leary saw most of his playing time in 1909 at third. With Moriarty nursing a muscle pull early in the season, O'Leary saw extensive action. While his hitting worsened to .203, Charlie's defense kept him in the lineup enough for him to go to bat 261 times during the year.[34] When Moriarty could not remain in Game 7 of the World Series, O'Leary ran for him and stayed in the game, but went 0-for-3.

O'Leary stayed in a utility role for the Tigers the next few years, but played regularly for the Cardinals at short in 1913. When St. Louis teammate Miller Huggins took over the managerial reigns with the New York Highlanders, he asked O'Leary to join him as a coach. He remained on the coaching sidelines for 19 years. Ironically, the weak-hitting O'Leary returned to action at the age of 51 in 1934 as, of all things, a pinch-hitter. He delivered a single in his final major league at-bat and scored a run. The base hit raised his career average to .226 and made him the last player whose career began before 1910 to appear in a game.[35]

Outfielders

Matty McIntyre

Left Field
Born 6/12/1880   Died 4/2/1920
Detroit Tigers 1904–1910   Major League Career 1901, 1904–1912

Matty McIntyre overcame a life-threatening bout of appendicitis in the offseason of 1908–1909 to reclaim his left-field job with the Tigers, but lost it late in the season to Davy Jones due to McIntyre's .244 season and Jones' late-season hot hitting. McIntyre batted only three times in the World Series in the Tigers' losing effort.

McIntyre broke in with Detroit in 1904, following a .342 season with Buffalo of the Eastern League in 1903.[36] He had previously played for the Philadelphia Athletics in the American League's opening season of 1901. While he put up respectable offense (.276), the A's did not retain him, reportedly because they did not feel he was fast enough for the major leagues.[37] McIntyre hit .253, but some saw him as the next baseball star, one going so far as to compare him favorably with Wee Willie Keeler.[38] McIntyre's batting, however, improved minimally the next two seasons before a broken foot sidelined him for all but 20 games in 1907.

During this time, Ty Cobb joined the Tigers and the two took an instant dislike to each other. Al Stump wrote that McIntyre ignored and baited the rookie.[39] While a reason was not given, it would be obvious that if Cobb were going to cut into a teammate's playing time, McIntyre would be a prime candidate to lose his job. McIntyre may have been the ringleader in the hazing of the young Georgian. He blocked the rookie from taking batting practice.[40] Matters worsened when McIntyre dropped a fly ball as Cobb had intruded on his fielding territory, with each accusing the other of messing up the play. McIntyre began feuding with management as well. He openly campaigned for a trade, but the Tigers refused to oblige. Although on the surface the player and team reconciled, things remained tense for the rest of Matty's tenure with the team.

McIntyre's best year in Detroit was for the 1908 pennant-winning club. Batting leadoff, McIntyre led the league in runs scored (105), hit .295 and boasted a .392 on-base percentage. McIntyre's fine season came during a year in which the American League was held to a .244 cumulative batting average and .303 on-base mark. Coupled with outstanding seasons by his outfield mates Cobb and Sam Crawford, who finished one–two in slugging, the Tigers boasted one of baseball's all-time great outfields. So impressive was their play that year that noted baseball sabermatician Bill James rates it as the second greatest of all time, behind only the Tiger ensemble of Cobb, Crawford and Bobby Veach in 1915.[41]

Following the season, McIntyre arranged a series of exhibition games in Cuba. Some key players, most notably Cobb who ignored the invitation, did not participate and the trip was not a successful business venture.

McIntyre's 1910 season stats were again disappointing and he no longer was considered a minor star, the Tigers finally sent him out of town, selling him to the White Sox. Coming back with a vengeance, McIntyre hit a career high .323 and for the second time in his career, scored 100 runs, but a .167 average escorted him out of the majors. Matty played and managed in the minors after that, enjoying some .300 seasons, but not another shot at big league play. McIntyre died young, at the age of 39, of Bright's Disease.

Davy Jones

Center Field
Born 6/30/1880   Died 3/30/1972
Detroit Tigers 1906–1912   Major League Career 1901–1904, 1906–1915, 1918

Nicknamed Kangaroo because of his habit of jumping teams for better opportunities early in his career, Davy Jones was an effective leadoff hitter, albeit one without much power. His best year with the Tigers was in 1907 when he scored a career-high 101 runs while batting .273. He also set a personal high with 30 stolen bases, but notched only 16 extra-base hits in 126 games. Jones had gotten everyday duty that year following an injury to Matty McIntyre, but when McIntyre came back healthy in 1908, Jones became the team's fourth outfielder and he batted only .207 with three extra-base hits in 121 at-bats. A late season surge in 1909, which featured a 17-game stretch in which Jones hit .420, brought his season average to .279 and earned Davy the chance to start in that year's World Series against the Pirates. Jones started despite the fact that he again showed minimal long-ball hitting, collecting just a pair of doubles and the same total of triples during the season.

Jones hit only .231 against Pittsburgh, but scored six times in the Series and ironically hit the only home run he would ever smack in his seven years in a Detroit uniform, when he drove one to center field off Babe Adams in a losing cause in Game 5.

Jones played semi-regularly for the next three years before he was sold on waivers to the White Sox, but appeared in only a dozen games in 1913. After spending most of that season in the minor leagues, Jones jumped once again, joining the Pittsburgh entry in the new Federal League. He was released in 1915 although he was hitting well (.327) after appearing in 14 games. Jones put in one more big league appearance, playing a farewell game at the end of the 1918 season for the Tigers.[42]

Looking at Davy Jones from a historical standpoint, he appears to be a man of contrasts and contradictions. Despite earning an associate's degree in law, he jumped to new ballclubs at least five times in his career.

Jones had forsaken a career in law to pursue life as a ballplayer. "I was a very poor boy, and the prospect of $85 a month right away, compared to years as a law clerk before I could start my own practice made it (a contract offer by the Rockford, Illinois, club in the Three-I League) hard to turn down."[43] The decision carried another price, however. The parents of the girl Jones was seeing at the time refused to let her date a professional ballplayer. "In those days, a lot of people looked upon ballplayers as bums, too lazy to work for a living." Nearly 60 years later, after Jones' first wife had passed away he met up with his earlier love once again. She, too, was widowed and they decided to rekindle their relationship and eventually married.[44]

Another interesting relationship in Jones' life was the one he held with Ty Cobb. "I was probably his best friend on the team. I used to stick up for him, sit and talk with him on long train trips, try to understand him."[45] Yet, Cobb walked off the team in 1910 after accusing Jones of missing hit-and-run signs on successive pitches, telling Hughie Jennings he wouldn't play with Jones again.[46] However, by late May 1912, Jones and Cobb apparently were back to getting along to some degree. Jones is said to have encouraged Cobb to attack a heckler in the stands. Jones also helped prevent onlookers from interfering as Cobb pummeled the man, who was missing parts of both hands.[47]

After retiring, Jones became a partner with his brother in several successful pharmacies. He was the last survivor of the 1909 World Series when he passed away at the age of 91 in 1972.

Ty Cobb

Right Field
Born 12/18/1886   Died 7/17/1961
Detroit Tigers 1905–1926   Major League Career 1905–1928

By 1909, Tyrus Raymond Cobb had established two facts about himself: that he was an extremely talented baseball player and an even more difficult human being. In the Tigers' third straight pennant-winning year, perhaps as in no other season, Cobb's reputation for both greatness and bedevilment showed like no other.

Cobb was only 18-years-old when he made his first major league appearance in 1905. The occasion should have been a high point in the young man's life. Instead, it was melancholy, for a few weeks before Cobb's mother had shot and killed his father. Cobb's father had suspected his wife of having an affair and, hoping to catch her with her lover, had told her he would not be home that evening. He later attempted to enter their home through their upstairs bedroom window. Cobb's mother, who would later claim she suspected a burglar was trying to enter the house, shot her husband. He died at the scene. Although Cobb's mother was acquitted of manslaughter, the incident haunted Cobb for the rest of his life. "My father had his head blown off with a shotgun when I was 18-years-old, by a member of my family," Cobb told biographer Al Stump near the end of his life. "I didn't get over that. I've never gotten over it."[48]

Cobb struggled with what must have been incredible grief, feelings he kept inside most of his life.[49] He also displayed a sense of loyalty, but perhaps unspoken questions about his mother's innocence and the rumors that she was unfaithful. Under these circumstances, Cobb became a very young member of the Detroit Tigers. Cobb felt he was treated cruelly by his new teammates. The other players, while admitting hazing the young man from Georgia, pointed out that razzing rookies was a common practice at the time, but Cobb overreacted. Parents will often tell their children who are being teased, "Ignore it and those kids will lose interest." Cobb couldn't ignore it. Biographer Stump reports some who knew Cobb felt he had issues even before

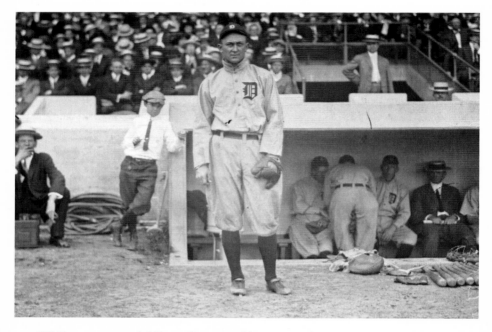

While a controversial figure for most of his career, there is no disputing the greatness of Ty Cobb. He is in the top 10 all-time in 20 categories, including hits
where he is one of only two men to eclipse the 4,000-hit plateau, and average,
where he holds the all-time best mark at .366 (courtesy of Library of Congress,
Bain Collection, Prints & Photographs Division, 13533u).

his father's killing, but the trauma Cobb experienced, combined with his
Southern pride and desire to somehow prove to his father that he had made
a wise decision in choosing an athletic profession over an academic or political
one, combined to make him determined, angry and paranoid. He rarely
backed away from an altercation. "Every rookie gets a little hazing, but most
of them just take it and laugh. Cobb took it the wrong way. He came up with
an antagonistic attitude, which in his mind turned every little razzing into a
life or death struggle. He always figured everybody was ganging up on him,"
Sam Crawford remembered.[50]

Davy Jones, who also was an outfield mate of Cobb's, said, "Trouble was
he had such a rotten disposition that it was damn hard to be his friend ... Ty
didn't have a sense of humor, see. Especially, he could never laugh at himself.
Consequently, he took a lot of things the wrong way."[51] Cobb saw considerable
action during the final weeks of the 1905 season, but hit just .240 with only
two stolen bases.

Expected to be a backup in 1906, Cobb overcame the emotional strain of his mother's trial to take over a regular spot in the Detroit lineup. The stress, however, overwhelmed him in midseason and he suffered a breakdown. The Tigers sent him to a sanitarium, where Cobb recovered well enough to return to the club in September. Amazingly, he finished the season with a .316 average in 98 games. Cobb played mostly center field that season, but ongoing problems with left fielder Matty McIntyre led manager Hughie Jennings to move Ty to right field so the two would not have to play side by side. As impressive as his hitting was in 1906, Cobb's final batting figures would remain above .316 for the rest of his career. He truly was just getting started.

The next two seasons, Cobb led his league in hits, RBIs and batting average both seasons. He also led the AL in stolen bases in 1907 and doubles and triples in 1908. Both times, he led the Tigers into the World Series. Cobb's play against the Cubs was mixed. He hit only .200 with one run scored and none driven in 1907, but led the Tigers with seven hits, four RBIs and a .368 average in 1908.

As devastating a player and uncontrollable a man and teammate Cobb had previously been (he had left the Tigers for a week during the 1908 pennant race to get married), 1909 saw Cobb's stardom and savagery hit new heights. His outstanding play led his team to its third World Series in three years. His off-field behavior may have destined the Tigers to their third straight loss. Cobb became the first American League player to lead his league in what would become considered the Triple Crown categories with a .377 average, nine home runs (all of which were hit inside-the-park) and 107 RBIs. Cobb's batting and RBI crowns were his third in a row and for the third consecutive season, Ty led the AL in hits with 216. He won his second stolen base title (76) and led the league in runs scored (116) for the first time. Cobb's entire league-leading statistics, except for runs batted in, represented career highs to that point. He was easily the best player in the American League and he had not yet turned 23.

Ty was far from being the only man who had a dangerous reputation on the basepaths, but over the years some players stated that Cobb was actually fair in his attacks on defenders. "Cobb never tried to spike anybody," Sam Crawford told Lawrence Ritter in *The Glory of Their Times*. "The base line belongs to the runner. If the infielder gets in their way, that's their lookout."[52] Honus Wagner echoed Wahoo Sam's sentiment. "But Cobb was a good sportsman. He wanted the baseline, demanded the baserunner's right of way, and usually got it. He sharpened his spikes, but then we all did that."[53]

However, when Cobb's hard slide opened Home Run Baker's leg in an August game against Detroit's chief contender, the Philadelphia Athletics, a cry went out for Cobb to be sanctioned. Some observers felt the play was dirty, but the incident happened during the heat of a pennant race. *The Sporting News'* Joe S. Jackson wrote in Cobb's defense.[54] In fairness to the Georgia Peach's defense, it must be considered that Athletics' manager Connie Mack's call for Cobb to be suspended could have been an attempt to put the best player of his team's chief competitor on the sidelines.

Cobb's controversial slide, however, paled in level of violence and potential consequences to the infamous off-field assault on a Cleveland hotel's house detective, George Stanfield. Charges were filed and a warrant was issued charging Cobb with aggravated assault with attempt to kill. Although the Tigers reportedly paid off Stansfield to drop the charges, the police decided to keep the case open.[55] This meant Cobb could be arrested if he returned to Ohio. During the World Series, Cobb had to travel first a circuitous route and later a clandestine one between Detroit and Pittsburgh. The extra travel likely took some of the heat out of Cobb's fire at a time when Cobb was playing head to head against the only man who would be mentioned with Cobb as the greatest baseball player in the world, Honus Wagner.

Cobb hit only .231 in what would be his final World Series performance and was out shined by the Flying Dutchman in the Series, but Ty did enjoy some fine moments.

After scoring the Tigers' only run in Game 1, adding a stolen base to the box score, Cobb stole home in Game 2, a 7–2 Tiger victory. In Game 3, he knocked in two runs with a pair of hits in a losing cause, but added another pair of RBIs in Detroit's 5–0 win in Game 4. At this point, Cobb was batting a respectable .286. Cobb also contributed a run-scoring double in Game 6, a game which the Tigers won by a scant run, but against Babe Adams in Game 7, Cobb went hitless. In fact, Cobb had a very difficult time against the Pirate rookie, going just 1-for-10 in the youngster's three victories.

Later, Cobb admitted he worried throughout the Series he would be arrested, particularly while he was on the field in Pittsburgh.[56] His teammates were unsupportive and grumbled that Cobb's legal issues had cost them a winner's purse for the Series. While he came home a loser in the World Series, Cobb came out a winner in his problems with the law. With the aid of a lawyer who was a former mayor of Cleveland, Cobb's charges were reduced to simple assault and battery. He paid a $100 fine.

Somehow, Cobb did not destroy his baseball career in the years beyond 1909. He only continued to advance his legend. He won nine more batting titles, topping the .400 mark three times, including one season when he finished second in the race despite hitting .401. He led the league in runs scored, hits, doubles, triples, slugging, on-base percentage and stolen bases multiple times during the last 19 years of his career. His 96 stolen bases in

1916 established a new modern record as had his 248 hits in 1911. Cobb, however, did not slow down in his intimidation of others. He continued to brawl with players, umpires and even fans. He did receive support from his teammates on at least one occasion. When Cobb went into the stands and beat up a reportedly verbally abusive, but physically disabled heckler, American League president Ban Johnson suspended him. The other Detroit players refused to take the field, expressing the belief that Ty was justified in his attack as the man, among other things, had insulted Cobb's female family members. Cobb encouraged his teammates not to strike as each player was facing the possibility of financial consequences. However, the Tigers stuck with Cobb. After a team of aging coaches and semi-pro players suffered a 24–2 loss at the hands of the Athletics, matters were worked out. Cobb was suspended 10 days and fined only $50 and the Tigers owner covered the striking players' fines.

Matters with teammates, while never great, softened as the players from the early 1900s retired, were traded or released. Cobb was named the Tigers manager in 1921. The club had one second-place finish under Cobb, in 1923, and after 1921 posted winning records in each of Ty's years at the helm. He helped some of the players, such as Harry Heilmann and Henie Manush, become better hitters, but still could be a hard man to work for.[57]

"I guess he was satisfied with the way I took his instruction. But he could be a tough man to play for. Very demanding. He was so great himself he couldn't understand why if he told players to do certain things, they couldn't do it as well as he did. He didn't seem to realize that it wasn't possible, and he got frustrated with a lot of guys. But if you had the talent, he could really help you. I think he made a fine hitter out of Manush, who pretty much followed Cobb's advice," Charlie Gehringer recounted in *Baseball When the Grass Was Real*. "Oh, he got tough with me. I was supposed to start the season in '26, but somehow in spring training I said something or didn't say something, that provoked him and he took me out of the lineup about a week before we came home, and I never got to start. He never explained it to me, and nobody else ever did. He wouldn't even talk to me. The only way I got into the lineup was because our second baseman Frank O'Rourke, got the measles. So, Cobb had no other choice but to put me in. But even then he wouldn't tell me to bunt or hit or to do his or do that. He'd tell the coaches to tell me what to do."[58]

Following the 1926 season, Cobb became embroiled in a scandal. Former pitcher Dutch Leonard, released by Cobb in 1925, claimed Cobb and Cleveland's superstar player-manager Tris Speaker along with Smokey Joe Wood and Leonard had conspired to place bets on a game between the Indians and Tigers that Speaker promised to lose so the Tigers could capture the third-place share of first division money. Cobb, Speaker and Wood were exonerated by Commissioner Landis, but Cobb and Speaker were removed from their posts as managers and released by their respective teams as players. Years later, Wood admitted bets had been wagered on the game, but said no one purposely played to lose. The former pitcher/outfielder had asked his admission be left out of the published version of *The Glory of Their Times*, but it was included in a release of tape recordings of Lawrence Ritter's interviews.[59]

Now 40-years-old, Cobb caught on with the Athletics and their owner/manager Mack, the same man who had pushed for Cobb's banishment in 1909 and at one point had remarked he would not allow Cobb to play for him even if Cobb played for free. Mack got one productive season from Ty as a full-time player as the Georgia Peach hit .357, scored 104 runs and drove in 93 in 1927. Playing less in his final season, Cobb batted .323 before retiring.

Cobb had become wealthy due to his wise investments. Although he made donations to charities and helped support old acquaintances from the game, he remained a solitary man to the end, often alienating those who attempted to befriend him. He married and divorced twice. When he died at the age of 74 in 1961, only three men connected with the game that had made his name a household word attended his funeral.

Sam Crawford

Center Field
Born 4/18/1880   Died 6/15/1968
Detroit Tigers 1903–1917   Major League Career 1899–1917

There are many debates about players and their worthiness for the Baseball Hall of Fame, but those arguments are not to be addressed here. Instead, the question we're addressing is who is the most underrated Hall of Famer. Our answer is Wahoo Sam Crawford, the longtime outfielder of the Detroit Tigers and one of the greatest hitters of the Deadball Era.

Establishing his star status with the Cincinnati Reds from 1899 to 1902, Crawford jumped to the Tigers for 1903. He was well sought out, given back-to-back .330 seasons during his final two years in the Queen City. The 22-year-old also showed he could hit with power, leading the National League with 16 home runs in 1901 and 22 triples in 1902. Crawford continued to thump the ball in his new digs, again topping .330 and leading his former rival league with 25 three-baggers.

Triples became Crawford's calling card. He led the AL in that category four more times and his career total of 309 is the highest in major league history. While his batting average fell for a couple of years, Crawford still came close to .300 in 1905 and 1906, seasons in which American Leaguers batted .241 and .249, respectively.

In 1907, Crawford's average moved up to .323 and he placed second in the batting race behind his young teammate Ty Cobb. Crawford's return to the .300 club coupled with Cobb's first truly outstanding season were huge factors in the Tigers winning 21 more games in 1907 than in 1906 and brought Detroit its first American League crown. Two more .300 seasons followed as did two more pennants. In 1909, Crawford led the league in doubles (38) while finishing second to Cobb in RBIs, slugging and total bases. His status as one of the AL's elite batters did not help him in the World Series, as he had nearly identical disappointing stats. Both years, he went 5-for-21 (.238) with one double in each of the Series against the Cubs. His power numbers improved some in 1909, when Crawford hit a home run and three doubles, but Wahoo's favorite son still managed just a .250 average and drew only one walk. Game 3 was particularly tough for Sam, as he popped up with two on to end the eighth inning with the tying runs aboard, and, coming to the plate representing the tying run in the ninth, Crawford grounded out to Honus Wagner. In Game 6, however, the big left-handed hitter redeemed himself with a two-out first-inning double against Vic Willis, which opened the Tigers scoring in what would be a 5–4 Detroit win, and a play he made at first base saved the victory. Manager Hughie Jennings had only moments before moved Crawford in at first after a collision had taken the team's regular first sacker, Tom Jones, out of the game. Crawford had played 17 games at first during the season and had appeared there 85 times over the previous three years, so he was not a stranger to the bag. George Gibson hit a groundball to Crawford, who threw out Bill Abstein trying to score the tying run. The game ended when Chief Wilson was thrown out trying to steal third as Ed Abbaticchio struck out. Moving to a new position was nothing new for Crawford. He was actually not a natural center fielder, and played the vast majority of his games in right, but Jennings had asked him to move to center in 1907 so that Cobb and Matty McIntyre would not have to play next to each other. Crawford, as did his teammates, went quietly in Game 7, going 0-for-4.

Crawford continued to play at a star level for the next seven years. Although his average fell to .289, Wahoo Sam won the first of his three RBI titles in 1910 with a career-high 120, and lead the league for the third time with 19 triples, but pitching issues and dissension took its toll on the Tigers whose three-year run as American League Champions came to an end. Crawford enjoyed a fantastic 1911 when he batted .378, the highest total of his career, and drove home another 115. But after appearing at the top of his game by again boasting the league highs for triples and RBIs in 1914 and 1915,

Crawford's playing time was limited to 100 games, including 15 as a pinch-hitter, in 1916. Crawford could still hit respectably, if not outstandingly, and led the American League with 8 pinch-hits. Sources vary on why the 36-year-old began to see less playing time. The emergence of another future Hall of Famer, Harry Heilmann, combined with Sam's declining outfield skills and Crawford's complaints about his salary as well as the friction between him and Cobb noted elsewhere, likely led to his release.

Crawford wasn't through as a ballplayer. He played four more seasons in the Pacific Coast League, leading the PCL in hits in 1919 before winning his final triples crown at the age of 40 in 1920.[60] Staying in southern California, Crawford later coached baseball at USC and umpired in the PCL during the 1930s.[61] He became an avid reader and spent his later years pursuing this passion and tending to his garden.

So why do we state Sam Crawford is the most underrated Hall of Fame ballplayer? While contemporaries praised Sam, time seemed to erase first the memories and then the perceptions of just how good he was. First of all, other than Crawford's record for career triples, playing in the Deadball Era held down his batting statistics. Ed Barrow, the man responsible for the signing of Honus Wagner and move of Babe Ruth to being an everyday outfielder, said that no one was a better hitter than Crawford.[62] Cobb, a man who once said Crawford couldn't stand being number two on the Tigers behind him, argued that Crawford would hit 40 home runs a year if he played during the Lively Ball Era.[63] Bill James, in the *New Historical Baseball Abstract*, uses a complex formula of statistical adjustments which figure Crawford would have accounted for around 494 homers if his career began 20 years later than it had.[64] In that context, Crawford would have hit more home runs than any player besides Ruth at the time of his retirement and would have finished his career with one more round-tripper than Lou Gehrig. Ironically, Barrow once was quoted as saying Crawford was the Gehrig of his time.[65]

Crawford's 97 career homers were hit during the Deadball Era, a figure surpassed only by two National Leaguers, Gavy Cravath and Wildfire Schulte, but it must be noted that Cravath enjoyed an incredible advantage given that his home ballpark was Philadelphia's Baker's Bowl with a right field wall only 250 feet away from home plate. In 1914, Cravath led the NL with 19 home runs, hitting all of them at home.[66] In contrast, Navin Field had a right-field foul line of 370 feet, a nice place for triples, but death for home runs. When Cleveland erected a 45-foot screen in right field, the team's owner boasted it was built to stop Crawford's long drives. The Tiger slugger made the investment look bad by driving the ball over the screen.[67] Other admirers of Crawford included sportswriters such as H.G. Salsinger, who claimed he saw

Crawford hit five balls in one game that would have cleared the fence if a lively ball had been in play.[68]

Unlike Cobb, who used to say he used a scientific approach to hitting, Crawford said he simply saw the ball and swung.[69] SABR's *Deadball Stars of the American League* reports Crawford was not a speed merchant, but he had to have had plus speed in order to accumulate not just his gaudy total of triples, but his 363 career stolen bases. He was considered a good right fielder in his day and had enough speed to play center field for pennant-winning teams. On top of this, Sam was seen as a genial player by just about everyone but Cobb.

Using a system devised by Bill James called the Black Ink Test (a system where a player receives weighted credit for leading the league in offensive categories), Crawford scored 33 points to rank fiftieth all time. Expanding this to the Gray Ink Test (where the player receives points for being among his league leaders), Crawford scores 330 points to rank ninth all time. The players rated ahead of him — Cobb, Hank Aaron, Stan Musial, Honus Wagner, Cap Anson, Tris Speaker, Babe Ruth and Willie Mays — are all unquestioned Hall of Famers.

Why then did it take the Hall of Fame over twenty years of balloting before inducting Sam in 1957? Amazingly, Crawford never scored more than 4.5 percent of the electorate's votes. Some of the players put in ahead of him included Tommy McCarthy, a lifetime .292 hitter, but who made about 1,900 hits less than Crawford and who played much of his career in the 1890s when batting averages soared; Fred Clarke, another player whose career statistics were bolstered by four seasons in which he hit between .325 and .390 in the '90s; and such glove men as Ray Schalk, Roger Bresnahan and Bobby Wallace who were only somewhat above average offensive players; and the trio of infielders who helped the Cubs defeat Crawford's Tigers in the 1907 and 1908 World Series, Frank Chance, Joe Tinker and Johnny Evers. It appears as early as 20 years after the Deadball Era ended, there became a substantial prejudice against hitters from that time. The Lively Ball Era of the 1920s changed the meaning of and thinking on offensive statistics. Suddenly, there regularly were .400 hitters again and the home run became a true weapon rather than an interesting, but relatively rare, display of strength.

Perhaps some of the romanticism of aging men who played in the 1890s or who were immortalized in verse or famed for some invention took precedent in the voter's minds. Surprisingly, it was Crawford's nemesis, Cobb, who petitioned the Veterans Committee to enshrine his long-time teammate. When Crawford was finally elected in 1957, his neighbors didn't even realize he was a former ballplayer until they saw reporters coming to interview him.[70] Finally, there was the factor of Crawford indeed having played most of his career as the second best player on his ballclub, or, as Smokey Joe Wood, a pitcher who faced both men in their prime, remembered as he spoke about Harry Hooper, "It's a real shame Harry was on the same club as Spoke (Tris Speaker), having to play all those years in his shadow. Just like Gehrig with Ruth and Crawford with Cobb."[71]

But the age of sabermetrics appears to have given fans of old-time baseball a greater appreciation of Crawford. Bill James rates Wahoo Sam tenth among all-time right fielders, between Paul Waner and Al Kaline.[72] Baseball.fever.com ran an interesting debate about who was a better player, Crawford or Reggie Jackson. While the votes of bloggers were fairly well split, several noted that Crawford probably would have been better able to adapt to today's game than Jackson would have had he been forced to play in the Deadball Era.[73]

Catchers

Charles Schmidt

Catcher
Born 9/12/1880   Died 11/14/1932
Detroit Tigers 1906–1911   Major League Career 1906–1911

The Tigers catching core featured only one holdover from 1908, Charles "Boss" Schmidt. Schmidt was in his fourth season with the team in 1909 and had hit .265 the previous season, the top figure among American League catchers. Schmidt also caught an impressive Deadball Era total of 121 games, second in the AL behind the White Sox's Billy Sullivan. Since the Cubs had run wild on him in both the 1907 and 1908 World Series, Jennings looked for better defense out of his backstop. A switch-hitter, Schmidt also had trouble hitting left-handers.[74] Still, Schmidt recognized he was still in a good position to bargain. Realizing the Tigers would not want to depend solely on rookies as they sought their third pennant in a row, he held out late into spring training.[75] However, in 1909 Schmidt struggled against all types of pitching and ended up batting just .209.

One area where Schmidt did not have any deficiencies was his toughness. He was said to have fought exhibitions against pugilists Sam Langford and the immortal Jack Johnson and once stopped Ty Cobb cold with a punch. Cobb had slapped the team's black groundskeeper Bungy Davis to the ground reportedly after Davis had attempted to shake Cobb's hand. When the groundskeeper's wife came to aid her husband, Cobb began choking her. It was then that Schmidt stepped in to put an end to the throttling.[76] A week later, Cobb and Schmidt clashed again and again Schmidt was the decided victor.[77]

Against the Pirates, Schmidt caught the majority of the games in the World Series. The Pirates continued to exploit his weaknesses as the Cubs had in the two previous Series, by stealing 15 bases against him. Schmidt added to his own embarrassment by committing five errors. His World Series was a strange one, indeed, as he collected only four hits, but drove in four runs in Game 2. His clutch double tied the game in the top of the second and he singled in two more runs with a two-out hit in the fifth to make the score 7–2.[78] Schmidt also made two outstanding defensive plays to in the final inning of Game 6. With two on and none out in the Pirate ninth, Schmidt fielded Chief Wilson's bunt and threw to first. On the play, Wilson collided with Tiger first baseman Tom Jones, knocking him unconscious. A run scored, and the Detroit lead was down to one run and Pittsburgh now had two men in scoring position. The next batter, George Gibson, grounded to the new first baseman, Sam Crawford, who threw home to nail baserunner Bill Abstein trying to score. Abstein spiked Schmidt at the plate, but the bloodied backstop not only held onto the ball for the out, but stayed in the game. Minutes later, Wilson, perhaps trying to take advantage of Schmidt's injury and assumed psychological state (considering his poor throwing in the Series and likely a good bit of anger due to being spiked), tried to steal third as pinch-hitter Ed Abbaticchio swung at a third strike, but Schmidt threw Wilson out to end the game.

The following season, Schmidt's hitting returned to a very respectable .259, but he played in half the Tigers' ballgames and in his final season, 1911, the 28-year-old catcher batted only 46 times. He finished his career with a .243 average in 477 games. Five years later, Schmidt's younger brother Walter debuted for the Pirates. Also a catcher, Walter became known for stellar defense and a keen ability to handle pitchers and in 1969 was voted the Buc's all-time catcher, and honor which has since passed on to Manny Sanguillen. Like his older brother, Walter knew his value as a ballplayer and became almost an annual holdout in his years in Pittsburgh.

Oscar Stanage

Catcher
Born 3/17/1883
Detroit Tigers 1908–1920, 1925

Died 11/11/1964
Major League Career 1906, 1908–1920, 1925

A defensive star by the second decade of the twentieth century, Oscar Stanage saw considerable playing time as a rookie in 1909. His defensive skills earned him promotion to the Tigers in 1908, although his hitting in the minors had been poor.[79] He did not appear in a game that season, but surprised at the plate with a .262 average as a freshman, which would turn out to be one of his strongest offensive years, but it was his impressive throwing arm that earned him playing time in 77 games.[80]

In the World Series, Stanage collected one hit in two games and allowed three stolen bases. Stanage went on to earn an ironman reputation, catching an American League record 141 games in 1911 and cemented his defensive reputation the same season with 212 assists, an AL record which has never been matched. The 1911 season was also Oscar's best offensive year as he boosted his highest average (.264) and RBI total (52). Stats LLC retroactively named Stanage the top backstop in the American League for that year.[81]

Stanage caught for the Tigers through 1920, then played a few years in the minors. He returned to catch one final game for Detroit in 1925. Ironically, Stanage's last job in baseball was as a coach for the Pirates during the 1926–1931 period.

Heinie Beckendorf

Catcher
Born 6/15/1884   Died 9/15/1949
Detroit Tigers 1909–1910   Major League Career 1909–1910

The Tigers' number three catcher was another rookie, Heinie Beckendorf. Appearing in only 15 games, Beckendorf hit a respectable .259, but drove in only one run. He did not appear in the World Series. After a 3-for-7 start in 1910, the right-handed hitting Beckendorf was sent to Washington for cash, where he played more often (37 games), but hit much less (.146). He never again appeared in a major league game.[82]

Joe Casey

Catcher
Born 8/15/1887   Died 6/2/1966
Detroit Tigers 1909–1911   Major League Career 1909–1911, 1918

One must wonder about the state of catching in 1909 as the Tigers employed a third rookie, 21-year-old Joe Casey in three games behind the plate. Casey went hitless in five at-bats and saw no action in the World Series. He did see some playing time for the Tigers the next two years, but his very week hitting (.178 average in a combined 38 games) led to his not appearing again in the major leagues until 1918, when he went 4-for-17 in a brief stay in Washington.

Pitchers

George Mullin

Right-Handed Pitcher
Born:7/4/1880   Died:1/7/1944
Detroit Tigers 1902–1913   Major League Career 1902–1915

As the Tigers' top pitcher during the Deadball Era, George Mullin had his greatest season by far in 1909. Mullin, who relied on a fastball and curve established a team record with 29 wins, a total no Tiger would top until Denny McLain became the last major leaguer to top 30 victories almost 60 years later.[83]

Mullin broke in with the Tigers in 1902. He was initially signed by Brooklyn, but like many players who were jumping back and forth between the two major leagues, George did not honor his contract, but his reason was more sentimental than most. Mullin chose to report to Detroit, not just for a few dollars extra, but because the city was closer to his hometown.[84] Mullin did not pitch effectively in his debut, but he did hit three doubles and earned a no-decision.[85] Mullin's slugging was a sign of things to come as "Wabash George" became one of the top-hitting pitchers in the league, finishing with a .325 average in his rookie season. For his career, Mullin hit .262 and was considered one of the best-hitting pitchers of all time.[86]

Mullin won in double figures every season prior to the Tiger's pennant-winning years and was a workhorse hurling as many as 382 innings (in 1904) and led the American League in starts (41) and innings (347) in 1905. He had problems with control, though, walking over 100 batters per season from 1903 to 1906, including leading the league for three consecutive years, after allowing 95 free passes as a rookie in 1902. After his first five years, Mullin's record stood at 91–93. While his record did not stand out, in four of his first five campaigns Mullin posted a better winning percentage than his team. His 2.25 ERA in his sophomore season was almost three-quarters of a run better than the league average while his 170 strikeouts placed him fifth in the league. Mullin's 2.40 ERA in 1904 was again below the league average of 2.60, but with the Tigers' offense finishing seventh in scoring, George would go only 17–23.

Ironically, Mullin could do no better than a .500 season, going 20–20 when the Tigers won their first pennant in 1907. Mullin pitched well in the World Series that season, but lost both his complete-game efforts. The powerful pitcher hurled his third complete World Series game the following year, this time coming out an 8–3 winner, which capped a season that saw George give up more hits than innings pitched for the first time since his rookie year.

He went 17–13, but had only the fourth-best winning percentage on his team. His 3.10 ERA ranked fifth among the club's top five pitchers.

Not one who prided himself on conditioning, Mullin worked hard in the offseason of 1908 and came into 1909 forty pounds lighter than the previous year.[87] When Jennings chose him to be his Opening Day starter, Mullin gave a preview of things to come by pitching a one-hitter. He won ten more before suffering his first loss. Regaining his position as staff ace, Mullin's 29–8 record was the American League's best. Although his strikeouts declined, Mullin was also now walking fewer men and his curveball was one of the most respected in the circuit.

The obvious choice to open the World Series for the Tigers, Mullin retired the first 11 men he faced before giving up a home run to Fred Clarke, which tied the game, 1–1. Wabash George was unable to keep pace with Babe Adams as shaky defense on the part of Mullin's teammates led to a 4–1 loss.

The next time out, in Game 4, Mullin took matters into his own hands, striking out 10 while pitching a five-hit shutout, which evened the Series. After the Pirates captured Game 5, Jennings sent his star back to the mound on only one day of rest. Noted as a cold-weather pitcher, Mullin started out cold, allowing three runs before recording an out. However, George proved Jennings' gamble worthwhile as he allowed only two hits over the next seven innings. By the ninth, Detroit led 5–3 and the game got no closer than 5–4 as the Pirates made two baserunning blunders, but it must also be noted that Mullin recorded a huge strikeout by fanning Ed Abbaticchio on a game-ending, strike 'em out, throw 'em out play.

Two days later, with Wild Bill Donovan ineffective, but the Tigers only trailing by a 2–0 score, Jennings again called on his ace, but Mullin gave up two more runs in the fourth. He finished the game, but was mostly ineffective as the Tigers lost, 8–0. No one could really blame George for not being on his game. He pitched a seven-game World Series record of 32 innings, a record that stands to this day.

Mullin had another strong campaign in 1910, although he was not as dominant as the year before. He finished fifth in the AL with 21 wins as the Tigers' run of pennants came to an end. His victories were most on the team, but his ERA was only fourth-best among Tiger starters. His win total dropped again, this time to 18 in 1911.

By 1912, George's success in Detroit was coming to an end, but he did have one more moment of glory left for the Tigers. Born on the Fourth of July, 1880, George set off another cause for celebration on his thirty-second birthday by no-hitting the St. Louis Browns. Also still able to swing the bat, Mullin collected three hits and two RBIs in the game.

In 1913, Mullin was sold to the Washington Senators in the midst of a 4–11 season. His last win for the Tigers was his 209th, a total surpassed only by Hooks Dauss in team history. After being sent back to the minors, Mullin returned to "major" league pitching in the Federal League and he won 14 games for Indianapolis as a swingman in 1914. He moved with the franchise to Newark the next year, but appeared in only five games before his major league career came to an end. Still not done with baseball, Mullin pitched and managed a few more seasons in the minors before becoming a police officer.

Ed Willett

Right-Handed Pitcher
Born: 3/7/1888   Died: 5/10/1934
Detroit Tigers 1906–1913   Major League Career 1906–1915

Right-hander Ed Willett's second season as a regular in the Tigers' rotation in 1909 turned out to be his best as he pitched his only 20-win season, finishing second in the American League with 21 victories against 10 losses. Despite his success, Willett was passed over by Hughie Jennings for a starting assignment in that fall's World Series.

Willett was described as "a Southerner, Virginia born and good-looking" who broke with the Tigers in 1906, around the time Ty Cobb was establishing himself.[88] Willett actually roomed with Cobb for a time, but in *Cobb: A Biography* author Al Stump reports, "Willett admitted that he had been warned by certain Tigers to find other housing or 'get hurt bad.'" Willett had been uncomfortable with Cobb carrying a gun with him and decided he would be better off with a different housemate. Cobb claimed Willett would be turned into a drunkard by his new friends and never forgave Willett for leaving.[89]

Willett's three main pitches, according to James and Neyer, were a sidearm curve, fastball and an under-handed floater.[90] The last pitch might have been used as a change up to keep hitters off pace. The authors note that George Moriarty felt Willett could have been more successful if he relied on his floater more often.

Willett was called on in relief of Ed Summers when Summers could not get out of the first inning of World Series Game 3; a poor defensive play by Willett allowed Tommy Leach to score to make it a 6–0 Pirate advantage. Willett's pitching in the Series, however, was effective, as he allowed only three hits in seven and two-thirds innings. Still, the sidearmer was bypassed in the later stages of the Series in favor of Bill Donovan and overworked staff ace George Mullin.

Willett pitched well again in 1910, winning 16 games with an ERA just

0.03 points higher than he had posted in 1909. He started to be less effective the following year. Willett pitched as a regular for the Tigers for three more seasons, but posted only a .500 record with 43 wins and 43 losses. Following 1913, Willett became the first Tiger to jump to the newly formed Federal League when he signed with St. Louis, but he was no longer very effective.[91] He won only four of 21 decisions in 1914 before pitching primarily out of the bullpen, posting a 4.61 ERA in 1915 before being given his release.

Ed Summers

Right-Handed Pitcher
Born: 12/5/1884   Died: 5/12/1953
Detroit Tigers: 1908–1912   Major League Career 1908–1912

An early knuckleballer who may have been the first big leaguer to successfully throw the pitch using his fingertips, Ed Summers was the number three man in the 1909 Tigers' rotation. As a rookie, Summers burst into the American League with a 24–12 record with a magnificent 1.64 ERA and five shutouts. As was common among players with native American ancestry, Ed was sometimes called "Chief," but was more specifically given the nickname "Kickapoo Ed" as a reference to his specific heritage.

Rob Neyer and Bill James hypothesized the 23-year-old rookie varied his signature pitch from the knuckleballs thrown by contemporaries Eddie Cicotte and Nap Rucker. Cicotte is generally given credit for inventing the knuckleball, but the pitcher, who became more famous as the Chicago White Sox pitcher who was banned from baseball for conspiring to throw the 1919 World Series, acknowledged it was partly due to Summers, a minor league teammate. Cicotte, as well as Rucker and others who threw the pitch, threw his signature pitch off his knuckles. Summers threw his off his fingertips so that the pitch was sometimes referred to as a "fingernail ball."[92]

Whether or not Summers had a unique pitch at his disposal as a rookie, he was not very effective against the Chicago Cubs in the 1908 World Series, losing both his decisions, allowing 18 hits in 14 and two-thirds innings with a 4.30 ERA. However, Summers and his fingernail floater came back strong in 1909, as the right-hander went 19–9. Summers' World Series performance against Pittsburgh, though, was even worse than his play against Chicago. He started two games and again went 0–2, this time with a ghastly ERA of 8.59 and 13 hits allowed in seven and one-third innings pitched. He was downright dreadful in Game 3 when he retired only one of six batters faced. Summers struggled in Game 5. This time control problems aided the Pirates as he walked in a run in the first and wild pitched in another in the second. After settling down for a few innings, Summers allowed a three-run homer to Fred

Clarke in the seventh, which broke a 3–3, tie and proved to provide the winning runs. But not all of Summer's big games were disappointing. Late in the 1909 season, Summers pitched and won both ends of a key doubleheader to clinch a tie for the pennant for the Tigers.

Summers' ERA rose each of the next three years and his victory totals dropped. He went a combined 24–23 in 1910 and 1911 before rheumatism forced him out of the big leagues after splitting a pair of decisions in 1912.[93]

Ed Killian

Left-Handed Pitcher
Born: 11/12/1876   Died: 7/18/1828
Detroit Tigers: 1904–1910   Major League Career: 1903–1910

An effective but sore-armed pitcher by 1909, Ed Killian was something of a tough-luck hurler in more ways than one, as despite posting the top ERA on the staff, an excellent 1.71 mark, he managed only an 11–9 record for a team that was the top scorers in the American League. A left-hander, Killian was a workhorse for the Tigers before his arm began giving him problems, pitching over 313 innings three times in a four-year span. Obtained after a 3–4 rookie mark for Cleveland in 1903, Killian went 14–20 with a weak Detroit squad in 1904, but turned his record around the following season, going 23–14 in 1905. Nicknamed "Twilight Ed" after throwing several extra-inning efforts, Killian led the AL with eight shutouts.[94] At times temperamental, Killian was suspended following a drunken tirade in the Tiger clubhouse in 1906, a season in which he finished 10–6.[95]

Killian apparently made peace with his employer in 1907 and enjoyed one of the greatest seasons ever by a Tiger pitcher. Not only did he go 25–13 with a 1.78 ERA, but he also won a league-high five games without a loss coming out of the bullpen. Perhaps starting to experience arm problems or simply fatigue, Killian was limited to one four-inning relief appearance against the Cubs in the World Series that fall. A sinkerball pitcher, Killian began to be used less often in 1908. His victory total dropped by over 50 percent as he won only 12 times and was unimpressive in his only Series appearance.

Killian began 1909 as seldom-used option for Hughie Jennings. Although his arm required nursing at times, on July 16, Killian once again earned his moniker of Twilight Ed as he pitched a complete game, 18-inning scoreless tie against Washington.[96] Not only was the start typical for the left-hander in that he earned no credit for his excellent work, it may have had an effect on the Tigers' World Series loss that year. Killian's opponent that day was Dolly Gray, at best a journeyman pitcher, who this day also held the opposition scoreless. It has been reported that National League president John

Heydler had witnessed Gray's fine performance that day and encouraged Pirate manager Fred Clarke to open the Series against the Tigers with Babe Adams, a pitcher Heydler felt pitched in similar fashion to the Washington twirler. Killian, on the other hand, did not pitch in the Series. Hughie Jennings would later face criticism for his decision not to use him. Whether or not Killian was able to pitch was not clearly explained. Perhaps it was a mystery best confined to the Twilight Zone. Now in the "twilight" of his career, Killian saw his effectiveness abandon him and after losing his last three decisions after taking four victories, Killian was sold Toronto and released the following year.

One further note of interest on the one-time Tiger star: Killian once went four seasons without allowing a home run, a span that covered a record 1,001 innings pitched.[97] In fact, Killian's rate of allowing only one home run for every 178 innings pitched is a record which likely will never be broken.

Bill Donovan

Right-Handed Pitcher
Born: 10/13/1876   Died: 12/9/1923
Detroit Tigers: 1903–1912, 1918   Major League Career: 1898–1918

Another one-time ace who suffered arm problems in 1909, Bill Donovan had accepted owner Frank Navin's offer to go to a Hot Springs spa to help rehabilitate his arm. Called "Wild Bill" because of his propensity for nightlife as well as handing out bases on balls early in his career, by the close of the first decade of the 1900s Donovan had established himself as a pitcher capable of dominating the opposition with his power pitching. After winning only one game in each of his first three seasons, posting a cumulative 3–10 record, Donovan won a league-high 25 games for Brooklyn in 1901. He fanned 226 that season, a career high, but still had not mastered control as he walked 152 batters. After a 17–15 campaign in 1902, Donovan jumped to the Tigers for 1903. The next three seasons, Donovan averaged 17 wins, but also nearly 16 losses while pitching for poor Detroit teams, before falling to a decidedly disappointing 9–15 season in 1906. For the first time since establishing himself as a starter, Donovan's ERA rose above 3.00 and his strikeouts dropped below 135, all the way down to 85. The 1907 season was a different story as Donovan stormed back with another 25-win season. He lost only four games all year, finishing with a league record for winning percentage of .862, a mark which would not be topped until Lefty Grove went 31–4 in 1931 for the Philadelphia Athletics. The ace of the Tigers' first pennant-winner pitched well in the World Series, but went 0–1 even though he allowed only 17 hits in 21 innings and posted a 1.71 ERA.

Donovan was a big contributor in 1908 as well, going 18–7, but lost two more games in the World Series during the Tigers' rematch with the Cubs.

Even during his banner year of 1907, Donovan sometimes was kept out of cold-weather games and this strategy for maintaining his health intensified in 1909. He pitched in only three games prior to June 21, when he tossed a shutout against St. Louis.[98] Wild Bill finished 8–7, just fifth on his team in wins, but his 2.31 ERA and four shutouts showed that when able, Donovan still was a capable hurler.

Donovan's money pitch was his fastball, which had both speed and movement.[99] As Donovan had pitched well down the stretch and had a strong pedigree, Hughie Jennings was not criticized when he announced his decision to start him in the second game of the World Series. Donovan rewarded his manager's faith with a 7–2 win. According to Fred Lieb, Donovan's actions almost led to a Detroit forfeit of Game 4.[100] In the second inning, Donovan relayed instructions to the Tigers' third base coach, walking out to the coach in order to do so. Umpire Bill Klem told Donovan to get back to the bench, but Donovan barked back, "I'm talking to this man. You go on with your umpiring business, and I'll look after my business." Despite an initial admonishment by Klem, Donovan would not leave the field. Klem then turned to Jennings and told him that if Donovan were not off the field in 30 seconds, the game would be forfeited to Pittsburgh. It was a promise Bill could not ignore.

As well as Donovan had pitched in Game 2, he was still not a consensus pick to start Game 7 as the weather had turned much colder and it was said Donovan could not get loose in cold weather. His control that day was dreadful, or as Honus Wagner remembered years later, "Wild Bill ... lived up to his name that day."[101] Donovan walked six batters and hit another, yet somehow left in the second inning with the Tigers trailing just 2–0. Mullin, who relieved Donovan, had run out of gas and allowed six more men to score before the game was ended.

Arm problems continued to limit Donovan's appearances, although he went 17–7 in 1910, but after a 10–9 season in 1911, Donovan made only three appearances in 1912. He began managing in the minor leagues and was named manager of the New York Highlanders in 1915. Donovan even called on himself to pitch a few times that year, but did not add any victories for his team, losing three. After a sixth-place finish in 1917, Bill was let go as manager. He coached under Jennings in 1918 and won the final game of his pitching career before managing again in the minor leagues. Donovan got his second chance to lead a big league club in 1921 with the Philadelphia Phillies, but was relieved of his duties before the end of the year.

On December 8, 1923, Donovan was traveling to Chicago for baseball's winter meetings.[102] Rumors had it he was going to be given the opportunity to manage the Washington Senators. Donovan never reached Chicago. The train crashed and Wild Bill was one of nine people who did not survive. One of his traveling companions that night was George Weiss, who later became the highly successful general manager of the New York Yankees.

Donovan continues to rate high among Tiger pitchers almost 80 years after his death. His 144 wins in a Detroit uniform ranks eighth all time and he finished his overall career with an impressive 186–139 record.

Ralph Works

Right-Handed Pitcher
Born 3/16/1888   Died 8/8/1941
Detroit Tigers 1909–1912   Major League Career 1909–1913

With the Tigers having rid themselves of veterans Ed Siever and late-season pickup George Winter after the two combined to go 3–11 for Detroit in 1908, Hughie Jennings' second-line pitching staff consisted of raw youngsters. The most successful in 1909 was the youngest of all, 21-year-old Ralph Works, who went 4–1 with a 1.97 ERA. Works was unimpressive against Pittsburgh in the World Series, allowing four hits and two runs in his only appearance. Unfortunately for the Tigers, Works was unable to pick up the slack when Detroit's pitching began to fail in 1910, going 3–6. While he went 11–5 in 1911, albeit with an ERA nearly half a run higher than the league average, he was again a .333 pitcher, going 5–10 in 1912 before he was sent to Cincinnati.

Ricks took his own life in 1941 in an apparent double suicide with his wife.[103]

Kid Speer

Left-Handed Pitcher
Born 6/16/1886   Died 1/13/1946
Detroit Tigers 1909   Major League Career 1909

Lefty George "Kid" Speer split eight decisions for the Tigers in his only big league season. Pitching 76 innings, the 23-year-old Speer fanned just 12 batters and opponents hit .293 against him, yet he showed good control, surrendering just 13 walks and posted a respectable 2.83 ERA.

George Suggs

Right-Handed Pitcher
Born 7/7/1882   Died 4/4/1949
Detroit Tigers 1908–1909   Major League Career 1908–1915

The one pitcher the Tigers would have been wise to hold onto who started the season with the team was George Suggs. Suggs had appeared in six games in 1908, going 1–1. In 1909, Suggs could manage just a 1–3 mark, but was pitching effectively with a 2.03 ERA and .228 opponents' batting average. Feeling Suggs was not going to provide enough support, Jennings dispatched him to Mobile in the Southern Association for Bill Lelivelt. The move proved shortsighted as Suggs resurfaced in the major leagues with the Reds in 1910 and, pitching for a mediocre (75–79) team, won 20 games. He added 15 more in both 1911 and 1912. After a bad year (8–13) in 1913, Suggs jumped to the Baltimore Terrapins in the Federal League and had one outstanding season, going 24–14 in 1914 before an 11–17 farewell tour in 1915.

Bill Lelivelt

Right-Handed Pitcher
Born 10/21/1884   Died 2/14/1968
Detroit Tigers 1909–1910   Major League Career 1909–1910

Bill Lelivelt, the man obtained for George Suggs, was not an improvement in 1909 or afterwards. He lost his only decision in 1909, appearing in four games with a 4.50 ERA. He made one more appearance, in 1910, losing a complete-game effort.

Ed Lafitte

Right-Handed Pitcher
Born 4/7/1886   Died 4/12/1971
Detroit Tigers 1909–1912   Major League Career 1909–1915

Ed Lafitte was yet another rookie to work for the Tigers in 1909. He was ineffective, pitching in three games, going 0–1 and allowing 22 hits and a pair of home runs in 14 innings. Lafitte did not play for Detroit in 1910, but returned in 1911 to go 11–8, but did not win again in the majors until 1914, when he was pitching for Brooklyn's Federal League entry. Enjoying his best "big league" season, Lafitte went 18–15 before finishing up with the league itself in 1915, posting an 8–11 record between Brooklyn and Buffalo.

Elijah Jones

Right-Handed Pitcher
Born 1/27/1882   Died 4/29/1943
Detroit Tigers 1907, 1909   Major League Career 1907, 1909

Elijah Jones, a right-hander, appeared in four games in 1907. More interesting than his 1–1 record in two starts in 1909 was his nickname, Bumpus, which was given to him in memory of the Cincinnati Reds' pitcher of the 1890s. The original Bumpus is the only man in history to pitch a no-hitter in his debut, his only appearance of 1892. In 1893, Jones developed a prehistoric version of Steve Blass disease, when he could not throw over the plate, walking 42 men in 32 and two-thirds innings and posting a 10.19 ERA. He never pitched in the majors again.

Coming to the Tigers

POS	Name	How They Came to Detroit
C	Boss Schmidt	Purchased from Minneapolis of the American Association in 1906
1B	Claude Rossman	Purchased from the Cleveland Naps in 1906
1B	Tom Jones	Traded by the St. Louis Browns for Claude Rossman in 1909
2B	Germany Schaefer	Purchased from Milwaukee of the American Association in 1904
2B	Jim Delahanty	Traded by the Washington Senators for Germany Schaefer and Red Killefer in 1909.
SS	Donie Bush	Purchased from Indianapolis of the American Association in 1908 for $6,000
3B	George Moriarty	Purchased from the New York Highlanders in 1909
OF	Ty Cobb	Purchased from Augusta of the South Atlantic League in 1905
OF	Sam Crawford	Jumped to the Tigers in 1903 from the Cincinnati Reds
OF	Davy Jones	Purchased from Minneapolis of the American Association in 1906
OF	Matty McIntyre	Traded by Buffalo of the Eastern League in 1903 with Cy Ferry for Ernie Courtney, Rube Kisinger and Sport McAllister.
C	Oscar Stanage	Purchased from Newark of the Eastern League in 1908
OF	Red Killefer	Drafted in the Rule 5 draft in 1906 from Kalamazoo of the Southern Michigan League
C	Heinie Beckendorf	Signed as a free agent in 1909
C	Joe Casey	Signed as free agent in 1909
1B	Del Gainer	Purchased from Grafton of the Pennsylvania–West Virginia League in 1909
1B	Hughie Jennings	Drafted in the Rule 5 draft in 1906 from Baltimore of the Eastern League
P	George Mullin	Signed as free agent in 1902
P	Ed Willett	Purchased from Wichita of the Western Association in 1906
P	Ed Summers	Signed as free agent in 1908
P	Ed Killian	Traded by the Cleveland Naps in 1904 with Jesse Stovall for Billy Lush
P	Bill Donovan	Jumped to the Tigers in 1903 from the Brooklyn Superbas
P	Kid Speer	Signed as free agent in 1909
P	Ralph Works	Purchased from Syracuse of the New York State League in 1908

POS	Name	How They Came to Detroit
P	George Suggs	Traded by Mobile of the Southern Association in 1909 with Frank Allen for Bill Lelivelt and $2,800
P	Bill Lelivelt	Signed as free agent in 1909
P	Elijah Jones	Signed as free agent in 1909
P	Ed Lafitte	Purchased from Springfield of the Three-I League in 1906

◆ 16 ◆

THE PIRATES BEYOND 1909

Following the memorable celebration of their world championship, the Pirates had scheduled a barnstorming trip, which they decided to cancel the trip due to projected bad weather. With the trip no longer on the schedule, the players split up, going their separate ways home for a well-deserved break, including Honus Wagner, who did in fact go with Ty Cobb on the hunting trip they both had talked about as the Series began. Both Hall of Famers went to Cobb's native Georgia for a bird hunting exposition in January 1910.

As the players rested and recouped, Pirates president Barney Dreyfuss looked forward to 1910, to what he thought would be the beginning of a second dynasty for the club, the first since the early days of the twentieth century when the Bucs captured three consecutive National League crowns from 1901 to 1903. Dreyfuss exclaimed to Fred Clarke when his manager visited the Steel City in the winter from his farm in Kansas, "Fred, I guess we have a team that'll stay up there for some time, like our team of 1901."[1]

Clarke was also just as confident and confided, "That's right boss. There are a few of us getting older, but those Cubs aren't getting any younger either. We're a great team, and there's nothing in sight that should finish ahead of us in 1910."[2] The Pirate manager's assessment was rosy for sure. After all, they had enjoyed sustained success since 1901, the worst season being an 87–66 mark in 1904, winning four National League crowns and, of course, were the reigning World Series champions. But one thing that seemed to be a measure of concern was the age of the club, since three regulars and three of their better pitchers were approaching their mid-thirties.

To stay on top, the Pirates needed an influx of youth. On the mound, youthful talent seemed to be in abundance as they were encouraged by the 1909 performance of fall classic hero Babe Adams. Howie Camnitz, Nick Maddox and Lefty Leifield were also in their early-to-mid-twenties. Because there were concerns with some of the staff, Dreyfuss and Clarke needed to find suitable replacements for thirty-three-year-old Vic Willis, who won 22 games, as well as Deacon Phillippe and Sam Leever, both of whom were 37 and were on the back end of their careers.

Some of the candidates included Chick Brandom, Bill Powell and Sam Frock. Brandom, an alumnus of the University of Oklahoma, spent the season with the big club during their championship run, pitching eleven games in relief with two starts, winning his only decision, with a sparkling 1.11 ERA. Physically he did have an issue, although it was one that was not expected to be a concern in 1910. His second toe lapped over his first and when he threw a pitch, it would press down painfully on the lower one. The constant rubbing of the one toe over the

After 16 years as manager of the Pirates, Fred Clarke decided to retire after a 73–81 finish in 1915. Clarke retired as the most successful manager in team history with a 1422–969 mark (courtesy of the Pittsburgh Pirates).

other caused the big toe to become swollen at various times. Despite the fact he tried different methods when he pitched to alleviate the situation, nothing seemed to work. Doctors wanted to perform an operation, which, in essence, would amputate the second toe to end the issue. If it did work, the Bucs might have another in a long line of outstanding pitchers.

Bill Powell was a tall man, 6'2", and was said to have a "deceptive delivery."[3] Powell also spent some time with the world champions in 1909, although only tossing seven and one-third innings, losing his lone decision. The issue that caused the tall Richmond native to see such limited action was an injury he received in his other love, basketball. A member of the Homestead club in the Central Basketball League, Powell was cautioned by Dreyfuss not to play in the offseason before the 1910 campaign, so he could be at full strength to help the Bucs defend their title.

Frock also spent the entire season with the Bucs in 1909, tossing 36 and one-third innings with a 2–1 mark and 2.48 ERA. Clarke had high hopes for the Baltimore native. Frock had an exceptional curveball and was considered to be a very smart pitcher.

Despite the issues with age, it was Adams who was considered the potential cornerstone of this staff, hopefully being able to continue the formidable legacy of Pirate hurlers in the early twentieth century. The World Series hero was expected to get a more important role in the team's starting rotation. He was also getting his fair share of adulation for his fall classic heroics in the offseason. Fans wanting to hear of his tales in the Series constantly approached him. A Chicago promoter tried to get him to commit to a barnstorming trip to Cuba, which he declined after conferring with Dreyfuss. (Dreyfuss was not a proponent of barnstorming trips in the offseason, thinking the players needed rest after a long campaign. He also had issues with players playing basketball and football, feeling these sports were too physical and players could get hurt.) Adams was given several banquets, including a smoker in Bethany, Missouri, where the local paper noted how level-headed Adams remained with all the attention. "Mr. Adams is very pleasing to talk to, and appears a gentleman in every sense. His fine record as a ball player has made no difference in his personal and social life. He is the same Charles Adams."[4]

He had to be the same Charles "Babe" Adams, if not a better one on the mound, if the team was to overcome one of Dreyfuss's offseason decisions that affected his pitching staff, the decision to release Vic Willis. Even though Willis had an amazing season for the world champions, winning 22 games, and was a member of the 20-win club for the team in each of his four seasons in the Smoky City, it was the thought that his drinking issues were excessive and that he was not the best influence on the young Pirate pitching staff.[5] Because of this Dreyfuss decided to sell the pitcher to St Louis, leaving a void that would be hard to fill.

While not as important as Willis to the framework of the 1909 Pirates, another hole in the team that Dreyfuss and Clarke had to address was one that was very apparent during the World Series, first base. Even though the fans gave Bill Abstein a big hand at the post-series celebration at Forbes Field despite his horrendous play against Detroit, the Pirate president was not pleased at all with his play and put him on waivers in January 1910.

One potential replacement for the bumbling first baseman was Bud Sharpe. The 28-year-old had played one season for the Boston Doves in 1905, and had been in the minors since, the last three seasons with Newark of the Eastern League. Not considered a strong hitter, as his .241 average in 1909 indicated, Sharpe nonetheless was considered one of the best glove men in minor league baseball. The thought was he could be a dramatic improvement over Abstein, who not only had a poor World Series defensively, but cost the club a few games by intercepting throws from Chief Wilson in right field instead of letting the tosses of the strong-armed right fielder go home.

There was also the suggestion of letting Wagner go to first and moving Abbatacchio to short. This was something that was a possibility, as Wagner had some experience at first, playing 75 games there in 1898 for Louisville and Abbatacchio was primarily a shortstop for the Boston Doves the first half of his career. Who to play at first base seemed like a sticky situation and

Pirate Hall of Fame shortstop Honus Wagner was a coach for the club later in his life (courtesy of the Pittsburgh Pirates).

was one that plagued Clarke all season.

Offensively, age was also a problem as the question of whether or not Wagner or Clarke would retire. While those rumors seemed to exist every year as the great shortstop aged, it was thought to be something concocted by some newspapers rather than anything Wagner confided to someone.[6] Another reason Wagner wanted to return was that the Chalmers Car Company decided to award a car to the player who had the highest batting average in the majors. Wagner, who had won six of the last seven National League crowns, wanted that car. He claimed that the auto "has the usual medals and loving cup beaten by a mile."[7] For Clarke, he put the rumors to rest quickly by stating he would man his usual post in left field to help his club defend their title.

The rest of the Pirate infield seemed set. Dots Miller, who had a fine rookie season with the Bucs in 1909, was a lock to retain is starting job. It was thought that he would be so much stronger with another year of experience. If he didn't go to first, Wagner was a sure thing at shortstop while Bobby Byrne manned third. The outfield of Clarke, Leach and Wilson was thought to be one of the strongest in the league. A young Vin Campbell, a 22-year-old phenom from Vanderbilt University, lurked in the background if any one went down to injury. Behind the plate there was no need for a phenom to be in the wings waiting, as the Bucs ironman backstop George Gibson certainly would take the majority of the assignments.

On paper it looked like the sky was the limit for this championship club, but as the old adage goes, that's why they don't play the games on paper. The season started out well enough with the Pirates leading the National League through May 23. Following a loss to the Giants that evening, Pittsburgh lost six games in a row to fall behind the Cubs and they never recovered. Dreyfuss would exclaim later, "Our 1910 team was my biggest disappointment in baseball. Never did I see a great team fold so quickly."[8]

Just about everything went in reverse in 1910. The Pirates scored one-third of a run less despite the fact they hit better, .266 compared to a 1909 average of .260. On the mound is where they really suffered. A spectacular 2.07 ERA in 1909 ballooned to 2.83 the following year. A 2.91 runs-per-game figure during their championship run became 3.74 in 1910.

Howie Camnitz, Lefty Leifield and Nick Maddox, who were so dominant during the championship run with 66 wins, became very average combining for a 29–29 mark. The three youngsters that Clarke was hoping would take over for the older pitchers, Brandon, Powell and Frock, provided the club with absolutely nothing. Powell and Frock were 4–6 (all decisions being Powell's as Frock tossed only thee innings) while Brandom never pitched for the Bucs again. The only good thing that came from the trio was the fact the Pirates were able to get Kirby White from Boston, who would win ten games for the Bucs, for Frock and Sharpe, another of Clarke's young guns who didn't pan out, hitting only .188.

On the positive end Adams lived up to his promise, winning a team-best 18 games with a 2.24 ERA, while the old man Deacon Phillippe went 14–2 in limited action for a National League best .875 winning percentage. It would prove to be the last hurrah for the 38-year-old veteran, who retired the following season after six unproductive innings.

Offensively the team was not as bad, although there were few bright spots there also. The situation at first base was confusing to say the least. Seven men during the season manned the spot at first. Purchased from St. Paul of the American Association in December for $4,000, John Flynn, enjoyed the most success at the position, hitting .274 over 96 games with a National-League-fifth-best six home runs. Ham Hyatt, Jack Kading, Bill McKechnie, Dots Miller, Wagner and Sharpe all took turns at first in 1910.

Miller had a horrific sophomore season as he was out for month with an injury as he hit a meager .227, while Leach and Clarke, both got off to horrible starts that they were never really able to recover from. Perhaps the worst issue came with the start of their Hall of Fame shortstop. After his average stood at just .238 on June 17, rumors and innuendoes hurt the sensitive Wagner as the season went on.

There was talk that Miller and Flynn engaged in fisticuffs. It was reported that Miller and Wagner were upset that Flynn was given the first base job over Sharpe. When the fight supposedly occurred, Wagner and Gibson stepped in to stop it and were both decked. In the book *Honus Wagner: The Life of Baseball's Flying Dutchman*, Arthur Hittner pointed out that the report came in a Pittsburgh paper that often specialized in sensational reporting ... and was owned by a unhappy Pirate stockholder. He also noted that Miller and Flynn were roommates and friends.[9]

There were also reports that Wagner's issues had to do with his obsession with automobiles and a developing drinking issue.[10] Whether they were true or not, it was affecting the sensitive shortstop. Eventually the Hall of Famer was successfully able to put the rumors behind him when he caught fire as

By the mid–1910s the Pirates had fallen from the ranks of champions to mediocrity. Pictured left to right are Honus Wagner, Cozy Dolan, Fred Clarke and Marty O'Toole, members of the 1913 team (courtesy of Library of Congress, Bain Collection, Prints & Photographs Division, 10375u).

the season went on, eventually breaking the .330 plateau, before settling with a .320 average for the campaign. While it was a tremendous finish, it wasn't enough to overtake Sherry Magee of the Phillies for the NL batting crown and far off from Napoleon Lajoie and Ty Cobb for the best average in the majors, both of whom shared the magnificent prize of a Chalmers Automobile instead of Wagner.

On the positive end there were two the bright spots in the lineup. Third baseman Bobby Byrne hit .296 with a league-leading 178 hits and 43 doubles while outfielder Vin Campbell was the one young player that Clarke was looking to for success in 1910 that actually succeeded, with a .320 average in 282 at-bats.

The club fell 24½ games below their 1909 output and was 22 games behind the Cubs in third place. The dynasty that Clarke and Dreyfuss hoped for never came to pass. Eventually trades by the club of names the likes of Miller, Leach, Byrne, Wilson, Camnitz and Leifield returned less successful ones such as Cozy Dolan, Bob Harmon, Ed Konetchy, Mike Mowrey, King Cole and Solly Hofman. By 1914 the club had fallen under .500 and Dreyfuss's predicted return to the World Series would take an additional 16 years. It was then a grizzled veteran hurler by the name of Charles "Babe" Adams had one last moment in the sun, as the only member of the 1909 championship club to win a second world championship for the Pirates in 1925.

Leaving the Pirates

POS	Name	Reason for Leaving
C	George Gibson	Put on waivers by the Pirates in 1916.
1B	Bill Abstein	Put on waivers by the Pirates following the 1909 campaign after his poor play in the Series
2B	Dots Miller	Traded to the Cardinals after the 1913 campaign with Art Butler, Cozy Dolan, Hank Robinson and Chief Wilson for Bob Harmon, Ed Konetchy and Mike Mowrey
SS	Honus Wagner	Retired in 1917
3B	Jap Barbeau	Traded in August 1909 with Alan Storke to the Cardinals for Bobby Byrne
3B	Bobby Byrne	Traded in August 1913 with Howie Camnitz to the Phillies for Cozy Dolan and cash
OF	Tommy Leach	Traded in May 1912 with Lefty Leifield to the Cubs for King Cole and Solly Hofman.
OF	Fred Clarke	Retired in 1915.
OF	Chief Wilson	Traded to the Cardinals after the 1913 campaign with Art Butler, Cozy Dolan, Hank Robinson and Dots Miller for Bob Harmon, Ed Konetchy and Mike Mowrey.
UT	Alan Storke	Traded in August 1909 with Jap Barbeau to the Cardinals for Bobby Byrne.

POS	Name	Reason for Leaving
UT	Ed Abbaticchio	Purchased by Boston Doves in July 1910.
UT	Ham Hyatt	Put on waivers following 1914 season.
OF	Ward Miller	Traded to the Reds with cash for Kid Durbin in May 1909.
C	Mike Simon	Jumped to St. Louis of the Federal League in 1914
UT	Paddy O'Connor	Released; went to Kansas City of the American Association in 1910
PR	Kid Durbin	Released; went to Omaha of the Western League in 1911
P	Vic Willis	Purchased by the Cardinals in 1910
P	Lefty Leifield	Traded in May of 1912 with Tommy Leach to the Cubs for King Cole and Solly Hofman.
P	Nick Maddox	Sold to Kansas City of the American Association in September 1910.
P	Babe Adams	Released; went to Springfield of the Western Association in 1927
P	Deacon Phillippe	Retired in 1911
P	Sam Leever	Released; went to Minneapolis of the American Association in 1911
P	Sam Frock	Traded to the Boston Doves in April 1910 with Bud Sharpe for Kirby White
P	Chick Brandom	Released; went to Kansas City of the American Association in 1910
P	Bill Powell	Sold to Kansas City of the American Association in July 1910.
P	Harry Camnitz	Released; went to Jersey City of the Eastern League in 1910
P	Gene Moore	Released; went to Galveston of the Texas League in 1912
P	Charlie Wacker	Sold to Milwaukee of the American Association in 1909
P	Howie Camnitz	Traded in August 1913 with Bobby Byrne to the Phillies for Cozy Dolan and cash.

◆ 17 ◆

THE TIGERS BEYOND 1909

The Tigers were still a young club, with players averaging only 26.3 years old, following their third consecutive American League championship in 1909, with their key player, Ty Cobb, only 22 years old. The future indeed seemed to be extremely bright for the Detroit Tigers. Their potent offense, which led the junior circuit in runs, hits, doubles, stolen bases, batting average, on-base percentage and total bases in 1909, was in tact so the club certainly was the odds-on favorites to reach the World Series for an incredible fourth consecutive time.

As the team was preparing for its defense, it set off for a barnstorming trip to Havana, Cuba. The ballclub stopped in Tampa before embarking on their final leg of its journey to the baseball-mad country. Playing a warm-up game there in a field with no bleachers, about 400 fans braved a torrid downpour to see the Tigers and Matty McIntyre, who became very popular in Tampa playing winter ball there for the two previous seasons. Bill Lelivelt tossed a fine game, leading the club to a 9–1 victory.

There were a few concerns for the club before the trip, the biggest one being the health of their feisty third baseman, George Moriarty. Injured in the seventh game of the just-completed fall classic, Moriarty had been walking with the help of a cane since the end of the Series. Despite the fact he was still hobbled, the Detroit third baseman was determined to play and made the trip to Havana. McIntyre, who was the manager on this excursion, had thought about putting the Detroit third baseman at first, but true to his stubborn nature, Moriarty started the series at his natural position.

While grateful for his third baseman's effort to make it to Havana despite the pain, McIntyre certainly had to be disappointed in those that did not make the trip. Second baseman Jim Delahanty stayed home in Cleveland, Oscar Stanage remained in Detroit with no explanation of why he wasn't accompanying the team, while pitcher Ed Summers declined due to illness.

World Series hero George Mullin originally committed to make the sojourn, but first wired McIntyre he'd be late joining the team, then later declined to go all together, claiming illness.

To make sure he had enough pitchers, McIntyre solicited the services of Lelivelt who was with the team for a while in 1909.

With the team in tow, the Tigers made it to their destination in Havana, winning the first two games to Cuban teams amid much controversy. There were several questionable calls, but one so egregious it infuriated the Detroit bench immensely. With no one on base, Ed Willett began his motion to the plate, then paused before delivering the pitch. With men on base it was a balk, but with no one on it should have been nothing according to the rules of the game. The Cuban umpire unbelievably sent the runner to first, prompting the Tigers to leave the field in protest. The police stepped in to convince the team to retake the field so the fans would not become unruly, and then overruled the umpire, prompting him to remove the runner from first and send him back to the plate to bat. The Tigers returned to the field and peace was restored.[1]

As the 12-game series between the Tigers and the Havana and Almendaras clubs (six games played against each team) began to unfold, it was apparent the depleted Detroit club was no match for their opponents. The Tigers dropped seven in a row after winning three of the first four, losing the series four games to eight.

It was a frustrating series. They forfeited their financial take due to the defeat, since many of their teammates did not show up; poor umpiring and questionable pitching were also issues. There was nothing left than to board their boat back to Florida and hope that 1910 would bring with it better times and another trip to the fall classic, in another effort to win that elusive world championship.

As the team was preparing for the season, there were several rumors of trades coming out of Detroit, the most prominent of which was a deal with Cleveland involving Nig Clarke. Clarke was a catcher with the Indians who once smacked a professional record eight home runs in a game in 1902 while playing for Corsicana of the Texas League, and hit .274 in 1909. The hope was he could stabilize Detroit's catching situation offensively, adding another bat to their already powerful offense. After Navin denied such rumors several times, the Tigers decided to go into the campaign with their lineup virtually in tact.

Like the Pirates, there were rumors of discord among the championship roster that Navin decided to go forward with. Unlike the situation in Pittsburgh, the rumors were all true and mostly focused towards one man, Ty Cobb.

Two of the greatest players ever to play the game were Ty Cobb (left) and Christy Matthewson (right). Cobb went onto play for the Tigers for seventeen more seasons after 1909, but never again played in a World Series (courtesy of Library of Congress, Bain Collection, Prints & Photographs Division, 09869u).

After his legal troubles that followed him through the 1909 Series, Cobb's anger led to another situation in 1910. His anger was notorious, even resulting in a bloody fight with an umpire in 1921. After being called out in two close calls at home plate, Cobb challenged Hall of Fame umpire Billy Evans to a fight under the grandstands in Detroit. Al Schacht, more well known as baseball's crown prince for his comical act during games following his short career with Washington, described the fight the following way. "When the game ended they both went under the grandstand while the members of both teams became spectators. Billy posed like a real fighter while Ty stalked him like a Tiger and then suddenly hit him in the jaw. Down went Evans with Ty on top of him. With his knee on Evans' chest, Ty held Billy by the throat and tried to choke him. We finally got him off Billy and that was the end of the fight."[2] In 1910, though, it was another situation in Cleveland when he knocked down an African-American waiter whom he felt did not show significant respect for "a white gentleman from Georgia."[3] These were the issues that led to the conflicts that took place between Cobb and his teammates.

The players were not only upset at the Tiger great for his legal issues in Cleveland that led to his excessive travel that sapped his strength in the recently completed World Series as well as the one that took place in 1910, but the fact that manager Hughie Jennings had apparently no rules for Cobb. According the Al Stump in his memorable biography on the Tiger great, the players had a difficult time dealing with Cobb's favored status: "Matty McIntyre, Sam Crawford, Davy Jones and other regulars criticized Hughie Jennings for not lowering the boom on 'his pet,' who reported to spring training camp on whatever date he wished, insisted on a set of batter-to-baserunner signs dictated and flashed by Cobb from the plate, and who required, and received, the only private hotel quarters provided team members when on the road."[4]

Crawford who played with Cobb for 13 seasons, explained how difficult it was to have him as a teammate by using an example from his rookie season in 1905. "He wrote an autobiography, you know, and he spends a lot of time in there telling how terrible he was treated when he first came up to Detroit, as a rookie, in 1905. About how we weren't fair to him and how we tried to 'get' him.... We weren't cannibals or heathens. We were all ballplayers together, trying to get along. Every rookie gets a little hazing, but most of them just take it and laugh. Cobb took it the wrong way. He came up with an antagonistic attitude, which in his mind turned and little razzing into a life-or-death struggle."[5] The great Tiger center fielder also remembered what used to get under Cobb's skin more than anything else, when Crawford had a better day than Cobb, an attitude that was not indicative of a consummate teammate. "One thing that really used to get Ty's goat was when I'd have a good day and he didn't. Oh, would he ever moan then."[6]

It wasn't just Cobb's teammates that had issues with the Tiger superstar in 1910, so did players in the rest of the league. Wagner wasn't the only player who looked forward to being awarded an automobile from the Chalmers Company for winning the batting title, so did Cobb. He was locked in a life-and-death struggle for the batting crown with the great Napoleon Lajoie down to the last day of the season. Both Hall of Fame players had far outdistanced their National League rivals in the race for the best average in the majors and the Chalmers automobile, a model 30 that was considered the ultimate in luxury for the time, that went with the honor.[7]

As the season came to a climax, Cobb seemed to pull away just enough with a .384 average, that he decided to sit out the final two games of what was turning into a disappointing campaign for the Tigers, due to an eye injury he had suffered with during the season. To win the car, Lajoie had to be just about perfect in a doubleheader the Indians played against the St. Louis Browns on the final day of the year. Browns manager Jack O'Connor was not a fan of Cobb and did not want to see him win the car he cherished. O'Connor allegedly instructed his third baseman, Red Corriden, to play so far back, inciting Lajoie to bunt, so the Indians great could get the needed hits to win the title by just bunting towards third.

A brilliant player, Lajoie took full advantaged of the maneuver as he was safe with seven bunt hits in the doubleheader, 8-for-9 overall, to apparently beat out Cobb for the car and batting crown by a fraction of a percent, according to several newspapers across the country. When American League president Ban Johnson released the official figures a few days later, Cobb and not Lajoie was the official winner, .38415 to .38411. (The ironic twist was that in 1981, *The Sporting News* discovered errors in box scores that credited Cobb twice for a 2-for-3 performance against Detroit. The final stats, officially credited 71 years later, had Lajoie winning the batting crown with a .384 mark compared to Cobb's adjusted figure of .383.)

Disgusted, Johnson investigated the claims of inappropriate behavior by the Browns, eventually insisting that O'Connor and pitching coach Harry Howell be dropped by St. Louis while he absolved Corriden from any wrong doing. O'Connor sued the club for the $5,000 owed to him from a contract that ran through 1911 and successfully recouped his money, but was out as the Browns manager. As far as the car went, the Chalmers Company decided to award both men a car to settle the controversy. But the situation was a reminder of how players around the game felt about Cobb.

It was that kind of conflict that filtered within the team and from outside, conflict that ended the club's three-year run of American League championships. The 1911 *Spalding Guide* referred to the conflict, also giving kudos to Jennings for getting the club to win as many games as it did in 1910. "Occasional rumors were heard that there was dissention on the part of the Detroit players. If this were the case the manager must be given credit for handling the differences with some diplomacy, for it was not until the season was in its extremity that Detroit could no longer depend upon beating the Philadelphia's (the Athletics)."[8]

Whether it was conflict or just a failure to play at the level they had been accustomed to the previous three seasons, there were various statistical comparisons between the two seasons that show why there was a decline in play. Offensively, after leading the league in nine offensive categories in 1909, the Tigers only emerged as the best in two in 1910, one being the most important of them all, runs scored with 679, thirteen more than in their championship season.

That being said, pitching was a source for their decline in 1910. George Mullin and Will Bill Donovan were the only two hurlers to remain dominant, with 21–12 and 17–7 marks, respectively. The club's 2.26 ERA in 1909 ballooned up to 2.82 the following season. They surrendered 89 more runs in 1910, 582, the sixth worst in the circuit compared to 493, which was third best in the American League in 1909. Walks also were significantly higher, with Tiger pitchers issuing 460 free passes in 1910 compared to 359 in 1909.

Bottom line, the illusive world championship which Detroit came so tantalizingly close to between 1907 and 1909, a championship that certainly should have come to pass due to the relative young age of the Tigers, took 26 years to become a reality. After Detroit fell to the Cardinals in seven games in the memorable 1934 fall classic, they finally gave Navin his first world championship the following season. That year the Tigers gained a long-awaited revenge against the Cubs for their World Series victories against Detroit in 1907 and 1908, by defeating Chicago in six games for their first World Series championship. A little over a month later after seeing his beloved club finally achieving his dream, Navin suffered a heart attack while horseback riding and died.

While Navin did finally get an opportunity to celebrate a championship, this era of the Tigers would not live that dream. Their best player, Ty Cobb, put the blame directly on Navin. When recalling that he knew the Tigers pennant chances would no longer be there following 1909, Cobb stated, "It wasn't hard for me to guess. Navin and his scouts couldn't make a good trade if it bit them."[9]

Writer Al Stump said it best, though, when he included Cobb's lack of being a consummate teammate, reportedly alienating one Tiger after another, as one of the reasons this team never lived up to its potential and win a title.[10] As incredible and perfect as his play could be on the field, his actions off it had to be a major contributor to the fact that Cobb would not only never experience the joy of a world championship, but also never participate in another fall classic, despite the fact he was only 22 years old in 1909 and had a career that would last until 1928.

Leaving the Tigers

POS	Name	Reason for Leaving
C	Boss Schmidt	Released; went to Providence of the International League in 1912
1B	Claude Rossman	Traded to the St. Louis Browns in August 1909 for Tom Jones
1B	Tom Jones	Released; went to Milwaukee of the American Association in 1911
2B	Germany Schaefer	Traded to the Washington Senators with Red Killefer for Jim Delahanty
2B	Jim Delahanty	Released; went to Minneapolis of the American Association in 1912.

POS	Name	Reason for Leaving
SS	Donie Bush	Put on waivers in 1921
3B	George Moriarty	Released; went to the White Sox as a free agent in 1916
OF	Ty Cobb	Released; went to the Athletics as a free agent in 1927
OF	Sam Crawford	Released; went to Los Angeles of the Pacific Coast League in 1918
OF	Davy Jones	Purchased by the White Sox in 1913. Came back to Tigers in 1918 where he finished his career.
OF	Matty McIntyre	Purchased by the White Sox in 1911
C	Oscar Stanage	Released; went to Los Angeles of the Pacific Coast League in 1921. Returned to Tigers in 1925 then ended his career with Evansville in 1926 in the Illinois-Indiana-Iowa League
OF	Red Killefer	Traded to the Washington Senators with Germany Schaefer for Jim Delahanty
C	Heinie Beckendorf	Purchased by the Senators in June 1910
C	Joe Casey	Released; went to St. Paul of the American Association in 1912
1B	Del Gainer	Put on waivers in 1914
1B	Hughie Jennings	Retired as a player in 1912. Returned for 1 game in 1918.
P	George Mullin	Purchased by Senators in May 1913
P	Ed Willett	Jumped to St. Louis of the Federal League in 1914
P	Ed Summers	Released; went to Providence of the International League in 1914
P	Ed Killian	Purchased by Toronto of the Eastern League in 1910
P	Bill Donovan	Released; went to Providence of the International League in 1912
P	Kid Speer	Released; went to Buffalo of the Eastern League in 1910
P	Ralph Works	Purchased by Providence of the International League in September 1912
P	George Suggs	Signed with the Reds in 1910
P	Bill Lelivelt	Traded to Mobile of the Southern Association with $2,800 for Frank Allen in July 1909
P	Elijah Jones	Released; went to Montreal of the Eastern League in 1909
P	Ed Lafitte	Released; went to Providence of the International League in 1912

CHAPTER NOTES

Introduction

1. Dennis DeValeria and Jeanne Burke DeValeria, *Honus Wagner* (New York: Henry Holt, 1995), p. 239.
2. www.baseball-reference.com.

Chapter 1

1. Cait Murphy, *Crazy '08* (New York: Smithsonian Books, 2007), p. 241.
2. Ibid., p. 252.
3. Ralph Davis, *The Sporting News*, 10/8/1908.
4. Ibid.
5. Ralph Davis, *The Sporting News*, 11/19/1908.
6. Ralph Davis, *The Sporting News*, 1/14/1909.
7. Ralph Davis, *The Sporting News*, 1/21/1909.
8. Ralph Davis, *The Sporting News*, 11/26/1908.
9. Arthur D Hittner, *Honus Wagner: The Life of Baseball's "Flying Dutchman"* (Jefferson, NC: McFarland, 2003), p. 177.
10. Ralph Davis, *The Sporting News*, 6/17/1909.
11. Ralph Davis, *The Sporting News*, 6/24/1909.

Chapter 2

1. Murphy, *Crazy '08*, p. 217.
2. Ibid.
3. Joe S. Jackson, *The Sporting News*, 1/7/1909.
4. Joe S. Jackson, *The Sporting News*, 2/24/1909.
5. Joe S. Jackson, *The Sporting News*, 5/27/1909.
6. Joe S Jackson, *The Sporting News*, 6/24/1909.

Chapter 3

1. DeValeria and DeValeria, *Honus Wagner*, p. 138.
2. Ibid.
3. Ibid.
4. Al Stump, *Cobb* (New York: Workman, 1994), p. 170.
5. Ibid.
6. Ibid., p. 172.
7. Ibid., p. 178.
8. Ibid., p. 177.
9. Ibid., p. 177.
10. David Pietrusza, Matthew Silverman and Michael Gershman, eds., *The Biographical Encyclopedia of Baseball* (Kingston, NY: Total Sports, 2000), p. 216.
11. William Cobb, ed., *Honus Wagner: On His Life in Baseball* (Ann Arbor: Sports Media Group, 2006), p. 139.
12. Brian Stevens, "Babe Adams," SABR Baseball Biography Project, http://bioproj.sabr.org/bioproj.cfm?a=v&v=1 &bid=888& pid=48.
13. Bill James, *The Bill James Guide to Baseball Managers* (New York: Scribner's, 1997), p. 42.
14. Frederick G Lieb, *The Pittsburgh Pirates* (Carbondale: Southern Illinois University Press, 2003), p. 140.
15. Stevens, "Babe Adams," SABR Baseball Biography Project, http://bioproj.sabr.

org/bioproj.cfm?a=v&v=1 &bid=888&pid=
48.
16. Pietrusza, Silverman and Gershman,
eds., *The Biographical Encyclopedia of Baseball*, p. 5.
17. http://www.baseball-reference.com.
18. *The New York Times*, 10/04/1909.
19. Pietrusza, Silverman and Gershman,
eds., *The Biographical Encyclopedia of Baseball*, p. 572.
20. *The New York Times*, 10/09/1909.
21. Pietrusza, Silverman and Gershman,
eds., *The Biographical Encyclopedia of Baseball*, p. 207.
22. DeValeria and DeValeria, *Honus Wagner*, p. 222.
23. Ibid.
24. Cobb, ed., *Honus Wagner*, p. 21.
25. Hittner, *Honus Wagner*, p. 185.
26. Ibid.
27. *The New York Times*, 10/09/1909.

Chapter 4

1. DeValeria and DeValeria, *Honus Wagner*, p. 223.
2. Merriam Webster Online Dictionary,
http://jaguar.eb.com/dictionary/quinsy.
3. Lieb, *The Pittsburgh Pirates*, p. 142.
4. Tom Simon, ed., *Deadball Stars of the
National League* (Dulles, VA: Brassey's, 2004),
p. 164.
5. Ibid., p. 163.
6. David Jones, ed., *Deadball Stars of
the American League* (Dulles, VA: Potomac
Books, 2006), p. 540.
7. DeValeria and DeValeria, p. 224.
8. Simon, ed., *Deadball Stars of the National League*, p. 173.
9. Lieb, *The Pittsburgh Pirates*, p. 143.
10. Frederick G. Lieb, *The Detroit Tigers*
(Kent, OH: Kent State University Press,
2008), p. 128.
11. *The Daily Courier*, Connellsville, PA,
10/10/2009.
12. *Baseball Library.com*, http://www.
baseballlibrary.com/ballplayers/player.php?
name=Boss_Schmidt_1880.
13. *Baseball Library.com*, http://www.
baseballlibrary.com/ballplayers/player.php?
name=Boss_Schmidt_1880.
14. Al Stump, *Cobb* (Chapel Hill: Algonquin Books of Chapel Hill, 1996), p. 179.

15. *New York Times*, 10/10/2009.
16. Bill James, *The Bill James Historical
Baseball Abstract* (New York: Villard Books,
1986), p. 118.
17. *The Daily Courier*, Connellsville, PA,
10/10/2009.

Chapter 5

1. Lieb, *The Pittsburgh Pirates*, p. 145.
2. Hittner, *Honus Wagner*, p. 186.
3. DeValeria and DeValeria, *Honus
Wagner*, p. 225.
4. *New York Times*, 10/12/1909.
5. DeValeria and DeValeria, *Honus
Wagner*, p. 225.
6. Hittner, *Honus Wagner*, p. 186.
7. *New York Times*, 10/12/1909.
8. Simon, ed., *Deadball Stars of the National League*, p. 175.
9. Ibid.
10. Al Stump, *Cobb* (Chapel Hill: Algonquin Books of Chapel Hill, 1996), p.
179.
11. *The Daily Courier*, Connellsville, PA,
10/11/2009.
12. Simon, ed., *Deadball Stars of the National League*, p. 173.
13. *The Daily Courier*, Connellsville, PA,
10/11/2009.
14. Lieb, *The Pittsburgh Pirates*, p. 146.
15. Ibid.
16. *New York Times*, 10/13/1909.
17. Stump, *Cobb* (Chapel Hill: Algonquin Books of Chapel Hill, 1996), p. 124.
18. Lieb, *The Pittsburgh Pirates*, p. 146.
19. *The Daily Courier*, Connellsville, PA,
10/11/2009/.
20. DeValeria and DeValeria, *Honus Wagner*, p. 227.
21. Hittner, *Honus Wagner*, p. 186.
22. DeValeria and DeValeria, *Honus Wagner*, p. 227.

Chapter 6

1. *The New York Times*, 10/13/1909.
2. Jones, ed., *Deadball Stars of the
American League*, p. 533.
3. DeValeria and DeValeria, *Honus
Wagner*, p. 227.
4. Simon, ed., *Deadball Stars of the National League*, p. 167.

5. Stump, *Cobb* (Chapel Hill: Algonquin Books of Chapel Hill, 1996), p. 180.

6. Hittner, *Honus Wagner*, p. 186.

7. Lieb, *The Detroit Tigers*, p. 132.

8. *The Detroit Tigers*, p. 132.

9. *The Daily Courier*, Connellsville, PA, 10/12/2009.

10. Jones, ed., *Deadball Stars of the American League*, p. 566.

11. *The New York Times*, 10/13/1909.

12. Hittner, *Honus Wagner*, p. 187.

13. *The Daily Courier*, Connellsville, PA, 10/12/2009.

14. DeValeria and DeValeria, *Honus Wagner*, p. 228.

15. *The New York Times*, 10/13/1909.

16. DeValeria and DeValeria, *Honus Wagner*, p. 228.

Chapter 7

1. *The Pittsburgh Gazette*, 10/13/1909, p. 10.

2. Pietrusza, Silverman and Gershman, eds., *The Biographical Encyclopedia of Baseball*, p. 5.

3. Jones, ed., *Deadball Stars of the American League*, p. 538.

4. FC Lane, *Hitting* (Cleveland: SABR, 2001), p. 6.

5. Ibid., p. 40.

6. Simon, ed., *Deadball Stars of the National League*, p. 157.

7. Lane, *Hitting*, pp. 214–215.

8. *The Pittsburgh Gazette*, 10/13/1909, p. 10.

9. Lane, *Hitting*, p. 4.

10. Lieb, *The Detroit Tigers*, p. 133.

Chapter 8

1. *The Pittsburgh Gazette*, 10/15/1909, p. 1.

2. Lieb, *The Detroit Tigers*, p. 134.

3. Ibid.

4. Simon, ed., *Deadball Stars of the National League*, p. 311.

5. Ibid.

6. Lieb, *The Pittsburgh Pirates*, p. 150.

7. Hittner, *Honus Wagner*, p. 189.

8. *The Pittsburgh Gazette*, 10/15/1909, p. 9.

9. Ibid.

10. Ibid.

11. Ibid.

12. Hittner, *Honus Wagner*, p. 189.

13. David Finoli and Tom Aikens, *The Birthplace of Professional Football: Southwestern Pennsylvania* (Portsmouth, NH: Arcadia, 2004), p. 60.

Chapter 9

1. *New York Times*, 10/16/1909.

2. DeValeria and DeValeria, *Honus Wagner*, p. 232.

3. Lieb, *The Pittsburgh Pirates*, pp. 152–153.

4. Jones, ed., *Deadball Stars of the American League*, p. 563.

5. DeValeria and DeValeria, *Honus Wagner*, p. 234.

6. *Pittsburgh Gazette*, 10/16/1909.

7. Hittner, *Honus Wagner*, p. 190.

8. Ibid.

Chapter 10

1. *The Pittsburgh Gazette*, 10/19/1909, p. 6.

2. Ibid.

3. Trey Strecker, "George Gibson," SABR Baseball Biography Project, http://bioproj.sabr.org/bioproj.cfm?a=v&v=1&pid=5072&bid=896.

4. *The Pittsburgh Gazette*, 10/19/1909, p. 6.

5. Ibid.

6. Ibid.

7. *The New York Times*, 7/29/1909.

8. Lieb, *The Pittsburgh Pirates*, pp. 152–155.

9. *The Pittsburgh Gazette*, 10/19/1909, p. 6.

10. DeValeria and DeValeria, *Honus Wagner*, p. 236.

11. Lieb, *The Pittsburgh Pirates*, p. 156.

12. Stump, *Cobb* (New York: Workman, 1994), p. 181.

13. Ibid.

Chapter 11

1. Ralph Davis, *The Sporting News*, 12/31/1908.

2. Ibid.

3. Ralph Davis, *The Sporting News*, 7/8/1909.

4. DeValeria and DeValeria, *Honus Wagner*, p. 211.

5. http://www.ballparktour.com/Former_Pittsburgh_2.html.

Chapter 12

1. http://www.baseballhalloffame.org/news/download/DreyfussTranscript.doc.

2. Robert Dvorchak, *Pittsburgh Post Gazette*, 7/20/2008, available online at http://www.post-gazette.com/pg/08202/898262-63.stm.

3. DeValeria and DeValeria, *Honus Wagner*, p. 89.

4. Ibid., p. 100.

5. Ibid., p. 104.

6. http://www.baseballhalloffame.org/news/download/DreyfussTranscript.doc.

7. http://www.baseballhalloffame.org/news/download/DreyfussTranscript.doc.

8. http://www.baseballhalloffame.org/news/download/DreyfussTranscript.doc.

9. Jones, ed., *Deadball Stars of the American League*, p. 536.

10. Stump, *Cobb* (New York: Workman, 1994), p. 189.

11. Lawrence R. Ritter, *The Glory of Their Times* (New York: Perennial, 2002), pp. 42–43.

12. Lane, *Hitting*, p. 91.

13. Lieb, *The Detroit Tigers*, p. 39.

14. Ibid.

15. Jones, ed., *Deadball Stars of the American League*, p. 536.

16. Stump, *Cobb* (New York: Workman, 1994), p. 323.

17. Ibid.

18. Ritter, *The Glory of Their Times*, p. 314.

Chapter 13

1. David Finoli and Bill Ranier, *The Pittsburgh Pirates Encyclopedia* (Champaign, IL: Sports Publishing, p. 279).

2. Angelo Louisa, "Fred Clarke," SABR Baseball Biography Project; http://bioproj.sabr.org/bioproj.cfm?a=v&v=1 &bid=893&pid=2513.

3. Ibid.

4. Lieb, *The Pittsburgh Pirates*, p. 74.

5. James, *The Bill James Guide to Baseball Managers*, p. 83.

6. Louisa, "Fred Clarke," SABR Baseball Biography Project; http://bioproj.sabr.org/bioproj.cfm?a=v&v=1 &bid=893&pid=2513.

7. http://www.thebaseballpage.com/players/clarkfr01.php.

8. Lane, *Hitting*, p. 44.

9. Ibid., p. 114.

10. Jack Gallagher, *Los Angeles Times*, 7/5/1925.

11. Jones, ed., *Deadball Stars of the American League*, p. 557.

12. Stump, *Cobb* (New York: Workman, 1994), p. 122.

13. Lane, *Hitting*, p. 11.

14. Ibid., p. 17.

15. Ibid., p. 179.

16. *The 1911 Spalding Baseball Guide*, p. 62; available online at the Library of Congress website: http://memory.loc.gov/cgi-bin/ampage?collId=spalding&fileName=00156/spalding00156.db&recNum=104&itemLink=r%3Fammem%2Fspalding%3A@field%28DOCID%2B@lit%28spalding00156div5%29%29%2300156428&linkText=1.

17. Stump, *Cobb* (New York: Workman, 1994), p. 250.

Chapter 14

1. Ralph Davis, *The Sporting News*, 11/26/08.

2. www.baseball-reference.com.

3. Ralph Davis, *The Sporting News*, 4/22/09.

4. Ralph Davis, *The Sporting News*, 9/23/09.

5. George Cantor, *The World Series Fact Book* (New York: Inside Sports, 1996), p. 36.

6. Ibid.

7. Simon, ed., *Deadball Stars of the National League*, p. 173.

8. Ralph Davis, *The Sporting News*, 4/29/09.

9. William Hageman, *Honus: The Life and Times of a Baseball Hero* (Champaign, IL: Sports Publishing, 1996, p. 107.

10. Finoli and Ranier, *The Pittsburgh Pirates Encyclopedia*, p. 336.

11. www.baseball-reference.com.

12. Ralph Davis, *The Sporting News*, 3/25/09.

13. Ralph Davis, *The Sporting News*, 6/10/09.

14. Ibid.

15. Hageman, *Honus*, p. 97.

16. Bert Soloman, *The Baseball Timeline* (New York: Stonesong Press, 1997), p. 154.

17. John P. Carmichael, *My Greatest Day in Baseball* (New York: Grosset & Dunlap, 1968, p. 172.

18. Lane, *Hitting*, pp. 43–44.

19. Ibid.

20. Carmichael, *My Greatest Day in Baseball*, p. 172.

21. Ibid., pp. 171–174.

22. Hageman, *Honus*, pp. 107–109.

23. Finoli and Ranier, *The Pittsburgh Pirates Encyclopedia*, p. 440.

24. Ibid., 249.

25. Ralph Davis, *The Sporting News*, 5/20/09.

26. www.referencecenter.com.

27. www.baseball-reference.com.

28. Simon, ed., *Deadball Stars of the National League*, p. 175.

29. Lieb, *The Pittsburgh Pirates*, p. 158.

30. Ralph Davis, *The Sporting News*, 11/19/08.

31. Ibid.

32. Ritter, *The Glory of Their Times*, p. 30.

33. Ralph Davis, *The Sporting News*, 5/17/09.

34. Ralph Davis, *The Sporting News*, 4/1/09.

35. Ralph Davis, *The Sporting News*, 4/22/09.

36. Simon, ed., *Deadball Stars of the National League*, p. 169.

37. Ralph Davis, *The Sporting News*, 4/1/09.

38. Simon, ed., *Deadball Stars of the National League*, p. 170.

39. Lieb, *The Pittsburgh Pirates*, p. 136.

40. Ralph Davis, *The Sporting News*, 3/25/09.

41. www.baseball-reference.com.

42. http://en.wikipedia.org/wiki.

43. http://en.wikipedia.org/wiki.

44. www.baseball-reference.com.

45. Finoli and Ranier, *The Pittsburgh Pirates Encyclopedia*, p. 441.

46. Lieb, *The Pittsburgh Pirates.*

47. Ralph Davis, *The Sporting News*, 11/5/08.

48. Ralph Davis, *The Sporting News*, 8/5/09.

49. Simon, ed., *Deadball Stars of the National League*, p. 164.

50. Ibid., p. 163.

51. Hageman, *Honus*, p. 110.

52. Finoli and Ranier, *The Pittsburgh Pirates Encyclopedia*, p. 308.

53. Simon, ed., *Deadball Stars of the National League*, p. 164.

54. Ralph Davis, *The Sporting News*, 2/11/09.

55. Rob Neyer and Bill James, *The Neyer and James Guide to Pitchers* (New York: Simon & Schuster, 2004), p. 428.

56. Finoli and Ranier, *The Pittsburgh Pirates Encyclopedia*, p. 308.

57. Simon, ed., *Deadball Stars of the National League*, p. 312.

58. Neyer and James, *The Neyer and James Guide to Pitchers*, p. 278.

59. Simon, ed., *Deadball Stars of the National League*, p. 167.

60. Neyer and James, *The Neyer and James Guide to Pitchers.*

61. Simon, ed., *Deadball Stars of the National League*, p. 167.

62. David Nemec, et al., *20th Century Baseball Chronology: A Year-by-Year History of Major League Baseball* (Lincolnwood, IL: Publications International, 2003), p. 38.

63. www.sabr.org.

64. Orel R Geyer, *Baseball Magazine*, 2/1910.

65. DeValeria and DeValeria, *Honus Wagner*, p. 220.

66. www.baseball-reference.com.

67. DeValeria and DeValeria, *Honus Wagner*, p. 64.

68. Finoli and Ranier, p. 281.

69. DeValeria and DeValeria, *Honus Wagner*, p. 64.

70. Ralph Davis, *The Sporting News*, 3/11/09.

71. Simon, ed., *Deadball Stars of the National League*, p. 146.

72. www.baseball-reference.com.

73. www.baseball-reference.com.

74. Ralph Davis, *The Sporting News*, 11/11/09.

75. www.baseball-reference.com.

76. www.baseball-reference.com.

77. Ralph Davis, *The Sporting News*, 7/29/09.

Chapter 15

1. Joe S. Jackson, *The Sporting News*, 5/27/1909.

2. Joe S. Jackson, *The Sporting News*, 8/26/1909.

3. http://en.wikipedia.org/wiki.

4. www.baseball-reference.com.

5. Jones, ed., *Deadball Stars of the American League*, pp. 551–552.

6. Ritter, *The Glory of Their Times*, pp. 35–36.

7. Ibid.

8. Jones, ed., *Deadball Stars of the American League*, p. 552.

9. Ibid.

10. Jones, ed., *Deadball Stars of the American League*, p. 562.

11. David S. Neft, Richard Cohen and Michael Neft, eds., *The Sports Encyclopedia: Baseball 1998* (New York: St. Martin's Griffin, 1998), pp. 44–45.

12. www.baseball-reference.com.

13. Jones, ed., *Deadball Stars of the American League*, p. 562.

14. Bill James, *The New Bill James Historical Abstract* (New York: The Free Press, 2001), p. 527.

15. Jones, ed., *Deadball Stars of the American League*; Philip Lowry, *Green Cathedrals* (New York: Walker, 2006), p. 559.

16. www.baseball-reference.com.

17. Pietrusza, Silverman and Gershman, eds., *The Biographical Encyclopedia of Baseball*, p. 153.

18. Finoli and Ranier, *The Pittsburgh Pirates Encyclopedia*, p. 444.

19. Ibid.

20. Jones, ed., *Deadball Stars of the American League*, p. 539.

21. Ibid.

22. Ritter, *The Glory of Their Times*, pp. 45–46.

23. Jones, ed., *Deadball Stars of the American League*, p. 560.

24. Ibid., p. 564.

25. Ibid.

26. Ritter, *The Glory of Their Times*, p. 28.

27. Ibid.

28. Pietrusza, Silverman and Gershman, eds., *The Biographical Encyclopedia of Baseball*, p. 803.

29. Donald Honig, *Baseball When the Grass Was Real* (New York: Berkley, 1975), p. 30.

30. Gene Karst and Martin J. Jones, Jr., *Who's Who in Professional Baseball* (New York: Arlington House, 1973), p. 682.

31. Ritter, *The Glory of Their Times*, pp. 329–330.

32. Pietrusza, Silverman and Gershman, eds., *The Biographical Encyclopedia of Baseball*, p. 803.

33. Karst and Jones, *Who's Who in Professional Baseball*, p. 682.

34. Joe S. Jackson, *The Sporting News*, 5/20/1909.

35. http://en.wikipedia.org/wiki.

36. www.baseball-reference.com.

37. Jones, ed., *Deadball Stars of the American League*, p. 544.

38. Ibid.

39. Stump, *Cobb* (Chapel Hill: Algonquin Books of Chapel Hill, 1996), p. 118.

40. Ibid.

41. James, *The New Bill James Historical Abstract*, p. 674.

42. Jones, ed., *Deadball Stars of the American League*, p. 559.

43. Ritter, *The Glory of Their Times*, p. 38.

44. Ibid.

45. Ibid., p. 41.

46. Stump, *Cobb* (Chapel Hill: Algonquin Books of Chapel Hill, 1996), p. 224.

47. Jones, ed., *Deadball Stars of the American League*, p. 549.

48. Stump, *Cobb* (Chapel Hill: Algonquin Books of Chapel Hill, 1996), p. 27.

49. Ibid., p. 96.

50. Ritter, *The Glory of Their Times*, p. 62.

51. Ibid., p. 41.

52. Ibid., p. 60.

53. Lieb, *The Pittsburgh Pirates*, p. 151.

54. Joe S. Jackson, *The Sporting News*, 9/2/1909.

55. Stump, *Cobb* (Chapel Hill: Algonquin Books of Chapel Hill, 1996), p. 172.
56. Ibid., p. 181.
57. Honig, *Baseball When the Grass Was Real*, pp. 28–29.
58. Ibid.
59. Ritter, *The Glory of Their Times.*
60. www.baseball-reference.com.
61. Karst and Jones, *Who's Who in Professional Baseball*, p. 206.
62. Ibid.
63. James, *The New Bill James Historical Abstract*, p. 795.
64. Ibid.
65. Lowell Ridenbaugh, *Cooperstown: Where Baseball's Legends Live Forever* (St. Louis: The Sporting News, 1983), p. 60.
66. James, *The New Bill James Historical Abstract*, p. 867.
67. Ridenbaugh, *Cooperstown: Where Baseball's Legends Live Forever*, p. 60.
68. Ritter, *The Glory of Their Times*, p. 47.
69. Jones, ed., *Deadball Stars of the American League*, p. 538.
70. Ritter, *The Glory of Their Times*, p. 63.
71. Ibid., p. 159.
72. James, *The New Bill James Historical Abstract*, pp. 794–796.
73. www.baseball.fever.com.
74. James, *The New Bill James Historical Abstract*, p. 117.
75. Joe S. Jackson, *The Sporting News*, 4/22/1909.
76. Stump, *Cobb* (Chapel Hill: Algonquin Books of Chapel Hill, 1996), p. 141.
77. Ibid., p. 144.
78. www.baseball-reference.com.
79. Ibid.
80. Jones, ed., *Deadball Stars of the American League*, p. 566.
81. Ibid., p. 385.
82. www.baseball-reference.com.
83. Neyer and James, *The Neyer and James Guide to Pitchers*, pp. 317–318.
84. Jones, ed., *Deadball Stars of the American League*, p. 533.
85. Ibid.
86. James, *The New Bill James Historical Abstract*, p. 135.
87. Jones, *Deadball Stars of the American League*, p. 534.

88. Stump, *Cobb* (Chapel Hill: Algonquin, 1994), p. 124.
89. Ibid.
90. Neyer and James, *The Neyer and James Guide to Pitchers*, p. 426.
91. http://en.wikipedia.org/wiki.
92. Neyer and James, *The Neyer and James Guide to Pitchers*, pp. 40–41.
93. http://en.wikipedia.org/wiki.
94. Pietrusza, Silverman and Gershman, eds., *The Biographical Encyclopedia of Baseball*, p. 606.
95. Ibid.
96. David Nemec, et al., *20th Century Baseball Chronicle*, p. 46.
97. Jones, ed., *Deadball Stars of the American League*, p. 542.
98. Joe S. Jackson, *The Sporting News*, 6/24/1909.
99. Neyer and James, *The Neyer and James Guide to Pitchers*, p. 188.
100. Lieb, *The Pittsburgh Pirates*, p. 148.
101. Honus Wagner in Carmichael, *My Greatest Day in Baseball*, p. 173.
102. Pietrusza, Silverman and Gershman, eds., *The Biographical Encyclopedia of Baseball*, p. 297.
103. http://en.wikipedia.org/wiki.

Chapter 16

1. Lieb, *The Pittsburgh Pirates*, p. 157.
2. Ibid.
3. Ralph Davis, *The Sporting News*, 11/11/2009.
4. Ralph Davis, *The Sporting News*, 11/18/2009.
5. DeValeria and DeValeria, *Honus Wagner*, p. 242.
6. Ralph Davis, *The Sporting News*, 12/16/2009.
7. DeValeria and DeValeria, *Honus Wagner*, p. 242.
8. Lieb, *The Pittsburgh Pirates*, p. 157.
9. Hittner, *Honus Wagner*, p. 194.
10. Ibid.

Chapter 17

1. Joe S. Jackson, *The Sporting News*, 11/11/1909.
2. http://www.baseballlibrary.com/ballplayers/player.php?name=Billy_Evans.

3. Lieb, *The Detroit Tigers*, p. 138.
4. Stump, *Cobb* (New York: Workman, 1994), p. 186.
5. Ritter, *The Glory of Their Times*, p. 62.
6. Ibid.
7. Baseball Hall of Fame website, http://www.baseballhalloffame.org/news/article.jsp?ymd=20090325&content_id=11534&vkey=hof_news.
8. *The 1911 Spalding Baseball Guide*, p. 62; available online at the Library of Congress website http://memory.loc.gov/cgi-bin/ampage?collId=spalding&fileName=00156/spalding00156.db&recNum=104&itemLink=r%3Fammem%2Fspalding%3A@field%28DOCID%2B@lit%28spalding00156div5%29%29%2300156428&linkText=1.
9. Stump, *Cobb* (New York: Workman, 1994), p. 189.
10. Ibid.

BIBLIOGRAPHY

Books

Bak, Richard. *Ty Cobb: His Tumultuous Life and Times.* Dallas: Taylor, 1994.

Cantor, George. *The World Series Fact Book.* New York: Inside Sports, 1996.

Carmichael, John P. *My Greatest Day in Baseball.* New York: Grosset & Dunlap, 1968.

Cobb, William, ed. *Honus Wagner: On His Life in Baseball.* Ann Arbor: Sports Media Group, 2006.

DeValeria, Dennis, and Jeanne Burke Valeria. *Honus Wagner.* New York: Henry Holt, 1995.

Finoli, David, and Thomas Aikens. *The Birthplace of Professional Football: Southwestern Pennsylvania.* Portsmouth, NH: Arcadia, 2004.

Finoli, David, and Bill Ranier. *The Pittsburgh Pirates Encyclopedia.* Champaign, IL: Sports Publishing, 2003.

Hageman, William. *Honus: The Life and Times of a Baseball Hero.* Champaign, IL: Sports Publishing, 1996.

Hittner, Arthur D. *Honus Wagner: The Life of Baseball's Flying Dutchman.* Jefferson, NC: McFarland, 2003.

Honig, Donald. *Baseball When the Grass Was Real.* New York: Berkley, 1975.

James, Bill. *The Bill James Guide to Baseball Managers.* New York: Scribner's, 1997.

_____. *The Bill James Historical Baseball Abstract.* New York: Villard Books, 1986.

_____. *The New Bill James Historical Abstract.* New York: Free Press, 2001.

Jones, Davis, ed. *Deadball Stars of the American League.* Dulles, VA: Potomac Books, 2006.

Karst, Gene, and Martin J. Jones. *Who's Who in Professional Baseball.* New York: Arlington House, 1973.

Lane, FC. *Hitting.* Cleveland: SABR, 2001.

Lieb, Frederick G. *The Detroit Tigers.* Kent, OH: Kent State University Press, 2008.

_____. *The Pittsburgh Pirates.* Carbondale: Southern Illinois University Press, 2003.

Lowry, Philip. *Green Cathedrals.* New York: Walker, 2006.

Murphy, Cait. *Crazy '08.* New York: Smithsonian Books, 2008.

Neft, David S., Richard Cohen, and Michael Neft, eds. *The Sports Encyclopedia: Baseball 1998.* New York: St. Martin's Griffin, 1998.

Nemec, David, et al. *20th Century Baseball Chronicle: A Year-by-Year History of Major League Baseball.* Lincolnwood, IL: Publications International, 2003.

Neyer, Rob, and Bill James. *The Neyer and James Guide to Pitchers.* New York: Simon & Schuster, 2004.

Palacios, Oscar A. *Ballpark Sourcebook: Diamond Diagram.* Skokie, IL: Stats, 1998.

Pietrusza, David, Matthew Silverman, and Michael Gershman, eds. *The Biographical Encyclopedia of Baseball.* Kingston, NY: Total Sports, 2000.

Ridenbaugh, Lowell. *Cooperstown: Where Baseball's Legends Live Forever.* St. Louis: Sporting News, St. Louis, 1983.
Ritter, Lawrence. *The Glory of Their Times.* New York: Perennial, 2002.
_____. *Lost Ballparks.* New York: Penguin Studio Books, 1992.
Simon, Tom, ed. *Deadball Stars of the National League.* Dulles, VA: Brassey's, 2004.
Solomon, Bert. *The Baseball Timeline.* New York: Stonesong Press, 1997.
Stump, Al. *Cobb.* Chapel Hill: Algonquin Books of Chapel Hill, 1996.

Newspapers

The Daily Courier (Connellsville, PA)
The Detroit News
The Los Angeles Times
The New York Times
The News-Palladium (Benton Harbor, MI)
The Pittsburgh Post-Gazette
The Titusville Morning Herald (Titusville, PA)

Magazines

Baseball Magazine
The Sporting News

Websites

http://en.wikipedia.org/wiki
http://memory.loc.gov/ammem/collections/spalding/index.html
www.ballparks.com
www.baseball-almanac.com
www.baseballcube.com
www.baseball.fever.com
www.baseballhalloffame.org
www.baseballlibrary.com/homepage
www.thebaseballpage.com
www.baseball-reference.com
http://bioproj.sabr.org
www.boxrec.com
www.pittsburghlive.com
www.pittsburghpostgazette.com
www.referencecenter.com
www.retrosheet.org
www.sabr.org
www.tycobb.org

INDEX

269